"IT HAPPENED. POW!"

Phillip's hands go to his face. Blood streams out through his fingers. "I'm looking at him and I see the blood coming out from underneath his hand. And the dude is screaming, 'Oh my God!' "

Brian puts the gun to Phillip's temple, looks up into the air and squeezes the trigger again. The bullet tears through Phillip's brain, carving a path of destruction.

Diana never screams. "She just stood there. Nude. The whole time, she watched. She didn't say a word. She had this look on her face, like, you finally got what you deserved all this time."

A DEATH IN SANTA BARBARA

MATTHEW HELLER

AVON BOOKS △ NEW YORK

A DEATH IN SANTA BARBARA is an original publication of Avon Books. This work has never before appeared in book form.

AVON BOOKS
A division of
The Hearst Corporation
1350 Avenue of the Americas
New York, New York 10019

Copyright © 1993 by Matthew Heller
Published by arrangement with the author
Library of Congress Catalog Card Number: 92-97477
ISBN: 0-380-76641-8

First Avon Books Printing: July 1993

AVON TRADEMARK REG. U.S. PAT. OFF. AND IN OTHER COUNTRIES, MARCA REGISTRADA, HECHO EN U.S.A.

Printed in the U.S.A.

RA   10   9   8   7   6   5   4   3   2   1

To my parents

Acknowledgments

This book would not have been possible without the cooperation of a countless number of people. From a high-school librarian in Visalia to a bartender in Colfax, they all helped put pieces in the puzzle.

I would like to single out for special thanks those who agreed to be interviewed for this book, often at the cost of reliving painful memories. I am also grateful to the public information officers who arranged the prison interviews and to the legion of court records clerks who helped compile the documentation for the book.

I was fortunate to have the cooperation of those on both sides of the justice system in the Bogdanoff case. On the defense side, Steve Balash and Michael McMahon helped me untangle the legal web. On the law enforcement side, I owe a huge debt to Russ Birchim, Fred Ray and Pat McKinley.

Finally, I would like to thank Jecky Barnard for her support; my agent Ellen Levine for her faith and encouragement; and my editor Tom Colgan for turning my manuscript into this finished product.

Prologue:
Where Creeks Go Dry

For most of its serpentine, twenty-mile course through the hills northeast of Bakersfield, California, Round Mountain Road is the only human imprint on a desolate landscape. Beyond the rusty sign that warns, "Unlawful to Dicharge [sic] Firearms in This Area," there are a few stray oil pump jacks and storage tanks, a ski ranch, and a radio transmitter atop the sixteen-hundred-foot summit of Round Mountain. Otherwise, the road twists a solitary path around hairpin bends, above sheer drops, through the parched brown hills that look like loaves of bread, offering an occasional glimpse of the patchwork fields of the San Joaquin Valley below. After a few miles, the road markings disappear. A cawing crow, a free-ranging cow, a passing pickup truck, are the only company for the traveler.

This is where a bunch of Bakersfield friends stopped one clear, moonlit night in September 1989. There were ten of them, in three cars. The youngest among the friends was sixteen, the oldest was twenty-five. They all pulled off the road where it bisects a canyon and parallels a dry creek bed. They had spotted cows on one side of the canyon.

Out of one of the cars, a cream-colored Ford Fairmont, stepped two guys. One of them, named Brian, was stocky, compact, and muscular; the other, Calvin, was tall, lithe, and limber. They were both black and wore flattop hairdos. They were both carrying sawed-off shotguns. Calvin had a twelve-gauge, Brian the twenty-gauge.

Out of another of the cars, a Toyota Celica, stepped Rickey, a lanky white guy with delicate features and long, center-parted, brown hair. He also had a weapon, a palm-sized, small-caliber pistol.

The rest of the group stayed by the cars. Some were smok-

1

ing marijuana; some were already high on a more potent drug, methamphetamine or, as they called it, "crank." They included Brian's girlfriend, Stephanie, a blue-eyed brunette, and Calvin's girlfriend, Jodie, a tiny peroxide blonde; two sets of brothers—Gator and Mike, and Chad and Travis; and a twenty-year-old called Sean.

One of the reasons they had supposedly come all the way out there was so Brian could teach Sean a lesson for not paying his drug debts.

But for now, the cows took priority. The free-ranging Herefords were perched on a hillside above the road. Brian and Calvin clambered down a brush-covered embankment and started firing at them from the creek bed. The detonation of shotgun shells echoed around the canyon, but the pellets sprayed away from their target. "I could have swore I got a cow. It was about this close," Calvin said later, indicating a few feet. "The cow looked at me and ran. I was sweating like a dog up there, shooting the damn shotgun."

Rickey's luck or marksmanship was no better. He crossed the creek bed and fired his pistol from a ridge connected to the cows' pasture by oil pipes. The nearest animals were about fifty feet away. He didn't have to waste time reloading—the gun was a semiautomatic—but nothing hit a cow.

The convoy of cars pulled out of the canyon, heading toward the summit of Round Mountain. With the two black guys and Jodie as passengers, Stephanie drove her Ford like a maniac, trying to keep up with the other cars. She screeched round the hairpins, scattering shotgun shells onto the floor.

They met up again about three miles later. There, cows were grazing in more open, accessible country. The hillsides roll gently like waves, crisscrossed by dirt trails, and dotted with feeding troughs and water tanks.

Brian and Calvin took off again with the shotguns, chasing cows. "It was funny watching them do it," Stephanie recalled. "It's like a cartoon. You can see somebody running up and down on the fields with guns, trying to kill these cows. They're not coming anywhere close, but they're chasing them in the middle of the night on these fields. You're on drugs watching this stuff and it's funny."

Stephanie and Mike tried to help by driving their cars up a hillside and herding the cows toward the firing squad. But the results were the same as in the canyon. Calvin thought they hit one. "It just didn't fall. It ran a bit too fast for us. I'm shooting, but nothing ain't falling." One cow escaped by running across the road and down a ravine.

Sean also escaped unharmed that night. When he finished cow hunting, Brian found out that Gator, his trusty right-hand man in what he called his "family" of friends, had already driven off with his human prey.

Phillip Bogdanoff was not so lucky. Shortly after their cow-shooting adventure, some of the friends mounted two separate expeditions to kill the man who was Stephanie's stepfather, the man her mother wanted dead. They traveled even farther afield, 150 miles away to an idyllic corner of Santa Barbara, California. On the first trip, they armed themselves with the shotguns but gave up after failing to find Phillip. But on the second trip—on September 21, 1989—they caught up with him. Brian put Rickey's .22-caliber pistol to Phillip's temple and shot him dead as he sunbathed naked with his wife on a secluded beach.

This is the story of how the friends of Bakersfield collided fatally with Phillip Bogdanoff, of how his wife was able to lure them to commit the ultimate crime as flippantly as they had stalked cows. It is the story of a moral landscape as dismal as that of Round Mountain Road, one on which basic human values make no imprint.

PART ONE

Unknown Currents

According to his first wife, Phillip Bogdanoff had "a pattern of doing what you asked him not to do." It wasn't that he was a rebel, just that what he was "not to do" was defined by such exacting standards. The standards were set by his family and his church. On two occasions, doing the forbidden led to his expulsion from both family and church. He spent the last phase of his life with a woman for whom such standards did not seem relevant. Because he essentially had no family or church to worry about anymore, he should have been more secure. But he still could not shake off his background, and the result was chaos.

Phillip grew up in an area as rural and isolated as the cow-shooting scene on Round Mountain Road. The thirty-three-acre farm he called home was on the other side of Bakersfield, beside a lonely crossroads in the district of Rosedale. Even today, the tide of tract homes has yet to swallow up the fields of cotton and alfalfa.

The geographic isolation of Phillip's childhood was comple-mented by the life-style of the obscure immigrant group from which he came. He was an American-born Russian Molokan, part of a group whose ethnic and religious identities are one and the same.

The Molokans came to America from czarist Russia after centuries of persecution. The poorest of peasants, they had made nuisances of themselves by railing against the moral excesses of the established Russian Orthodox clergy. They were derisively known as Molokans, literally "milk drinkers," because they refused to observe the Orthodox taboo against drinking milk during fasts. But more than milk drinking, what set them apart was their manner of expressing religious ecstasy. When infused with the Holy Spirit, some Molokans, even the elderly, would leap high into the air. This group called themselves "Spiritual Christians of the Sect of Jumpers."

In the late 1880s the czarist regime imposed conscription, starting the first trickle of Molokan emigrants to the United States. The trickle became a flood as Russia and Japan moved toward war in 1904. Some fled to the San Francisco area, and some to Baja California, Mexico. The majority of them ended up in "the Flats" of Los Angeles—a neighborhood of run-down buildings, old warehouses, and junkyards near what is now the East L.A. freeway interchange.

In 1912 an estimated thirty-five hundred Molokans lived in southern California. There, on the cutting edge of progress and Western mores, the Molokans began a struggle that consumes them to this very day: how to resist assimilation into the dominant, "heathen" culture. Their weapons in this struggle have been the same as in Russia—the absolute conviction that theirs is the true Christian church, and a strict separation from the outside world. Even today, they jealously guard the secrets of their faith from outsiders.

Phillip Nicholas Bogdanoff—pronounced with the stress on the first syllable—was born May 27, 1940, in Los Angeles, the younger son of Nick and Jennie. His father, then thirty-seven, came to southern California from Armenia in 1911; his mother, thirty-four, grew up in Baja California. Nick worked at a tire shop and drove a garbage truck. But after work, it was back to the close-knit community of Molokans in the Flats, where the men tied braided cords around peasant-style shirts, and the women wore triangular lace head shawls.

In 1947 Phillip's asthma prompted the family to move across the Tehachapi Mountains to the Bakersfield area, then a relatively undeveloped, rural backwater, devoted to small-scale agriculture. Nick bought the Rosedale farm and started growing cotton and alfalfa. It wasn't easy scratching a living from the often scorched soil, and the farm never made Nick rich. "He was what you call a real dirt farmer," said Elaine Kosareff, a relative.

Like other Molokans, the Bogdanoffs emphasized the values of family and community over materialism, and in the fields of Kern County, Molokan life could at least bear a passing resemblance to the Russian model. The community was almost an extended family, its members always looking out for one another's interests. When cotton plants needed thinning, Phillip's mother, her sister, and an elderly, one-armed man and his wife would go from farm to farm, wielding their hoes. Phillip helped out on the farm after school, driving the tractor or setting siphon pipe.

Molokans have a saying: "The man is the head, and the woman is the neck." To that, women respond, "Have you ever seen the head turn if the neck wouldn't let it?" Jennie made the most of being the neck in the Bogdanoff family. "She was the one in the more dominating role," said Kay Bogdanoff, Phillip's first wife. "[Women] knew where their place was in the religious part of life. They're taught to be caretakers of the house." It didn't matter that Jennie could neither read nor write. She didn't have to read a recipe to be able to cook, bake, or pickle.

His parents, Elaine Kosareff said, gave Phillip a "good, clean, calm, quiet life."

But beneath this bucolic surface lurked undercurrents of tension and conflict. By the time he started attending high school, Phillip was moving away from the Molokan fold and embracing the life of a Californian teenager. "He just wanted to be one of the guys," recalled a high school friend. The problem was reconciling being one of the guys with being one of the Molokans.

It is difficult to pinpoint the nature of Phillip's predicament—memories of his non-Russian acquaintances are vague, and relatives such as the Kosareffs refused to discuss his attitude toward being Molokan. But in a 1932 study of the Los Angeles colony, Pauline Young put it well when she described Molokan youngsters as "cultural hybrids" who, "cut off from the anchorage of habitual modes of action . . . drift at the mercy of unknown currents."

Being Molokan involved all manner of customs and prohibitions that made it difficult to be one of the guys. Their insular society was one in which the Bible governed all aspects of daily life, in which there was no separation between the religious and the secular. It was a society where emotion and prophecy

pushed aside reason and science. The religious service, usually held in barely furnished meeting halls and conducted in
Russian, was an outpouring of ecstasy, of chantlike singing,
weeping, and, of course, jumping. It included the "brotherly
kiss"—worshipers, men and women, kissing one another on
the lips.

Unacceptable behavior included poor religious attendance,
going to movies, and associating with non-Molokans. Most rep-
rehensible were drinking, drug use, promiscuity, and "marrying
out." Some of the more conservative married couples insisted
on having separate beds when the wife was menstruating.
That way, she would not contaminate the marriage bed or
the husband.

The diversions available to Phillip in rural Kern County were certainly less insidious than those he would have
encountered in urban Los Angeles. But he, too, drifted "at
the mercy of unknown currents."

In his high school years, Phillip hung out with a group of
American friends, enough to win parental disapproval. One
friend recalled meeting Phillip's parents and getting "a definite
message that you weren't welcome. They didn't talk to you too
much. They looked at an American like you were going to lead
their son astray."

The American influence is even apparent in Phillip's looks
as a teenager. Bushy eyebrows, deep-set blue eyes, and broad
nose reveal his Slavic roots. But in an echo of Elvis, he allowed
a lock of hair to curl onto his high forehead.

According to one friend, Phillip "didn't do a lot more than
anyone else. But everything he did . . . he'd either get caught
or get in trouble." In October 1958 he got sixty days in county
jail for driving his father's pickup while drunk. Another time,
he loaned Nick's new Oldsmobile to some friends, who then
wrecked it.

Phillip's brother, George, ten years his senior, was also
nonconformist as a young man. According to Kay Bogdanoff,
he dated American girls, drank alcohol at parties, and raced a
dragster at the local track. But George returned to the Molokan
fold, marrying a Russian girl and devoutly following the religion. Phillip never found that Russian girl, and those girls
he did meet made his break from the Molokan community
irrevocable.

"The religion thing was hard for him to deal with to the extent that if he dated a person outside the church, the woman was automatically no good," recalled Tommy Byford, Phillip's closest high school friend. "It was the worst thing he could do."

After he graduated from Bakersfield High School in 1958, he became so smitten with one American girl that he followed her to Los Angeles. As a result, his family disowned him. He then returned to Bakersfield after the girl left him. In a deep depression, he sliced his wrists but ran cold water on them to reduce the bleeding. As he recovered in the hospital, his parents relented and came to see him. "I didn't think you cared about me," he told them.

The whole experience—the ostracism from his family, the pain of rejection—fueled an insecurity that became a constant in his life and was obvious to Kay when she met him a few years later. "I didn't really care for him at first . . . When we went places, you had to direct your attention totally to him. He'd make insecure, jealous remarks. It was like he owned me."

Phillip had his generous side—he was "one of those guys who when he was good, he was really good"—but Kay might not have married him if she hadn't got pregnant. They were married in May 1962, and their daughter Nicki was born the following July. "It was the best thing to do, I guess. I felt that if I didn't marry him, the jealousy would get worse. If I did, maybe he'd relax."

For the Molokans, the marriage was another act of flagrant rebelliousness. Not only was Kay American, but she was also twice divorced and had two children (a son and a daughter) from her past marriages. When Nick found out about the marriage, he hit Phillip and split his lip.

His parents started visiting Phillip and Kay again after Nicki was born. But there was no returning to the Molokan community. Phillip and his new family would soon convert to a faith quite foreign to that of his Russian ancestors.

The marriage did not enjoy much of a honeymoon period. Of course, Phillip had enormous responsibilities for a man in his mid-twenties. In August 1963 the couple had twin daughters, leaving Phillip—just starting a career with the state transit agency (Caltrans)—with a wife and five children to support. But no amount of stress could excuse Phillip's behavior, especially when it became violent. ┐

In the worst incident, Phillip beat Kay so severely that she spent a week recovering in the hospital. The couple separated, the children were placed in foster homes, and Phillip saw a psychiatrist. "What gives you the right to beat your wife?" the analyst asked him.

"She's my wife," he replied.

Kay said the psychiatrist told her that Phillip was "one of the most insecure men he had ever met, that he had a need to prove he was a real swinger, he was macho."

Phillip and Kay reconciled after six weeks, but it wasn't psychiatry that helped relieve their problems. While they were living in a Los Angeles suburb, Kay opened the front door to a Jehovah's Witness. Soon she was attending Kingdom Hall meetings, and one Sunday, she took Phillip along. They studied the Bible together, and by 1968, they had both been baptized in the church.

For Phillip, the Jehovah's Witnesses were a vast improvement on the Russian Molokans. Of course, in common with other fundamentalist sects, they both adhered to a strict moral code and separation from the wider world. But where, so Phillip believed, the Molokans clouded their faith with tradition, mysticism, and hypocrisy, the Witnesses relied solely on the Bible, the "Truth." Whatever the problem, a Witness only needed the Bible—or one of the church's myriad publications—to find the answer. "Phillip wanted answers, and he got them," Kay said.

According to Kay, the answers gave them ten years of marital contentment. "When we came in the Truth, that gave us common ground. Our relationship improved one hundred percent . . . He and I worked very hard to make those changes, have a good family life for our kids. A very strong motivating thing in our marriage was a good family life. The Truth revolves around that, and that cinched it."

They appeared to be a model Witness household, a facsimile of the radiant families depicted in the pages of *The Watchtower*. On Saturdays they went door to door, looking for new converts; on Monday evenings they had an hour of family Bible study; they taped themselves singing Witness songs.

Association with non-Witnesses was kept to a minimum; the children could not date until they turned sixteen, and then had to be chaperoned.

Phillip was the dominant figure in the household, but that accorded with Witness belief. In a publication called *Making Your Family Life Happy,* wives of Witnesses were told, "Above all, don't try to usurp his [the husband's] headship! If you succeed, you won't like him; and he won't like you or himself." Discipline of the children was swift and painful—a favorite tool for spanking was the track from a Hot Wheels racing set—but Witness parents were told that "a spanking may be a lifesaver to a child."

According to the Bogdanoff children, everything was not as it seemed. "They never had a good marriage," said Cindy Cook, Kay's daughter by her first husband. "A lot of times he'd get home from work and be in a bad mood. The marriage was, when's dinner?" The couple never exchanged "a wink across the table, nothing. They were not friends." Kay, an attractive woman with a lively sense of humor, found it hard to communicate with a man who took himself so seriously.

There was also Phillip's drinking habit. The Witnesses allow drinking of alcohol, but only in moderation. "True Christians realize that they cannot glorify God if their senses are confusingly dulled by immoderate use of alcohol," cautions the Witness publication *Awake!* Phillip tested the definition of "moderate," coming home regularly from work with a six-pack and finishing it by bedtime.

The tensions were held in check until around 1978. By that time the family had moved from Los Angeles to Shingle Springs, a rural community forty miles east of Sacramento. Now established as a Caltrans engineer, Phillip bought a twenty-acre parcel on which he built an impressive home—two stories, with the upper one devoted to the master bedroom, picture windows for the views of Sierra Nevada foothills, and a gravel driveway leading up from the road.

Phillip had achieved material comfort, but spiritually, he was unraveling. "It was real obvious he was having a struggle with that part of his life," Kay told me. Church activities—going to meetings, proselytizing, even praying—were a chore. "He didn't act like God's Spirit was on him anymore. He acted like he was having a problem with his conscience."

There may have been a bit more to it than that. Many Witnesses felt an anticlimax when the expected dawn of the thousand-year Judgment Day did not transpire in 1975. In the buildup to this moment, the church had become still more conservative, widening the boundaries of aberrant behavior. When the payoff of earthly paradise failed to materialize in 1975, some disillusionment was inevitable.

Local church elders tried counseling Phillip, particularly about his drinking. It was to no avail. "I think he gave up," Kay said. "It was like, 'I ain't fighting no more, I'm going to do what Phillip wants to do' . . . Trying to live as a true Christian was a strain because he was sidetracked with constantly wondering if he was attractive, if he could really turn girls on if he was running loose. When you toy around with things like that, you can't talk to God."

In October 1981 everything finally disintegrated. Kay, Nicki, and the twins went to Hawaii to celebrate the twins' high school graduation, but Phillip stayed behind. When they returned, he wasn't at the airport and he wasn't at home. He had taken some of his belongings and cleared out.

After a month, Phillip resurfaced, saying he needed to talk to the family. "I want to live my life the way I want to do it," he explained to them. "If I don't want to go to meetings anymore, if I want a drink, I'll do it."

"It was like he had raised us, and we didn't need him anymore," Christy, one of the twins, said later.

Jehovah's Witnesses call it "disfellowshipping," the expulsion from the church of those who "though claiming to be Christians, engage in serious wrongdoing and who fail to show a genuinely repentant attitude." Phillip qualified simply on the basis of "immoderate" drinking. But he also committed the sin of adultery. While the family was in Hawaii, Phillip visited a local bar and met Barbara Klos, a divorcée living in nearby Diamond Springs. Less than a week later, they spent the night together at her home.

It was Phillip's misfortune that the Witnesses had just stiffened their guidelines on treating the disfellowshipped. From the 1950s through 1974, the organization took a rigid line, decreeing that members could not even say hello to anyone expelled from the church. In 1974 they conceded that although there should be no "mixing in company" with the disfellowshipped, that "does not prevent us from being decent, courteous, considerate, and humane."

Such tolerance evaporated in *The Watchtower* of September 15, 1981. The church announced that refusal to associate with a disfellowshipped person "on any spiritual or social level reflects loyalty to God's standards and obedience to his command." Saying hello was once again dangerous. Witnesses were told that "true Christians realize that they cannot put family before God." In the case of an expelled relative living outside the family home, there would be "some limited need to care for family matters," but church members should "strive to avoid needless association, even keeping business dealings to a minimum." Even inviting the relative to a family wedding could be a problem.

"The fact is," *The Watchtower* concluded, "that when a Christian gives himself over to sin and has to be disfellowshipped, he forfeits much . . . including much of the association he had with Christian relatives."

In January 1982, Phillip, who was hoping to stay in touch with his children, visited Cindy Cook and her husband. Jim Cook took him outside the house and walked him through the September 15 article. "We can't even eat with you," Jim told him.

"By God, I'm the father of these kids," Phillip objected.

"Phil, this is nothing new."

Phillip returned home in tears. Going his own way had cost him his wife and his church. For the second time in his life, it had also ostracized him from his family.

Phillip picked up the pieces. He spent the next four years with Barbara Klos, marrying her in April 1983. The couple moved about ninety miles north to Oroville in Butte County, where they bought a ranch-style home on two acres with a swimming pool. But these were difficult years for Phillip.

First, he fought a lengthy battle with Kay over their divorce settlement. "He didn't want to give me nothing," Kay said. "It got real bitter, mean, and hateful."

The main hurdle was the fate of the Shingle Springs house and the surrounding acreage, which had been subdivided into several lots. Eventually, in a settlement approved in April

1983, Phillip and Kay split the proceeds from the sale of one acre, while he kept two five-acre lots, which were rented out at $286 a month. Kay got the house, but that saddled her with mortgage payments she couldn't make, and she had to sell out. She won only fifty dollars a month in child support.

Phillip also battled illness and injury. While involved with Barbara, he broke his ankle while tree-trimming, separated his shoulder twice water-skiing, and lost parts of two fingers in a lawn mower. Most seriously, he was diagnosed as having a cancerous tumor in his chest. The pain of the illness was compounded by what he saw as further rejection by his family. While he was in the hospital to have the tumor removed, none of his children visited him. "He told me that if he died, he didn't want the kids at his funeral," Barbara said. (The children say they were unaware he was having surgery at that time.)

When Phillip was not in the hospital or the emergency room, there were problems at home. Like Kay, Barbara could not escape his insecurity. "Any affection or attention you'd show anyone else would detract from him," she said. "For him to function as a whole person, he had to be the hub of the wheel." Barbara, a spirited, self-possessed woman, didn't take kindly to Phillip's controlling behavior, whether it was objecting to her joining a mixed bowling league or trying to get her to go topless on a boat on Lake Oroville. A couple of times, he roughly grabbed Barbara by the hair, although he never hit her.

Some photographs capture Phillip during his relationship with Barbara. A stocky man, about five foot ten and 175 pounds, he had a full, Rasputin-type beard that enveloped most of his spherical face. In three of the shots, he is smiling broadly. But the most striking image has Phillip standing in front of a trailer, wearing his trademark peach-colored tank top. His arms are crossed firmly over his chest as if defying anyone to come near him. The lugubrious expression in his blue eyes evokes a police mug shot.

Less than eighteen months after moving to Oroville, Phillip and Barbara split up. During the fall of 1986, they discussed reconciling and spent a few weekends together. But there was no going back. In fact, by that time, there was a new woman in Phillip's life, a third wife on the horizon.

The Shady Glen

Colfax, California, is not the sort of place where most people would choose to make a fresh start. The Placer County town has been dormant since its gold mines were exhausted. The population has hovered around one thousand since before World War II. The shabby main street beside the railroad tracks boasts only two bars, a diner, a deli, video and drugstores, and a savings and loan housed in a converted railcar. Many of the houses do not have street numbers. If it weren't for Interstate 80, which connects Sacramento to Lake Tahoe and runs past Colfax's doorstep, the town might not have survived at all.

But Colfax was where Phillip, then forty-six, retreated after his separation from Barbara. His residence was a trailer in a mobile home park, the Shady Glen, mostly occupied by senior citizens; his place of work—a bridge over the Bear River which Caltrans was widening—was just down the hill from the park; his place of entertainment—the Shady Glen Inn—was just up the hill.

Regulars at the Inn, a simple, unadorned tavern with barstools at the counter, a few tables, and a small stage and dancing area, remember Phillip as a solitary type. He would keep to himself, preferring to sit by the window rather than at the counter. "He was very quiet," recalled Bruno Ricci, the bartender at the time. "He was a loner, he didn't talk much."

But in the early summer of 1986, Phillip emerged from his shell long enough to meet another Shady Glen patron.

Like Phillip, Diana Wymore was trying to build a new life in Colfax. Then thirty-eight years old, she had recently broken up with her second husband. She was living in the center of town with the three children from her first marriage.

17

To support them, she drew welfare and worked as a kidney dialysis technician.

According to Martha Campbell, Diana's sister and a Colfax resident, it was "love at first sight" for Diana. She thought Phillip "was the greatest thing in the world."

After only a few months of dating, Diana decided in January 1987 to move with Phillip to Bakersfield, where he would pay her to nurse his mother, who was dying of cancer. Stephanie, her youngest child, came with them, but the others, Christine and Bryon, went their separate ways. Martha tried to counsel her sister against what she considered a rash move. She quoted Diana as saying, "I know it's only been a few months, but I really love the guy. I know he'll be really good to me. He's got a good, steady job."

Others believe Diana's motives in taking off with Phillip were less pure and that her love for him was expedient at best. Ask Bruno Ricci, an elderly Colfax version of Sam Malone of "Cheers," if they cared the same way about each other; he immediately shakes his head. "It could have been [love] with him, but not her," he told me one night at the tavern.

Diana was notorious at the Shady Glen. Sometimes she would show up with one man and leave with another. "She had a bad habit of being with a person and leaving that person and going home with another person," said Ricci.

She made herself unpopular with other female patrons by going after their escorts. "I don't have anything good to say about her," said one woman. "She was flirtatious with the fellas. It didn't matter if he was yours or anybody else's." Even after she met Phillip, Diana would still see other men when he was out of town.

Ricci thought Diana was looking for a man who could give her "an easy way of life where she didn't have to work." He said Diana was tired of being crammed into the ramshackle, one-bedroom cottage she shared with her children. "She said she wanted a nice house . . . She wanted to have better things than other people. That's why she left [Colfax]."

Another acquaintance in Colfax had a similar impression. Diana "complained about working a lot . . . She just wanted to forget it all and go party all the time." When she had been drinking, Diana would blurt out, "I want a man with money."

* * *

A jury would ponder the same question years later: Was Diana loving and devoted or mercenary and manipulative? Even more puzzling, how could that question even be asked of someone of such apparently righteous pedigree?

Godly Living

Diana was conditioned to be the loyal, dutiful wife and mother. In the world of the fundamentalist Christian church in which she was raised—a world every bit as cloistered as that of the Russian Molokans—she was given very little choice. Like Phillip, when she was finally exposed to the outside world, she fell into a very different life-style that compromised the values of her upbringing. Unlike Phillip, she appeared willing to forget all about her background and be whatever she wanted to be—never mind the consequences.

Diana Jo McCowan was born February 19, 1948, in the Los Angeles suburb of Lynwood, only a few miles south of the Molokans of Boyle Heights. The youngest of the six daughters of James and Josephine McCowan, she was of mixed Scotch-Irish ancestry with a dash of Cherokee Indian. Her parents had moved to California twenty years earlier—James from his family's tobacco farm in Kentucky, and Josephine from Colorado—and had met and married in Tijuana, Mexico.

At Diana's birth, James McCowan was thirty-nine and a salesman for the Triangle Grain Company, responsible for a territory that included part of the San Joaquin Valley. He had an alcohol problem and, under the influence, physically abused his wife. But when Diana was still a toddler, her father experienced a religious rebirth that changed the family's lives.

According to his daughter Kathy Markwell, he was driving through the Valley one day when he picked up a hitchhiker, who testified to him about "baptism in Jesus' name." He went to the church the man attended in Bakersfield, and soon was baptized himself. Josephine told her daughters that he "completely changed and made a good husband." He was also "completely delivered from alcohol when he found the Lord."

After this transformation, McCowan moved his family to the farm town of Visalia, part of his sales territory and sixty miles north of Bakersfield. It was, as Diana later described it, a "quiet, family-oriented community." There, secluded from the fast life of the big city, he set about raising his daughters in the church that had saved him: the United Pentecostal Church.

The UPC, based in the St. Louis, Missouri, area, was formed in 1945 but traces its roots to the great Pentecostal revival at the turn of the century. It shares mainstream Pentecostal doctrine—that the Bible is the "infallible word of God," speaking in tongues is a sign of receiving God's Spirit, and Jesus will come again. It also enforces the austere Pentecostal moral code, which had a particular appeal to people like the McCowans.

Like so many other rural migrants to large industrial cities, they had experienced problems adapting to their new surroundings, to a society in which, as a biographer of Oral Roberts put it, "moral lapses and sexual promiscuity constantly threatened to undermine the family." With its moral code, the UPC offered an alternative to adapting—you set yourself apart from that society.

In recent years, as Pentecostal churches have tried to widen their membership and dispel the "Holy Roller" image, some have loosened the moral ties. But not the UPC. It still maintains a strict separateness in the belief that "moral delinquency plagues every level of society" and "the only effective antidote for sin-enslaved people is the gospel of Jesus Christ."

The church's Articles of Faith include: "We wholeheartedly disapprove of our people indulging in any activities which are not conducive to good Christianity and Godly living, such as theater, dances, mixed bathing, women cutting their hair, make-up, any apparel that immodestly exposes the body, all worldly sports and amusements."

James McCowan, who was known in the family as "Chief," followed this credo to the letter. Roller-skating was taboo because the girls would have to wear pants. So was television because of the evils it supposedly portrayed. The girls could not cut their hair, they could only date after they turned sixteen, and then it had to be a double date. "All the things you'd do as a kid, they were forbidden," a friend of the family said.

If the girls broke the rules, their father applied the biblical adage "Spare the rod and spoil the child." "We got spanked often as children. It seemed like daily to me," Markwell said. "After being married several years, I told my husband that I didn't think he loved me because he didn't spank me."

Diana seemed to fit happily into this environment. "She was a real sweet person. I don't remember her being moody, temperamental, anything like that," said one close school friend. Every Sunday and every Wednesday evening were spent in church, and during the summer, it was off to Bible camp. At high school she was an unremarkable student whose few extracurricular activities included Future Business Leaders of America. In the group's 1964 yearbook portrait, she stands at the end of one row, almost completely obscured by the beehive hairdo of another future business leader.

During her childhood, there was one chink in the Pentecostal armor: her mother. James, who commonly worked over twelve hours a day, wasn't around much of the time. In his absence, Josephine did not crack quite the same whip with the girls. "It was like, 'When Dad's not home, you guys do what you want,' " said Robert Allen, Diana's former brother-in-law.

Quite naturally, that appears to have been even more the case with the baby of the family, Diana, whom they all called "Joey." "Her mom let her do some stuff," recalled the family friend. "She went swimming a few times. Her father wasn't to know this."

Steve Allen, her first husband, put it more forcefully: "If she broke the rules, her mother always covered up for her. She cut her hair one time, and her mother fixed it all up so her dad wouldn't find out." If Diana sneaked out at night, "her mother would cover for her."

"She was different from me," said Martha Campbell, the sister closest to Diana in age. "She was more outgoing. She wasn't afraid to speak out. She'd argue with [her father] at the dinner table [about going out]."

Still, Diana's transgressions were minor, and she stayed on the Pentecostal path. In her senior year she attended Western Apostolic High School, part of a UPC-run facility in Stockton, California, which included a Bible college. There she met

Steve Allen, a student at the college who was three years older than she. They were married on August 25, 1966. Like her sisters before her, she was an eighteen-year-old bride.

It looked like the perfect match. Both Steve's parents were ordained Pentecostal ministers, and he was being groomed to follow in their footsteps. The Allens knew the McCowans from the time both families lived in the Los Angeles area, and Diana's oldest sisters had baby-sat Steve.

According to Steve, his parents voiced one objection about his new wife. Knowing how comfortably off the McCowans were, they were afraid it "would be tough to keep that standard up, to be able to give her everything that her dad had given her. My dad was a body and fender [repair] man . . . We didn't have the kind of money they had."

"We had a comfortable home, bills always paid, a nice car," Josephine McCowan recalled. The home was a three-bedroom stucco tract house amid plum orchards on what was then the southern edge of Visalia. "He made very, very good money," Steve said of his father-in-law. "I remember seeing one of his [annual] bonus checks. It was more than I made the entire year." The girls were taken on regular trips to the area's better stores to buy brand-name clothing. James invested in farmland near Visalia. "I don't know how many thousands of dollars he spent on that property just trying to get it so it would grow something," Steve said.

Steve noticed one thing about Diana from the very beginning—how she would make a beeline for jewelry displays and raptly examine the sparkling wares. "Other women in our organization wouldn't do that. There was always that little draw there."

Even if the church had approved of jewelry, Steve and Diana could not have afforded it in their first years of marriage. He was just starting out as an engineer for an electrical company in Visalia, and they soon had to support two children—Christine, born in 1967, and Bryon, born in 1970. After Bryon's birth, they moved to Paradise in northern California's Gold Country to live with Steve's parents. Steve turned to photography, calling his business Emanon ("no name" backward) and shooting church functions and directories, but he still struggled financially.

On September 18, 1971, a third child, Stephanie Joy, was born in Paradise. The day Stephanie was brought home, Diana looked every bit the model Pentecostal wife and mother. She wore her Sunday best, and her long hair was piled up into a bun, making her look older than her twenty-three years. She cradled the baby and beamed at the camera, showing a set of small, widely spaced teeth that looked like a picket fence.

Within four years, the model image would bear little relation to reality.

Around 1972, the family moved another eighty miles north to the city of Redding. There Steve worked for a lumber firm and assisted the local UPC pastor. When the pastor announced his resignation, Steve was a candidate to succeed him and become a fully ordained minister. But the congregation decided to bring in new blood, and Steve was overlooked.

Disappointed by the rejection, the Allens moved again in 1974, this time to Lynnwood, Washington, a Seattle suburb where Steve's parents were starting a ministry. Soon Steve noticed a distinct change in his wife. "It was just a hundred-eighty-degree turn. It was like hitting a brick wall and bouncing back. She was an entirely different person coming back than she was going." The change was first apparent in a general detachment. "It was, 'Here I am, hello, good-bye.' There wasn't a real interest in anything as far as the family."

Steve Allen, a somewhat dour man with pale blue eyes, thinning hair, and a bass voice, still couldn't explain the transformation during an interview in July 1991. "I can't tell you what started the whole thing because I don't know. She told me later I was dull because I didn't go out and party. But she was just as dull for all those years . . . She was the one that really didn't want to do anything."

The demise of Steve's pastoral prospects may have been partly responsible. The ministry of the Redding church, which had many wealthy, tithing members, would have given Steve and Diana the stability they badly needed. She would have enjoyed the prestige that comes with being the pastor's wife. Presiding over musical evenings, cake bakes, and church socials, Diana could have been a big fish in a small pond. Now there was no ministry: The pond was drained.

"In the first few years of working in the church, you're motivated by someday having your own church," explained Steve's brother Robert, who is an ordained UPC minister. "The dream is there, the push is there . . . I think she just lost all hope of becoming that dream."

On top of that, Diana started working at a K Mart store in Kent, Washington, where she got her first real taste of the outside world. "That was a big thing," Steve said. "She had ambitions there. She hadn't worked there very long, and they made her a department manager." She would work until late in the evening at the store—or at least that's what her husband presumed she was doing.

Dwylene Allen, Robert's wife, recalled Diana giving her a tour of the K Mart and telling her there was "a lot of hanky-panky going on at the store." Diana also told Debra Brown, the family's baby-sitter at the time, that senior managers at K Mart expected female employees with managerial ambitions to sleep with them.

That sort of atmosphere may have unleashed her vanity. Her features were somewhat plain—close-set brown eyes, thin lips, rather prominent nose, and auburn hair. She was petite, only five foot three, but her legs were short in relation to her torso. She looked like a small-town librarian or a game show contestant. But Brown recalled her saying "she knew she was very pretty. She wanted other people to think she was pretty."

Said her second husband: "She had a hang-up about wanting to be told how beautiful she was."

Diana's daughter Stephanie had the simplest explanation for her transformation. "I believe she did it because she wanted to break free from the Pentecostal life. She wanted to experience things . . . It was more curiosity than anything. I think she just wanted to try it, see what it was like out there."

In 1975 Diana made a bid for freedom. She asked Steve for a divorce, telling him she had been having an affair with a sailor. But Steve, who was still in love with his wife, refused to give her the divorce. "I can remember walking into my dad's room and he was kneeling by the water bed and he was crying and he was praying," Stephanie said, recalling an early memory. "He was crying because he didn't want my mom to go. I believe he really did [love her]."

Steve and Diana sought counseling from a UPC pastor, but that didn't help much. According to Steve, the next five years were a roller coaster. "It would do just fine for a while, come back down, go back up." And when Diana came back down, she made no secret of it.

"I'd see her come home with different guys," her son, Bryon, said, recalling his childhood. "It was very clear to me what was going on. She'd pull right up in the middle of the driveway, give the guy a kiss as my dad's standing on the front porch watching her."

Diana would later say that she did not begin drinking until her second marriage. But Steve said that, during the roller coaster period, she drank heavily and frequented various taverns. When she did not come home after the bars closed at night, Steve would go looking for her.

"I'd lay [at home] and wait and wait. Finally, two-thirty or so, I'd get up and go the route I figured she'd take to try to find the car. Most of the time I'd find her on the road coming back; sometimes I didn't find her at all. More than once I'd find the car parked behind the tavern. Nobody around. Usually I'd just head home because I figured she'd be back tomorrow. She'd gone off with somebody."

On one occasion, Diana boasted to Steve about a man she had gone home with and about how he had "this beautiful house down on [Puget Sound] and all about how big and beautiful this place was."

Diana's open dissatisfaction with Steve extended to complaining about their financial straits. "She used to say things like, 'It's so tiring not having any money,' " said Dwylene Allen. "On holidays she would ask Mom Allen to take her shopping, and Mom Allen always bought everything."

Diana would unfavorably compare her situation to that of her sisters. Colleen and Betty were married to affluent businessmen and lived in tidy suburban ranch-style homes; Margaret was a minister's wife. "Look at Bill, he makes this much money," she would say to family members, referring to Betty's husband. "Steve, he can't even hold a job."

In 1977 Steve was hired as an engineer by Boeing, the aviation giant, but his professional advancement came too late to save the marriage. On May 12, 1980, the couple filed jointly for a divorce, which became final three months later. "I could see no light at the end of the tunnel. I was just worn out with it," Steve explained.

Something Diana told him during one of their discussions about divorce may also have influenced his thinking. According to Steve's sworn testimony, he had just mentioned that he wasn't at all happy about getting divorced.

"You're lucky you're still alive," Diana replied. "I tried to hire two men to kill you."

"Where would you find somebody to do that?" Steve asked, incredulous.

"I go to places where these guys are at and I tried to find two men to do the job. I offered them five hundred dollars each to do the job, and they turned me down."

He took his wife seriously. A woman who flaunted her affairs was capable of killing him, he thought. He went so far as to drop his wife as the beneficiary of his life insurance policies, which, depending on the circumstances of his death, were worth as much as $250,000. The children became the new beneficiaries.

Steve and Diana never discussed the matter again. But Diana allegedly couldn't resist telling somebody else that divorce was not her only way out of the marriage.

Shocking Dwylene

Dwylene Allen was hardly Diana's confidante. Apart from anything else, they rarely saw each other, living most of the time some 150 miles apart. But Diana had this habit of dropping the most personal of bombshells in her sister-in-law's lap, and she didn't seem to care if Dwylene kept them secret or not.

These confidences didn't come very often, but when they did, they were major ones. They usually exploded at family gatherings when the sisters-in-law were alone in the kitchen and Dwylene would ask Diana how things were going. Then came the bombshell. If Dwylene said she must be kidding, Diana stood firm. "There was no shame," Dwylene recalled. "It was never like a joke. It was always matter-of-fact, like she just informed me."

Diana would say things like, "Steve and I are having trouble. It's bad. I'm going to bars." Or she'd say how she didn't love Steve and then boast of his sexual prowess.

One time, toward the end of Diana's marriage to Steve, she and Dwylene got onto the subject of an abortion Diana had recently had. Dwylene, whose eyes boggle at her memories of Diana, said her sister-in-law asked her, "You know why I had that abortion, don't you?"

"Yeah, you had medical problems."

Diana laughed. "No, it was a black baby."

"Oh, come on," Dwylene replied, her mouth falling open.

"It's the honest truth. I didn't want it."

"What are you saying?"

"You know. I've been running around. I've been to bed with all kinds of guys."

"You mean, you went to bed with a black guy?"

"Sure I did."

"Joey, stop, stop, please stop!" Dwylene gasped. "The reason you took it was because it was a black baby?"

"That's right. I don't need any more babies."

"So you could kill the little thing just because?"

"I wouldn't want that thing."

"You're so cold."

Diana laughed again. "I hate kids anyway."

(According to Steve, Diana told him after their divorce that the baby's father was black.)

Maybe she just wanted to shock Dwylene with these "confessions"—which wouldn't be very difficult. A native of Mississippi and seven years younger than Diana, Dwylene seems untouched by the evils of the outside world. With her cherubic features, she looks like she has just flown in from a Renaissance fresco. "It was like she would try to shock me out of my wits," Dwylene said. "She thought that was so funny. If she could see my eyes get big and my mouth drop, she just thought that was so cool. This naive sister-in-law of hers, that's the way she felt about me."

Dwylene would relay Diana's revelations to her husband, but that's as far as they went. She didn't feel close enough to Steve to tell him, and as for his parents, it might be construed as trying to compete for their affection. Mom Allen, in particular, seemed fond of Diana. "I didn't feel they would have believed me. It would have been like I was trying to get their approval over Diana . . . I think she knew I wouldn't dare [tell Mom Allen]."

Dwylene also liked Diana herself. "She was very likable. She never gave any of us any reason not to like her . . . She had a very winning personality."

Steve Allen isn't so sure that Diana was simply playing with Dwylene's mind. She wanted a divorce, and maybe this was her way of showing the family that the fault wasn't all on his side. "There'd be no reason for a mind game," he said. "She's not a person to just do things frivolously. There's got to be a reason behind what she does."

Diana saved her most startling revelation for a family celebration of Thanksgiving in November 1979. The scene was the home she and Steve were then renting from the UPC in

Puyallup, a town in the shadow of Mount Rainier. They were playing host to his parents, brother, and sister-in-law. The guests had come up from Portland, Oregon, where they were all assisting Steve's uncle in the ministry of a UPC church. Robert and Dwylene brought their six-month-old baby.

Dwylene, then well aware of her hosts' marital problems, noticed they didn't sit by each other during the meal and didn't talk to each other much. "It was a little bit strained, but nobody made a big deal of it."

After the meal, Diana and Dwylene went into the kitchen to do the dishes while the others sat down in the living room. While Dwylene washed, Diana rinsed. And they looked out the window and talked. The following is Dwylene's recollection of the conversation as recounted in court and an interview for this book:

"How are you and Steve getting on?" Dwylene ventured.

Diana shrugged. "Well, I found somebody to knock him off."

"What?" Dwylene could have toppled into the sink, she was so surprised. Diana repeated herself.

"Where would you find somebody to do that?" Dwylene said, trying to compose herself.

"Oh, at a bar," Diana continued as if she were discussing a conspiracy to buy a dress, not commit a murder.

"How much would you have to pay someone to do that?"

"Oh, five hundred bucks."

"You are kidding. You have got to be kidding."

"No, I am not."

Dwylene paused. "Why would you do something like that?"

"I don't love him."

"If you don't love somebody, well, good grief, just divorce him. But have him killed?"

Diana just shrugged her shoulders. "Why don't you just leave him?" Dwylene asked.

Again, a shrug. Dwylene looked out the window, struggling to think of what to ask next. Everything was quiet. It was as if Diana was waiting for the next question. Dwylene's heart pounded.

"Why would you have him killed?"

"Oh, insurance."

Diana mentioned a figure, but to this day, Dwylene cannot remember it.

That night, as they lay in bed at the Puyallup house, Dwylene told her husband what Diana had said. Robert was skeptical. "Oh, she wouldn't do that!"

"I didn't say she would, but that's what she told me."

They decided not to go to the police. They weren't going to tell Steve or his parents either. Instead, they would wait until the next family gathering at Christmas, and Dwylene would ask Diana about the state of her plot. "She wouldn't be able to do anything before then," Robert presumed. "She couldn't possibly do anything that fast."

The family celebrated that Christmas at the senior Allens' in Portland. Again, Diana and Dwylene were doing the dishes. After Mom Allen left the kitchen, Dwylene whispered, "Are you still going to go through with that?"

"No."

"How come?"

"It wasn't worth it."

Dwylene put the dishes down and hugged her sister-in-law. "I'm so glad to hear that," she gushed.

The Devil on One Shoulder

When Diana divorced for the first time in 1980, she did not suffer any religious repercussions. Financial and custodial matters were her main headaches.

The property settlement was straightforward: They had no property. Diana did not ask for alimony. She and Steve divided up assets worth a total of only $5,655. She got a 1971 Ford pickup, two horses and a horse trailer, and some household goods. Value of her share: $3,125.

The custody matter was more complex. According to Steve, when she first asked for a divorce in 1975, she didn't want any of the kids. Now they agreed she would have Stephanie, and Steve would take the others. However, in a clause of the original divorce agreement filed in a Tacoma, Washington, court, Diana requested custody of her older daughter, Christine. "If Christine should decide to live with her father, I wish custody of Stephanie," she wrote.

Strangely, Steve did not remember that clause when interviewed for this book. But judging by family members' recollections of Diana's relationships with each of her children, it would have been quite consistent for her to make Christine her first choice.

According to family members, Christine was the only child to whom she would demonstrate natural maternal affection. "Diana never had time for Stephanie or Bryon," Dwylene Allen said. "They both irritated her. She would say [of Bryon], 'I can't stand that kid.' "

She continued: "Stephanie would try to sit by her mom, and her mom would shoo her away—'Go on, go play.' But if ever Christine came to her mother, her mom would hug her, hold her, talk to her. She would say, 'This is Mama's favorite.' "

According to Robert Allen, Diana only paid attention to her younger children in return for favors. "They'd come to her wanting attention. She'd say, 'Why don't you get me a glass of water?'" When they got it, "she'd give them a hug and they'd be on their way. It was totally that way all the time. She never did that to Christine."

Years later, Bryon Allen still smarted when asked about his mother's attitude toward him as a child. "She could always talk to Chris, but if I tried to strike up a conversation with her, it was like, 'You don't know what you're talking about.'"

He recalled how "she would always go out of her way to put new clothes on Chris's back. She'd give Stephanie the hand-me-downs from Chris. She'd go to a secondhand store to get me clothes. I went to school in checkered pants and fucking flowered shirts."

Stephanie did not recall such favoritism, which may reflect her age at the time. She did know that her mother "didn't want to leave any of us. I think she took me because I was the youngest. I always felt special because of it."

Diana did not have much security to offer her nine-year-old daughter after the divorce. The child support from Steve was seventy-five dollars a month. She had to sell Stephanie's horse to raise cash, promising that she would pay her back. Her desperation is apparent from her next move—with Stephanie, she took off for her parents' new home in backwoods Kentucky.

After retiring and selling the Visalia house, "Chief" McCowan had revived his farming dream and moved back to the family homestead. "I remember the big tomatoes and not being able to wear bathing suits because my grandparents were real strict," Stephanie said. "I went to a little school with a bunch of country kids."

It must have been a bracing experience for Diana back in the world of her parents, and it didn't last long. Before winter set in, she and Stephanie returned to Washington, where she started building a new life with a new man.

One story has Diana saying that Steve Allen's replacement better have a beard, hair, and a motorcycle. Garald Wymore, known as Gary, fit those criteria perfectly.

Wymore, who is shorter but more hirsute than Allen, met Diana at a Puyallup tavern. Noticing his pumpkin-colored bike outfit, she asked him if he had a motorcycle. The next day, he took her out for a ride. The forty-year-old Tacoma native became a regular escort even before her divorce was final and while she was still living with Steve. He would chat with Steve when he came by to pick Diana up.

On July 30, 1981, Gary and Diana married, one month after his divorce from his first wife. They agreed that the first five years would be a struggle, at least financially. That soon proved accurate.

Not only did Gary have to support his new family on his salary as a trucker for a company that processed slaughterhouse waste, he was also paying four hundred dollars a month support for two children from his first marriage. The strain was such that he illegally supplemented his income with unemployment benefits. In December 1982 he was charged with drawing $3,450 in benefits during a six-month period starting just before he married Diana. The following May, he was placed on ten years probation.

But a report on Gary filed by his probation officer painted a rosy portrait of his marriage to Diana. It noted that the couple, who were living in the Puyallup area, were attending a fundamentalist church and receiving ministerial counseling. "Gary and Diana have worked hard to avoid some of the pitfalls of their former marriages and at this time are getting along 'beautifully.' "

"We were very happy when we were in the church," Gary said. Diana would think nothing of helping those in distress. "I'd come home and she'd say, 'Gary, there are some people right now that are really hurting. I think we ought to go over there and pray for them.' So we did. She had a gift of helping other people." Gary's sister recalled how when she and her husband were separated and she had no money for Christmas presents, it was Diana who came around and helped out. His daughter Stacy Stewart said Diana made a dress for her, and took her shopping when she was sick.

While she was married to Gary, Diana started to use this gift vocationally. She completed a three-week course in Seattle to qualify as a kidney dialysis technician.

But as soon as she drifted back into the darker corners of the outside world, she turned into a different person. "She'd go to church and be all this Christian and then turn around and just be the opposite," said Kathy Johnson, a friend of Gary and Diana's at the time.

Gary Wymore graphically expressed the dichotomy: "She's got the Devil sitting on one shoulder and she's got God sitting on the other."

By late 1983 Diana was back in the bars, and Gary was, like Steve before him, having to drag her out of them. When he found her, she would introduce him to the man who had just been buying her drinks. She used to tell him, "I never bought drinks. Men always bought me drinks."

Gary suspected one man was having an affair with his wife. One day, as he went to fish Diana out of a bar, he confronted the man outside. The man denied sleeping with Diana. Two friends joined him. "Is there a problem here? Do you want us to take care of it?" they asked him.

Gary wasn't about to step down. "You guys just get back in there and mind your own business."

A fight was averted. Later when he asked Diana what she was doing there, she replied: "I just stopped to have a couple of drinks before I come home."

It wasn't only Gary who experienced this side of Diana. His daughter Stacy lived with Gary and Diana for about six months when she was seventeen years old. She became aware that her stepmother was going to bars after some of Diana's collection of Hummel dolls disappeared from the house. According to Stacy, Diana told her she was selling the dolls to a man she knew at a bar. "She said, 'Don't tell your dad I'm doing this. We need the money.'" Stacy said neither she nor her father saw any of the proceeds.

Then there was the time in the fall of 1983 when Gary's sister and twenty-two-year-old niece took a four-day trip with Diana to central Washington to pick apples. According to her companions, Diana flirted with the Mexican laborers in the orchards and arranged for the men to take her and the niece out drinking. Gary's sister had to forcibly stop them from going. During the trip, Diana also regaled them with the story of how she once picked up two truckers and had sex with them all night in their rig. (She told Gary the same story before they were even married.)

Diana did not stop at merely cheating on Gary. As with her

first husband, she allegedly schemed against him.

According to Gary, toward the end of the marriage, Mike Banauch, a friend and coworker, told him of an offer he got from Diana. She would pay Banauch seventy-five dollars to beat Gary up. At the time, Gary didn't take his friend seriously, so he did not confront Diana with it.

Interviewed by police in December 1990, Banauch stated that he had "never been approached or solicited by Diana or anyone else to make any attempts on Gary Wymore's life or anyone else's life." There was no reference to any plan to beat Gary up.

If that scheme is difficult to substantiate, there was another that Diana allegedly concocted during her marriage to Gary that appears more convincing. That one involved a house, a will, and a life insurance policy.

Diana's idea was allegedly to enlist Gary's sister, Donna Hasenbalg, to persuade him to take his first wife, Janice, off his will and life insurance. Diana would be the new beneficiary. She also wanted to find a way to make Janice lose the house she had shared with Gary and which she had won in their divorce settlement. If her sister-in-law could talk Gary into going along with all this, Diana would split any profits with her.

That is what Hasenbalg told a defense investigator in February 1990. (She declined to be interviewed for this book.) She also said she notified Gary and his first wife of the plot and refused to have anything more to do with Diana. The scheme was "so indicative of Diana's amorality in general that this witness could no longer abide being associated with her," the investigator reported.

Gary said he had never heard of the plot when I asked him about it. He did, however, recall Diana pressing him to make her the beneficiary of his life insurance and his will. He refused, he said, because he didn't trust her. "She was pretty upset I didn't have it changed."

The whole thing is convoluted in the extreme, and it is not clear how Diana could have profited unless she also meant to get rid of Gary. But complexity was a hallmark of Diana's schemes.

"She always felt she was very clever," Steve Allen told me. "If it was buying something on time or whatever, she always felt she could come up with a clever way of getting it done. Not necessarily illegal, but a clever way of doing something. I can't think of one of them that made any sense.

"She was not a brilliant person when it came to being able to rationally lay out something . . . She could never see the end . . . It was, 'Build this fence right here.' 'If I build the fence there, fine, how am I going to put the tractor through there?' 'Well, I don't know.'

"That's the kind of approach she had . . . It was an everyday thing. She'd put an elaborate idea together but never looked to see what the outcome was going to be. She couldn't say, 'Oh yeah, but if I do that, this is what's going to happen.'"

Moreover, her scheme involving Gary's property is consistent with her continuing dissatisfaction over her material circumstances—a feeling all too familiar from her first marriage.

One incident was particularly revealing. Wes Johnson, one of Gary's friends, and his wife, Kathy, had built a new home on the west shore of Puget Sound. Their high-school-age sons, however, did not want to disrupt their education by moving. "I'm torn, all upset over this," Kathy recalled. "So I move back to my old house. She [Diana] didn't think that was right. She said, 'This is a beautiful house. Why would you want to go back there for them?'"

In addition to finances and philandering, there was another source of tension in the marriage of Gary and Diana.

Gary's probation report of May 1983 described Stephanie, then eleven years old, as "very bright, alert and personable." With freckled cheeks, almond-shaped blue eyes, and an infectious laugh, she seemed as wholesome as a Washington apple. Her mother's pet name for her was "Snuffy." "She was the most adorable and sweet little thing," Dwylene Allen said.

The probation officer also stated: "Gary's wife reports that he and the stepdaughter get along quite well and that the daughter respects his authority." But it was not as simple as that. Gary found himself unable to have much paternal influence on Stephanie, largely because of her strange, symbiotic relationship with her mother.

On one level, Diana was sometimes indifferent to her daughter, and when she did exercise supervision, did so arbitrarily.

According to Gary, if Diana wanted to be alone with him, she would tell Stephanie to leave. "You're going to your dad's," she would order.

"I don't really want to," Stephanie would reply.

"It doesn't make any difference what you want. You're going." And so Stephanie would troop off to her father's.

Donna Hasenbalg remembered that things always had to be done Diana's way. She wrote in a court document: "Stephanie was reading a book one night in bed, became sleepy and laid the book on the floor. The next morning Diana became extremely angry because she was vacuming [sic] and the book was on the floor.

"Diana was still angry days later when they came to visit. I finally asked her what was the big deal, one lousy book on Stephanie's own bedroom floor. She became even more angry and said that Stephanie knows the rules and that ... the book on the floor interferred [sic] with her vacuming [sic] schedule and was a deliberate act of disobeidence [sic] and disrepect [sic]."

On the other hand, if Gary tried to reprimand Stephanie, Diana would protect her. He recalled an incident when he saw his stepdaughter get off the school bus with a cigarette in her hand. This was not long after he had been assured that she had stopped smoking. Stephanie looked up, saw Gary, and threw the cigarette in the ditch.

When Gary got home, he found Stephanie standing on a chair in his and Diana's bedroom, smoking a cigarette out of the open window. "What are you doing smoking in our room?" he demanded.

"I didn't smoke in your room."

As Gary pressed her, Stephanie changed her story. "I really wasn't in the room. I had my head out the window."

Gary accused her of lying to him, but Diana stepped in. "That's only half a lie," she said.

"Excuse me, what's half a lie?" Gary exclaimed.

Similarly, Stephanie would come to her mother's defense when Gary thought Diana was deceiving him. "On more than one occasion, Stephanie lied to me in an attempt to cover up for her mother and protect her from being found out in a lie."

Stephanie admitted as much to me. "I made excuses for my mom a lot. I'd cover up stuff. She'd cover for me a lot."

For example, she would tell Gary that her mother had been shopping "when really maybe she was doing something else. But nothing major like she was out with somebody and didn't want Gary to know."

"Why did you do that?" I asked her.

"She's my mom," Stephanie replied matter-of-factly. "She asked me to. Sometimes I would just do it because I didn't want to hear them fight, and sometimes I would just do it to be doing it, and sometimes it was for things, like an outfit or going to movies with my friends."

"Do you think it was manipulative?"

"I don't quite understand why she had to hide things all the time. In a sense I do believe it was."

In Gary's view, the mother-daughter relationship was "one of exchange of favors. If Stephanie would do what Diana wanted, she [Stephanie] would be allowed to go do the things she wanted to do." Diana, he felt, was teaching her daughter "how to lie and manipulate people."

The marriage finally collapsed in October 1984, only three and a half years after it began. Gary and Diana filed for divorce, and it became final the following February.

From the settlement, Diana emerged no better off than she had done with Steve. Gary kept a 1970 pickup, his motorcycle, and a quarter horse. Diana got household goods including a water bed and a freezer, and a 1973 Ford sedan.

After this divorce, Diana did not have a new man waiting in the wings to take care of her and Stephanie. Nor did she have an extensive network of family or friends to fall back on. The only one of her sisters she appears to have been close to was Martha—the only one to have also experienced divorce and renounced some of the church's taboos. All Diana and Stephanie had now was each other. Their mutual dependency could only intensify.

During the first year or so after the divorce, Diana tried to reconcile with her ex-husband at least three times. Each time they broke up, she would move all the way to Placer County in northern California, living mostly in the county seat of Auburn, near Martha. "Several times, she came here when they weren't getting on," Martha recalled. "I wouldn't have any notice of it until she was here." When a new round of talks with Gary beckoned, she would pack up the car and Stephanie and drive back to Washington.

The last attempt at reconciliation, in the winter of 1985–86, illustrates the deep flaws in Diana's relationship with Gary, and Stephanie's role as her mother's aide.

This time, Diana and Stephanie joined Gary in Auburn, Washington, a town between Tacoma and Seattle where he rented a home. According to Gary, Diana begged him to remarry her. He told her no, he couldn't trust her. She promised him things would be better.

After they had been together about three weeks, Gary said, he got back from work one day, and Diana wasn't home. He quickly found her in a bar. "This is it," he told her. "I'm going to move back in with my son." He had paid the next month's rent, but after that, she was on her own.

"Gary, you're making a big mistake," she replied.

Gary did move in with his son, but three days later, decided to stop by and see how Diana was doing. Again, she wasn't there. Stephanie was, baby-sitting for a neighbor. "Where's your mom?" he asked her.

"She's staying in Federal Way," Stephanie said, referring to a nearby community.

"I'd like to talk to her."

"Well, Mom really doesn't want to see you now. She'll be back in a couple of weeks."

It turned out Diana was in Hawaii, and Stephanie had covered for her again. She had been taken to the islands by Dick Corey, a businessman over twenty years older than she whom she dated after her divorce from Gary and who had tickets for the NFL's Pro Bowl game in Honolulu.

When she got back, she made no secret of the trip, telling Gary that she didn't have to pay for anything. Corey even bought her clothes before they left. "I like the color of money and I like the glitter," Gary quoted Diana as saying. "You really don't have anything to offer me. You're getting old, you're getting gray, you're getting fat. You don't have nothing."

"Nothing Was Perfect"

Phillip Bogdanoff was two years younger than Gary, his hair was still a golden brown, and his body was muscular and well toned. He also had a lot more than nothing.

When he met Diana Wymore in the summer of 1986, he had nearly twenty years of experience at Caltrans. Although his career as a state engineer was not a recipe for spectacular wealth, he had built a tidy nest egg. He had joint title to the rustic home that he had shared with his second wife in Oroville. He was collecting rent from property in Shingle Springs and Bakersfield. The property in Bakersfield was the house next door to his parents', which he and Barbara had acquired in 1983 for thirty-nine thousand dollars. In January 1986 she quitclaimed her interest to him. Phillip also owned several vehicles, including no fewer than three trailers.

He couldn't have come along at a better time for Diana. Physically, the years were closing in fast as she edged toward forty. People who knew her then remember her as being somewhat portly. (Gary Wymore said she reached 150 pounds during their marriage.) Anything over 130 pounds on her petite frame would threaten her figure. The weight also went to her face and neck. A double chin was looming. Possibly because of her alcohol intake, her fleshy nose was taking on a bulbous shape.

Financially, she had a lot more cause for concern. Diana was now one of a growing horde of single mothers, one of the forgotten have-nots of the Reagan-era economic boom. With no longer even a foothold on the American dream, she had fallen into a poverty-level world of subsistence on welfare

programs with strange acronyms. Like about a third of single
mothers in Placer County at the time, she was living around
the poverty line.

During the first year after her divorce from Gary, Diana
worked as a part-time dialysis technician. The duties of such
technicians involve hooking up patients to the machines and
monitoring them. Under the supervision of a nurse, they can
draw blood. However, they earn about half as much as a
registered nurse—these days, they start at around eight dollars an hour at the type of clinic where Diana worked. Her
son, Bryon, recalled her getting around five dollars an hour
in 1986.

She was forced to supplement her income with benefits
from the AFDC (Aid to Families with Dependent Children)
program. The average benefit in Placer County in June 1986
was less than $450 a month. Her child support from Steve
Allen was still only $75 a month. She was sued by a grocery
store in September 1985 for bouncing a check worth $103.39.
A minuscule amount, but it suggests how little of a financial
cushion she had. That was when she only had Stephanie to
worry about.

By the summer of 1986, according to her sister Martha, she
was working full time in dialysis. But now she had an additional burden. The one-bedroom cottage in Colfax—hardly bigger
than a garage—that she shared with Stephanie became home
to her two older children. Christine shared the bedroom with
her mother, while Stephanie and Bryon made do with daybeds
in the living room.

"I don't remember being really hard up until Colfax when
we had our own place," Stephanie said. "Then she [Diana] had
my brother and sister come live with us, and that was crazy.
She had a lot of responsibility at the time that she couldn't
handle."

Why Christine and Bryon made the move from Washington is
a matter of dispute. Steve Allen's version suggests another of
his ex-wife's manipulations.

He said Martha Campbell called to ask him "to do something because Stephanie was in danger. Diana was bringing
men home with her from these bars who were not the most
desirable characters in the world." (Martha told me she never

made such a call, but Stephanie corroborated it.) Steve hired an attorney to explore suing for custody of Stephanie.

Then Stephanie called him to say "she was ready to move up because one of these men had indeed tried to molest her, and she was afraid for her life." But she stayed only two or three weeks before returning to her mother. Her siblings followed her. Steve said he found out later that Diana had dispatched Stephanie to Washington "with the sole purpose of trying to convince the other two children to move down to California because her mother wanted them down there with her." She wanted Bryon—a hulking sixteen-year-old over six feet tall— to protect her from any importunate men.

Bryon did not have to use his muscle. "There was never any big problem," he said. A few times he intercepted men coming up to the house whom Diana didn't want to see, but "there was never really anything that got out of hand."

There shouldn't have been much of a problem with strange men because, by this time, Phillip was already on the scene. Bryon remembered meeting him a couple of days after arriving in California. "My mom said, 'This is Phil. He's a good friend of mine.'"

Diana dated several other men while she was in Colfax. Bruno Ricci, the bartender, recalled her having "quite an affair" with a man he could only identify as Jim. Even after she met Phillip, he was not the only man in her life. Around August 1986, she took off with her children for a few days in Reno, Nevada, where she had arranged to meet Dick Corey. According to Bryon, she and her old beau from Washington shared a suite on the top floor of a casino-hotel. Corey "gave her two thousand dollars in playing chips the first day we got there," Bryon said.

Phillip also spent much of that fall with his estranged wife Barbara as they flirted with a reconciliation. But after Thanksgiving, the romance between Phillip and Diana does appear to have picked up steam. Diana would often stay overnight at Phillip's trailer in the Shady Glen park. Bryon Allen saw "a spark there, something there between them . . . They just got along real well. It really looked like she was enjoying herself."

Diana's sister Martha only recalled meeting Phillip a couple of months before they left town together. But her impressions were not favorable.

"She'd bring him over here. He'd say one little thing, and she'd jump. 'Do this, do that' . . . He never came here without a beer . . . He had this violent jealousy thing. I could see it. I told her, 'You go with this guy, you'll have nothing but trouble.' The look in his eyes is what it was. You could see a meanness."

Diana's children did not see Phillip that way. He was a friend, an unpretentious guy ready to have a good time. He smoked pot and would compete with the kids' friends to see whose truck stereo was the loudest. "Him and I got along great," Bryon said. "He'd let me drive the four-by-four, and we'd go up in the mountains."

"I liked him," said Stephanie. "He taught me how to drive his truck. I had a great time. He always knew how to push the right buttons to make you like him." After a pause, she added, "At the beginning."

According to Stephanie, Phillip also helped her mother financially while they were in Colfax. With Bryon working at a restaurant-lounge, the family was now just about making ends meet. "It was tough getting by, but we made it," Bryon said. "I have to say it was one of the happiest points in my life."

But his fifteen-year-old sister wasn't so happy. And the closer her mother and Phillip seemed to get, the unhappier she seemed to get.

Stephanie had been showing signs of waywardness for some time. Martha Campbell said her niece ran with "a bunch of rough kids" when she lived down the road in Auburn. She was caught stealing fake fingernails from a store in Auburn in 1985 and was fined three hundred dollars. Diana's reaction was muted. "My mom told me, 'There went your money to go to your dad's this summer.' I was struck; it killed me. She wasn't all that mad, but she knew how to push my buttons by telling me I couldn't go to my dad's, because I wanted to see him, my brother, and my sister."

This sort of behavior was no doubt influenced by all the disruption Stephanie had experienced since her mother's second divorce. "I didn't like being moved back and forth," she said. "It was real hard for me in school." She would complain to her mother about moving. "I was never an up-and-go type of person."

But the rebelliousness continued after the family became relatively settled in Colfax. Stephanie was now partying with an older crowd—one of her boyfriends was twenty-four. She was drinking and experimenting with drugs, including marijuana and crank. "I was a little crankster there . . . I knew people who made [crank] and sold it, so I always had access."

"She was on [crank] when I got there," said her brother, Bryon. "It wasn't so much the crowd [she was in], it was just the town itself. Everybody and their brother does something there . . . Pot is like a way of life. It was just something we all fell into. I had it in a lot worse way than either of my sisters did."

Stephanie told me she was reacting against her mother's desertion and what she considered the complete lack of a normal family life.

"My brother and sister were living with us, and she wasn't paying me no attention anymore. She was never home. In a way, I didn't like the way I was living. I wanted to be a kid again, I wanted to be normal. You've got your brother and sister living with you in this little one-bedroom house. Your mother's never home, she's always with Phillip. She comes home after work, fixes us dinner, leaves, and comes back the next day."

Stephanie resented having to clean up after her brother. "He'd lay on the bed in the living room and smoke cigarettes and throw them on the floor." Diana would tell him to do his chores, but she was never there to supervise anything. "I just really rebelled against the fact that nothing was perfect. It was all a mess."

The strangest thing was Diana's attitude toward Stephanie's behavior. Without actually condoning it, she seems to have done little to correct or reprimand it.

In fact, she allowed the cottage to become a popular teen hangout. "There were always people over there all the time," said a friend of both Christine's and Stephanie's. There was a party at the house "just about every night." Bryon recalled a Fourth of July party attended by over one hundred teenagers and liberally supplied with alcohol and drugs. When Diana came home during the party, all she said as she waded through the milling, drunken hordes, was, "Where's my beer?"

Diana encouraged the drinking and partying "although she made occasional pretenses not to like the drugs," Bryon said. Both Stephanie and Christine were sexually active, and his mother "couldn't seem to do anything about it."

Phillip didn't set much of an example, either. In August he was arrested for driving under the influence near Colfax. He was sentenced to probation and five days in jail, to be served as part of a weekend work program.

Martha Campbell believes that Diana simply spoiled her youngest daughter. "She probably felt guilty about moving her back and forth. She thought she could make up for it by letting her get away with things parents normally don't. It got to the point where Joey lost control."

Alternatively, Diana's attitude could just be a further variation on the theme of maternal indifference that others had observed while she lived in Washington. Doris Moreheart, a friend of Stephanie's from Auburn, recalled that Diana "was never around. Every time I was with Stephanie, she was either here or I was at her house, and her mother was not around . . . They were never together, ever."

The problems with Stephanie exploded into the open at the end of 1986 when her mother started talking about breaking up the family and moving away with Phillip.

According to Martha, she had Diana, Phillip, and Stephanie over for dinner on Christmas Eve. In the middle of the meal, Stephanie got up to say she was going out. "Sit down, you're not going anyplace," Phillip objected.

"You can't tell me what to do," Stephanie shot back. "You're not my father."

Furious at Diana's inability to control her daughter, Phillip stormed out of the house.

A few days later, Stephanie had a major fight with her mother. One issue was Bryon's laziness. "I told her it was either Bryon or me, he had to go or I was leaving, that I just couldn't handle it anymore," Stephanie recalled. The other problem was Phillip—"he was taking my mother away from me. She would rather be with him than come home and be a mother to me." Stephanie wanted to stay in Colfax and live with friends, not leave with her mother and Phillip.

Thinking she was messed up on drugs, Diana called the police. That prompted Stephanie to jump out the window. As police searched in vain for her, she spent a week living in a car with a drug dealer before returning home.

Diana and Phillip proceeded with their plans. They would take Stephanie with them to Bakersfield, where his mother was terminally ill and where he would pay Diana fourteen hundred dollars a month to nurse her—almost certainly more than she was getting from dialysis. As for Diana's other kids, Christine would move in with her boyfriend in Colfax; Bryon would have to go back to his father in Washington.

The memory of the family breakup infuriates Bryon today. "My mom very politely put it to me that it would be best if I went back to my dad's. The next thing I know, I'm on a bus back home. She said, 'We're moving to Bakersfield. Pack your shit; you're going to your dad's.'

"I was hot. I wanted to beat the shit out of everything I saw, including her and Phillip."

Whatever the emotional fallout, Diana had made her decision to start a new life with Phillip. She and Stephanie left the rolling, piney Sierra foothills for the arid checkerboard plains of the southern San Joaquin Valley, where Phillip was raised. As they left, the Placer County district attorney charged her with bouncing another sixty-five dollars worth of checks.

PART TWO

The Town

*Don't go, I say, if you've got any brains,
You'll stay far away from the San Joaquin plains.
—Anonymous nineteenth-century ballad*

If any place in California could serve as a study in paradox, it would be Bakersfield, the seat of Kern County and the hub of the southern San Joaquin Valley.

Far from being a California paradise, it is one of the state's most notorious eyesores. Shut off from the coast's cooling breezes, it swelters for most of the year in a glaring heat. During the winter, the landscape is often shrouded for days in the funereal "tule" fog. Yet the city has exercised an attraction for migrants from all over the world as powerful as any other area of the state. Its rate of population growth during the 1980s was more than twice that of the state as a whole.

Its appeal has made Bakersfield a melting pot of dozens of ethnic groups. Yet it is one of the most racially segregated cities in the state.

Bakersfield prides itself on its industriousness, conservatism, and "family" values. "We respect and love America, its flags and symbols," Mayor Donald Hart said in the late 1970s. "We believe in paternalism, a strong family . . . and the merits of good old hard work." In 1990 it was voted an All-America City by the National Civic League. Yet the city has crime, poverty, and unemployment rates well above the state average.

In residential neighborhoods, a common sight is a trim stucco bungalow with a manicured front lawn, next door to a ramshackle frame cottage whose tenant has turned the front yard into a dump for old sofas, kitchen appliances, and beaten-up automobiles.

Bakersfield has maintained this dual image almost from its inception. Colonel Thomas Baker, who founded the city

51

in 1869, marveled at its potential: "This is God's country. Someday, it will be filled with happy homes . . . The place is rich in future possibilities." But one early observer wrote of Bakersfield: "In summer, a cloud of dust . . . and in winter knee-deep in mud. Flies, flies, mud and dust. Board sidewalks, saloons, men at tables, odor of beer, cards, chips, gold, expectoration, sawdust, cuspidors." During the oil boom at the turn of the century, it became known as "the worst in the West for prostitution, gambling, drunkenness and vice."

The themes of promise and ugliness, of hard work and hard play, resounded in the experience of the city's most celebrated wave of migrants. During the 1930s some three hundred thousand refugees from the dust bowl states of Oklahoma, Arkansas, and Texas jalopied their way to Kern County in search of labor in the cotton fields of what was already one of the richest agricultural areas in the world.

As *The Grapes of Wrath* chronicled, the California dream of the "Okies" often degenerated into a nightmare of disease-ridden shantytowns and abusive bosses. Locals heaped scorn and prejudice on the newcomers. They were "ignorant, filthy people" and "shiftless trash who live like hogs." Okie youths, reacting to the exclusion they suffered, acquired a reputation for rebelliousness. Local teachers polled for one study said the youths "pride themselves on being 'tough,' " cultivate a "fighting spirit," and "hold others in disdain."

A sign outside a movie theater in Bakersfield delivered the ultimate insult: "Niggers and Okies upstairs."

Some Okies gave up and went home, but others gritted it out, picking cotton in backbreaking conditions for three dollars a day. Sticking to the soil like cottonwoods, they integrated so thoroughly into the community that their subculture became dominant. Their children became lawyers, doctors, and bankers; their nasal southwestern twang became the Bakersfield accent, and their hard-driving country music became the "Bakersfield sound." "What are the first three words an Okie baby says?" went one joke. "Mommy, Daddy, and Bakersfield."

Despite its new respectability, the Okie culture was still built on paradoxes. As James Gregory said in his recent book, *American Exodus,* it was "oriented on the one hand around stern-minded religiosity and on the other hand around hard-drinking irreverence—a community of churches and saloons, of churchgoers and good old boys." Okies attended the most rigorous of Protestant churches, from Southern Baptist to Pentecostal. But outside church, the battle against sin was often a losing one.

Another paradox was one common to many ethnic groups once regarded as inferior themselves. Despite the prejudice they suffered, Okies inflicted it on others, particularly the blacks who began migrating to the area after World War II. An Okie bar in Bakersfield hung a NO NIGGERS sign on its door; the Ku Klux Klan was active in many Kern County communities; blacks were virtually shut out of the oil fields where so many Okies worked.

While Phillip Bogdanoff was growing up in Bakersfield, the community was small and rural enough for these tensions to be held in check. As late as 1960, a population of fifty-six thousand could still enjoy views of the Tehachapi Mountains and swim in the rushing waters of the Kern River.

Now a population of 174,000, many of them new arrivals from more expensive areas of southern California, can hardly see the mountains through some of the nation's worst smog, and the river has virtually dried up. A tourist guide calls Bakersfield an "unmitigated assault on your senses of sight and order: stucco, asphalt, concrete, dust and barely a tree in sight." Its scenic drive presents a polluted Saharan vista of oil storage tanks and pump jacks pecking at the earth like huge crows. Tract home subdivisions sprawl over thousands of acres of what were once cotton fields and fruit orchards.

With rapid growth have come urbanlike problems that threaten the precarious balance between the righteous and the rowdy. Bakersfield has three times as many churches as San Francisco but one of the highest crime rates in California. "Come on Vacation: Leave on Probation" is one local police adage about the city. In gang-controlled neighborhoods, drive-by shootings are commonplace.

Family life in Bakersfield has an increasingly urban complexion. One in five families is headed by a single mother—double the ratio of a decade ago. Overall, some 10 percent of families live below the poverty line. The number of families on welfare in Kern County has increased by 140 percent since 1980.

Racial discrimination is less overt but perhaps more insidious. A recent survey in *USA Today* of twenty-two California
communities found that only Los Angeles–Long Beach was
more segregated than Bakersfield. Across the Kern River, the
Okie stronghold of Oildale is virtually off limits to blacks.
Only forty pioneering blacks intrude on a total population of
over 26,500.

Most threatening to Bakersfield's social fabric is the aliena-
tion of the young. One in three fail to make it through high
school, and many who do have rudimentary academic skills
that leave them with few employment options beyond fast-food
restaurants and service stations. A recent county ordinance
imposing a nighttime curfew on minors spoke of a "severe
and increasing problem" with juveniles engaged in vandalism,
usage of drugs and alcohol, public disturbances, violence, and
drive-by shootings.

In this kind of atmosphere, Mayor Hart's values seem to be
no more than an anachronism.

When Phillip returned to Bakersfield with Diana and Stephanie
in early 1987, they settled in one of its better neighborhoods.
They rented a two-bedroom apartment in a gray stucco, slate-
roofed complex in the southwest part of the city. Located at
the intersection of Planz Road and Hughes Lane, it was a mile
from South High School, where Stephanie was enrolled, and
from the house of Phillip's parents.

Nick and Jennie had sold the Rosedale farm in 1967. They
now lived on the 2100 block of South Eye Street in a frame
house that was an echo of Bakersfield's fading rural past with
its clapboard exterior, creaky front porch, and spacious yard.
Over the years, Phillip had reconciled with his parents and
become particularly close to his mother.

Diana was a combination nurse and maid for Jennie, who
was eighty, bedridden, and in the last stages of lung cancer.
The work was constant and demanding. She gave Jennie her
medication; she had to be there to help her sleep or deal with
the pain. She also cooked and cleaned for her and bathed
her. "When my wife was sick, Diana hardly slept at night,"
Nick told me in January 1990. "She took such great care
of her."

"He [Phillip] couldn't just hire anybody," Diana said. "He

had to have a certain type of person that could walk into a
Russian home when they don't speak Russian and eat Russian
food . . . And my personality, I guess, was perfect for the
situation."

As an added convenience, Phillip, who spent most of the
week working out of town, later gave up the Planz Road
apartment. Diana moved into his parents' house, and Stephanie
got a trailer parked in the yard.

Of course, Nick and Jennie would not have approved of their
son dating one woman while he was still married to another.
But that was no doubt outweighed by their gratitude toward
Diana. On May 5, according to Diana, they gave her union
with Phillip "their blessing." Because his divorce wasn't final
yet, she said, they considered that their marriage. "As far
as we were concerned, we were married May the fifth of
eighty-seven by his mom and dad." In fact, Barbara had not
even filed for divorce by then.

A few weeks later, Jennie's condition became so grave that
she had to go to the hospital. Diana told police that "she was
laying there and she said, 'Phillip, I want you to get my ring,
my wedding ring.' He said, 'Why, Mom?' She said, 'I want
you to give it to someone that means a whole lot to you.' She
looked over at me and winked at me."

The eccentric arrangement—Phillip away a lot of the time,
Diana and Stephanie taking care of his mother—seemed to be
working, and the Colfax discord was a dim memory. Maybe
Phillip's absences helped, but the three of them could get along
when they were together. Stephanie even had a nickname for
Phillip, calling him "Boogie."

One night at the Planz apartment, Stephanie found her moth-
er and Phillip struggling to roll some marijuana joints. "You
should have seen them! Oh, man, I just laughed my head off.
They tried to hide it. I said, 'You don't even have to try that.'
They were just like, 'You need to go back to sleep.' I said,
'You guys want help rolling that?'

"Phillip, he's missing fingers and so he can't roll. My
mom's never been around this stuff, so she never learned.
The combination, it didn't work. So I rolled them a couple
of joints and went to bed."

If there was tension in the family, it usually involved

Stephanie's social life. The freckle-cheeked child had developed into an attractive girl, with a slim, five-foot-six-inch figure, her oval face framed with curly, brown hair. Gregarious and easygoing, she met plenty of boys. The problem was that many of them were black.

While they were not virulent racists, Phillip and Diana shared the visceral distaste for blacks among middle-class whites that was as much a part of the Valley scenery as pump jacks and cotton fields. A friend of the McCowans recalled that the family commonly used the word "nigger." "It seemed to me they were prejudiced," the friend said. On top of that, when Diana's daughter Christine was about sixteen, she was allegedly raped by two blacks.

"She [Diana] had told me that if I ever went out with a black guy, she would disown me," Stephanie said.

Stephanie's first sexual experience was with a black in Washington when she was eleven. She had white boyfriends in Colfax, but in Bakersfield she started dating blacks. One of the first was Shalamar Fields, who turned eighteen in April 1987 and boasted a long criminal record as a juvenile.

Shalamar recalled Stephanie as "a respectable person" at that time. "She didn't do drugs, she didn't drink." He only met her parents once, and it wasn't comfortable. "I introduced myself, turned around, and walked out. White parents have a tendency to get real uppity about [interracial] relationships."

Phillip and Diana were uppity. They took Stephanie out of South High, she said, after they "came and picked me up from a dance and saw that it was all black people." Using Tommy Byford's address so she could qualify as a resident of the district, they arranged for her to transfer to West High, which was several miles from home.

The enrollment at West was more homogeneous, but it didn't make much difference to Stephanie's social life. There she met Jodie Davis, an elfin waif of a girl with craggy features and a nasal, high-pitched voice who looks as if she emerged from a poster for *Les Misérables*. Barely over five feet and one hundred pounds, she was two months younger than Stephanie but older in terms of domestic turmoil and drug abuse. Her parents divorced when she was an infant, and her father was killed in a motorcycle accident when she was eight. When she was in sixth grade, her mother left her stepfather and took her to live with an aunt. By eighth grade, she was sporting a black and white Mohawk hairstyle that she said made her look like a skunk; she was a regular pot smoker and had also snorted crank.

Apart from having a similarly turbulent history as Stephanie, Jodie also favored black boys. Among those she dated briefly was Brandon McLeod, a striking, athletic, soft-spoken youth from southwest Bakersfield who went by the nickname "Poo-Poo." One night Jodie took her new buddy Stephanie to a party at Brandon's. Stephanie and Brandon, also fifteen, spent the night together, and he would become what she calls "the love of my life."

It wasn't all smooth sailing at the beginning, however. Stephanie always had to conceal Brandon from her mother. If Diana was looking after Phillip's mother, Brandon would sneak over to Planz Road and stay overnight with Stephanie; if she was home, Stephanie would come out and talk to him in the parking lot; if Diana came home to check on Stephanie, Brandon would hide in the closet. "She said her mother didn't like blacks," Brandon said. He also heard Phillip was "real prejudiced," although he never met him.

And then, after only a few months in Bakersfield, it was time for Stephanie to be uprooted again.

The House

On June 10, 1987, Jennie Bogdanoff succumbed to her illness in her bed at South Eye Street. Her nurse was nowhere around. Instead, she died in the arms of fifteen-year-old Stephanie. "I'd been there twenty-four hours a day for six months caring for this woman, and then to have her die in my daughter's arms alone, it was horrible," Diana lamented.

So where was Diana? Phillip was back in town, and they were over at his friend Tommy Byford's apartment, she said. Stephanie remembered differently: Phillip and Diana were spending the night in a motel room.

Jennie's death caused enormous stress. Stephanie was so traumatized that she did not attend the funeral and went to stay with her father in Washington for two weeks. To make matters worse, Diana took a trip after the funeral that threatened her relationship with Phillip. Again Hawaii was the destination, and her host was Dick Corey.

In an interview for this book, Corey denied ever taking Diana anywhere except Reno. There were no trips to Hawaii. He said he never dated her, just met her at a bar and befriended her because "she was down and out." He added: "I have no real friendship there . . . I could probably pick out another thousand people I knew as well."

Corey is contradicted by an interview he gave to police on October 28, 1989. He told them that he began dating Diana after she divorced Wymore and that they were "quite close." He also gave an account of the second Hawaii trip.

Phillip was supposed to come with Diana so they could recuperate from the death of his mother, he said. They were all going to stay with another male friend of Diana's from Washington. But work prevented Phillip from getting away.

Corey said Phillip called while they were out having dinner and was furious that he only got an answering machine. When he eventually reached Diana, he ordered her to fly back at once. He also demanded she return his mother's ring.

Did Phillip really know in advance what Diana was up to in Hawaii? Given his possessive and insecure nature, it would be inconceivable for him to countenance her spending any time with any other man, let alone two. It would be about as likely as him agreeing to let her run a brothel.

A measure of Phillip's anger is an extraordinary note he wrote to Diana at this time, which was discovered in his car shortly after his death. Written in a printed hand in a spiral notebook, it went:

1. I love you as much as any man can love a woman. I thank you for everything.
2. Please let me call Sephenie [sic] Allen and thank her. I promise she will not be forgotten.
3. Please send me my mother's ring. It's very important & my ring.
4. Do not come by the house—ever.
5. I will tell my dad you will not be back again. He'll understand.
6. Do not suck or fuck my friend in Bakersfield please.
7. Where do you want the Buick to be parked?
8. Deposit 8,700. Anything else is yours unless you feel you have more coming.

Once Diana was back on the mainland, Phillip's anger abated and they patched things up. Free from the responsibility of his mother, they all moved in August 1987 to neighboring Tulare County. Phillip worked on a highway in Springville, where he lived with Diana in his trailer. Stephanie was assigned to a virtual stranger in Visalia, over forty miles away, until they found a permanent home.

Judy Chojnacki, a mousy woman with high cheekbones and wavy brown hair, was Diana's childhood friend. They had lived around the corner from each other and gone to school together. They had been out of touch for some time until their twenty-year high school reunion in 1986. Judy, who had recently divorced, had enough space at home to accommodate her friend's teenage daughter. The hard part was accommodating Stephanie's life-style.

According to Chojnacki, six weeks after Stephanie arrived, she began to play truant from Mount Whitney High, her mother's alma mater. She was also sneaking out of the house at night, and there was not much Judy could do about it. "For most of the time I lived in Visalia, I was sneaking out of windows," Stephanie said. "I was a serious sneaker-outer." On Friday and Saturday nights, there was no way she would miss out on cruising down Visalia's main strip with her friends. There were parties to go to and a new drug, LSD, to try.

Judy told Diana that "Stephanie was doing badly at school . . . She was really needing to be with her mother." By November, Diana was in a position to do something about it. She and Phillip had found a home in Visalia for them all. And it wasn't any old home, either: It was the very one that Diana grew up in with all her sisters.

Diana's return to 1620 Tulare Avenue in October 1987 was such a pivotal event in her life that she turned it into a story of mystical significance. That the story apparently bore little relation to reality didn't matter to her.

"It was so freaky the way it happened," she told police in September 1989. She and Phillip were just driving by the house one day when they spotted the owner in the yard. It was Ron Wachel, a divorced man who had purchased the house from her parents. "We got to talking, and he just insisted that I bring Phillip in and show him around."

The house had not changed much since she was a girl. It still had three bedrooms and two bathrooms, with a living room backing onto a covered patio in the rear. There was a garage and a driveway with enough space for two vehicles. Wachel had put in new drapes and carpets and redone the exterior in yellow stucco. But he had left the same wallpaper and hardly even used the family's old dishwasher.

What had changed was the surroundings. Visalia was no longer a slumbering farm town but a bustling county seat. Since Diana was a teenager, its population had quadrupled to over sixty-five thousand. Subdivisions had engulfed the plum orchards, and Tulare Avenue no longer marked the town's southern boundary but bisected its center. From the kitchen window of number 1620, you could watch a steady stream of traffic.

That didn't bother Phillip and Diana. After a tour of the house, they started talking to Wachel in the kitchen. According to Diana, Phillip asked him, "You wouldn't be interested in selling this house, would you?"

Turning to Diana, Wachel replied: "You know, I have to tell you this. I'm so glad when you said that you were who you were . . . I had a dream the other night that your mother called me and asked if they could buy the house back. Ever since then, I've been looking around."

Then he turned to Phillip. "I can just see her eyes are dancing. If you want this house, I'll sell it to Diana."

Wachel "bent over backwards" to make sure they got the house, Diana said. He had bought it for sixty-nine thousand dollars, she said, and now was so eager to have them live in it, he sold for only seventy thousand dollars. "He just wanted someone that was happy to be here."

In an interview for this book, Wachel, the owner of a pest-control business in Visalia, told me a very different—but equally bizarre—version of how he came to sell the house. "I never had a dream about it," he said. What he did have was a severe case of bad vibes.

"I hate to talk about that house," he said with a shudder in his voice. "In the last months I had it, it was a weird house. You may think I'm crazy, but I think it was possessed by an evil spirit." He would hear passing footsteps, doors creaking, floors squeaking. Pictures fell off the walls. He would keep the lights on all night, but he still couldn't sleep as fierce winds would gust through his bedroom. Wachel said he didn't want to sell the house, "but it just got unbearable to live in there."

Then Diana and Phillip show up and ask if he would be interested in selling. Funny they should ask, he told them, but he had just mentioned to his daughter that he was thinking about it. A few days later, he called Phillip and invited him to make an offer. "Whatever they offered me, I just said, 'Okay, fine.' "

The sale closed on October 30. Wachel wasn't quite as generous as Diana claimed. The deeds show that he bought

the house for sixty-one thousand dollars in 1979 and sold it
for seventy-five thousand.

Phillip had other financial responsibilities, including the payments on the Oroville house. After his mother's death, he had
also acquired her interest in the South Eye Street home. Why
did he agree so quickly to take on this additional burden for
someone to whom he was not even married?

According to Diana, "He really pushed hard to get this
home . . . because he wanted to do that for me. He knew I
wanted it real, real bad. And I had been willing to do for
him, so it was give and take, just like any marriage is a lot
of give and take."

But Phillip had already rewarded her generously for her help
with his mother. In addition to her salary, he bought a 1984
Audi sedan to replace her aging Buick and gave her joint title
to it. Maybe taking on the house was his way of really showing
Diana that he loved her "as much as any man can love a woman." According to Wachel, Phillip told him "he was really happy about buying this house. He said he'd do anything for her."

To help finance the house, Phillip stopped making payments
on the Oroville home, where Barbara was still living. "Let her
make them if she was going to live in it" was his philosophy,
according to Diana. Barbara couldn't handle it for long: The
house was foreclosed at the end of November.

Phillip also arranged for Diana to work as a flag person on
the Springville highway project. It actually paid much better
than K Mart or kidney dialysis—about fifteen dollars an hour
for nonunion labor. "He told me, 'We'll save every penny that
you make for a down payment on that house,' " Diana said
later. "And we put twenty thousand dollars cash down on that
house in order to get the loan."

There was one other important detail about the house. When
they purchased it, Phillip had sole title.

Title or no title, Diana finally had something material to
shout about. She had got her purchase on the American dream.
Maybe now she could even compete on equal terms with all
those sisters of hers who had those nice houses. If 1620 Tulare
Avenue was not most people's idea of a mansion, compared
with where Diana had been living in Colfax only a year before,
it was Hearst Castle.

"For them to buy that house . . . made her feel she'd really accomplished something, finally achieved some security," said a friend of Diana's. "It was the family home, and she was proud to get it and keep it in the family," agreed her sister Martha.

Diana could not, however, make 1620 Tulare Avenue into a home for her daughter. Stephanie was gone after only a few months, and she and Diana would not live under the same roof again until they were both in jail.

A Substitute Mom

Stephanie Allen recalled the final blowup in Visalia as if the sound of Phillip shouting still rang in her ears.

It was around April 1988. She was planning to spend the night at her friend Amy Baca's but had to go home with Amy to pick up some of her things.

"I walked through the front door and my mom and Phillip were having sex on the floor in the living room. I didn't think that nothing like that was ever going on, you know. I mean, the door wasn't locked or nothing."

According to Stephanie, Phillip reacted as if he had just been exposed on national television. A verbal donnybrook erupted between them, with Diana caught in the cross fire.

"You should knock before you come in the house!" he yelled.

"I can come home, I can walk into my own house without knocking on the front door," Stephanie screamed back.

"Get out, get out! I don't want you here. Pack up your stuff and get out!"

Stephanie was ready to oblige. "You know what, I'll be out of here. As soon as school is out, I'm gone."

Diana tried to act peacemaker. "Go ahead, go to your friend's," she pacified her daughter. "Come back tomorrow and everything's going to be all right. He's just been drinking and he's upset and you embarrassed him."

"No, I'm going to leave," Stephanie insisted. "Something has to be done, because I'm not staying here."

Again, Stephanie felt let down by her mother. "Instead of defending him, she should have been defending me," she said later. "She always defended him, *always*."

*   *   *

This incident capped a marked deterioration in the relationship between Stephanie and Phillip. To her, he was no longer "Boogie," but the bogeyman, an interloper who had no right to discipline her and come between her and her mother; to him, she was an insolent tearaway who needed a dose of the medicine he gave his daughters when they were teenagers.

Part of the problem was that once they moved into the Visalia house, Phillip and Stephanie saw each other daily instead of occasionally, as was the case in Bakersfield. Moreover, while she was living with Judy Chojnacki, she had become settled in the "sneaker-outer" life-style. After the freedom she was used to, there was no way she was going to be home by ten o'clock at night as Phillip directed.

Stephanie was quite open about her proclivities. "He knew that I got high," she told me. "I'd come home high almost every day from school. My eyes were bloodshot. I was like, 'Don't fuck with me.' "

She had other scholastic talents apart from getting high. For example, she sang well enough to join the Women's Glee Club at Mount Whitney. But because of her poor class attendance, she was moved to a continuation school. There she had only four classes a day, and usually skipped two.

Phillip tended to confront Stephanie indirectly. Her sister, Christine, who stayed at the Visalia house for a few weeks in early 1988 after having a baby, said: "He would always go through my mom instead of coming out directly to Stephanie. He'd yell at my mom about what Stephanie was doing that he didn't like." But even if Diana had changed her ways and tried to crack down on her daughter, it would have been too little, too late.

"I was a brat, I really was a brat," Stephanie told me from the perspective of later days. "I just really got rebellious."

She described her attitude as: "I'm going to do what I want to do now. I'm sick and tired of moving all around the country and meeting new people. I want to live the way I want to live, and if it takes the drugs and everything else to be part of it, that's the way it's going to be."

*   *   *

A final ingredient of tension was stirred into the caldron in February 1988 when Phillip became Stephanie's new step-father—or, at least, nominal stepfather.

Quite why Phillip and Diana decided to get married on Valentine's Day is unclear. They obviously did not put much thought into it. For one thing, Phillip was still legally married to Barbara. It was not a matter of being stuck in red tape—he had not even responded to the petition she filed in July 1987 or retained a lawyer.

They decided to get married in Reno and invite Martha Campbell and her husband along for the ride. But the whole thing was so rushed that they didn't give the Campbells any notice, just showed up on their doorstep in Colfax on their way up the interstate. They didn't bother telling Stephanie about the wedding until after they got back. They soon found out it wasn't legal, but never told her that either. All she knew was that she now had a stepfather, and it was this stepfather who, after she disturbed him making love to her mother, forced her out of the house.

It was later claimed that Phillip literally threw Stephanie onto the street. That wasn't the case. The original plan was for Stephanie to find an apartment in Bakersfield with her friend Zandra Crisel. When Zandra decided she wasn't ready to leave her parents' home, Phillip made another arrangement. After school broke up for the summer, Stephanie moved to a trailer in the yard of Nick Bogdanoff's house.

If Stephanie was the teenage equivalent of a Scud missile, surely Phillip wouldn't launch her at his worst enemy, let alone his own father? It seemed so incongruous. There was Nick, eighty-five years old, who, with his full gray beard, stooped posture, weathered hands, and deep-set eyes, looked like a character from a Tolstoy novel. He had become an elder in the Molokan church and had the aura of probity and dignity to befit his status. If anything, his moral code would be stricter than his son's. How could he be expected to control this sixteen-year-old girl with an authority problem, a girl whose fashion statements included pinning not just one, but a galaxy of studs to one ear?

In a funny way, it worked out. "She was like the only daughter to him," Diana said later. And he became "Grandpa," the source of unconditional love she lacked. They had forged a bond while she and her mother took care of his wife. For all her teenage self-indulgence, she still had qualities of warmth and empathy that could make her relate to an old man like Nick.

Things weren't all that stable in Nick's yard: Stephanie had to change trailers twice while she lived there. But she made each of them into cozy homes, equipped with color TV, stereo, posters, and stuffed toys. Sometimes she stayed in the house itself, using the spare bedroom. For meals, Nick served her homemade Russian cuisine. "He always had food ready," she recalled. "He cooked up a storm. We used to eat all kinds of stuff." He always kept ice cream or Dr. Pepper, her favorite soda, in the fridge for her. Stephanie had a job at a local McDonald's, but it paid only minimum wage. So if she needed a few dollars here and there, Nick would help out.

Nick even came up with a novel way of letting Stephanie know she had a phone call in the house—he would stick a bicycle horn outside the kitchen door and honk it.

"I was good to her," he said later. "It cost me money, but what the heck, I don't want to take it with me."

"He spoiled me, he really did," Stephanie agreed. "He made up for a lot of things I was missing out with from my mother . . . He was a substitute mom, that's what he was."

Nick had some rules. For example, he told her to keep the trailer door open if she had a visitor. "I have a reputation in the church," he said. She wasn't supposed to stay out late or ditch classes. But according to his granddaughter Nicki, he had mellowed since his wife's death. When Nicki visited her grandparents, "everything was so proper, so regimented, so restricted . . . With Stephanie, it was *so* different, so loose and different."

Stephanie also had no problem evading his rules. For one thing, Nick was very hard of hearing. So when she wanted to go out at night, she'd wait for him to take his hearing aid out. "I'd just say good night, go into my trailer, and I'm off as soon as he goes to sleep."

Stephanie, as gregarious and personable as ever, fitted into Bakersfield's youth scene as if she'd never been away. There was always a party to go to, a crowd to cruise with, a place to "kick back."

Her pal Zandra, she said, "would come over with her friends in cars and pick me up, and we would go party. They'd have music and beer and weed. We'd have a blast. Other times we would cruise Chester, grab beer, and go to a park with a bunch of guys, just kick it and have fun, talking. We always found something to do . . . If you knew the right people, [Bakersfield] could be a lot of fun."

She also kept busy pursuing her romance with Brandon. They picked up where they left off the night she returned to Bakersfield. Thanks to Nick's deafness, Brandon could sneak into her trailer to see Stephanie. "He could be standing right there and I'd sneak right past him," he said. One time, Brandon had to hide in Stephanie's closet. "I was in there fifteen minutes, sweating, and he's talking to Stephanie the whole time."

"Poo-Poo" was no Boy Scout. He was a party animal who could walk into a room full of people and be greeted with a chorus of "Poooooh." He can regale a listener with stories of selling pot as a South High freshman and beating up a "white dude" who came after him with a knife. But he was essentially a good-natured kid and had given up drug dealing after almost being arrested with fifty joints in his underwear. He was also close to his mother, Bertha, a respiratory therapist, and stepfather, Lonnie, a trucker. They were salt-of-the-earth types who gave him a backbone of authority and always welcomed Stephanie in their home.

Stephanie became particularly close to Brandon and his parents after he was seriously injured in a car accident in July 1988. "She went to the hospital that night and she practically never left," Bertha said. Brandon recalled that when he regained consciousness, "she was holding my hand, crying on the bed."

There was a tougher side to Stephanie that Brandon and other friends glimpsed. Far from being a doormat, she was capable of acting aggressively to protect what she saw as her rights and those of others. One time, Brandon said he and Zandra got in an argument, and she called him an asshole. "Stephanie said, 'Uh-uh, I can't have that.' Pow, she hit her in the eye."

Heather Malone, another friend, told me about an incident at a video arcade. While she and Stephanie were playing the video games, they noticed some older girls picking on a younger kid. Stephanie interceded.

"Why don't you leave her alone?" she barked. "You just leave her alone. It's not fair to gang up on her."

Then one of the girls tried to hit Heather. Without hesitation, Stephanie grabbed her and pushed her away as if she were a shopping cart.

"She had a really strong personality," Heather said. "She could take care of herself . . . She was never afraid to say what she wanted to say. She wasn't quiet or subdued. If she didn't like somebody, she'd say it."

Behind the Trailer Door

Despite the freedom she enjoyed with her substitute mom, Stephanie still needed the real one. But Diana was now farther away, physically as well as emotionally. Instead of being an hour's drive up Highway 99, she was 150 miles away, beyond the Tehachapi Mountains, beyond Los Angeles. In the picture-postcard setting of Santa Barbara, she and Phillip fashioned a world for themselves that was quite different from anything either had experienced before.

In early June 1988, Phillip got a new assignment from Caltrans, one so desirable that he could not afford to turn it down—an assistant bridge engineer on a major $32 million project on the crosstown U.S. 101 freeway in Santa Barbara. The project was expected to take three and a half years. Phillip would make some sixteen thousand dollars a year in per diem expenses alone. If he saved enough of that, his gross salary of thirty-eight thousand dollars, and the income from his real estate, he would be on the way to being able to retire when he turned fifty-five.

Diana supplemented the household income by signing on with the construction workers' local. There was always plenty of demand for occasional flagging, so most weeks she was out on the freeway brandishing her sign.

The couple maintained the Visalia house. They would return there occasionally for weekends and had neighbors keep an eye on it during their absences. But Santa Barbara was where they spent most of their time. Instead of toiling away in the dusty heat of the Valley, they were in one of southern California's breezy oceanfront nirvanas, where Phillip used to take his first wife and family on vacation every year. "He was licking his chops, saying, 'Hey, this is great money and I'm at the beach,' " recalled Scott Mawhinney, a Caltrans colleague.

"My dad always wanted to be in Santa Barbara," said his daughter Christy. "He loved Santa Barbara."

As the five million or so tourists who visit the city every year can testify, Santa Barbara is an easy place to love. From the summit of San Marcos Pass, it sparkles like a diamond bracelet sandwiched between the mountains and the ocean; from the bell tower of the famous Spanish-Moorish courthouse, it looks like a sea of unblemished stucco and red tile. Its glamour has made it the stuff of "Lifestyles of the Rich and Famous," of a daytime soap opera.

A visitor can hardly imagine any vestige of modern-day urban ugliness spoiling Santa Barbara. Its manicured streets lined with palm and jacaranda trees, ornate Spanish-style courtyards, and pristine beaches provide an apparent oasis from random violence, street gangs, and crack dens. This is still a place that, by any indicator, represents something close to the apex of California living—so much so that its residents are accused of suffering from a "paradise complex."

As a result of strict development controls, population growth has been minimal compared with the rest of the state. In 1960 the city was larger than Bakersfield. Now, at eighty-five thousand people, it is less than half as large. Crime, unemployment, and poverty rates are also roughly half that of the Kern County city. The most recent figure for median housing value ($129,200) was double that of Bakersfield.

Like sea gulls skating along the tips of waves, Phillip and Diana hovered on the periphery of Santa Barbara. With the mortgage payments on the Visalia house, they couldn't afford an apartment in the city itself. So they resided in the $250-a-month El Capitan Ranch campground some eighteen miles north of town. Home was Phillip's newest travel trailer, a twenty-nine-foot 1986 Jayco.

They took on few of the attributes of their new surroundings. You wouldn't find them enjoying the symphony at the Arlington Theater, browsing New Age literature at the Earthling Bookshop, brunching at the Biltmore Hotel, or sipping "inka" coffee substitute at the Green Dragon.

That may have largely been Phillip's doing. He was still the loner who sat by the window in the Shady Glen, the frugal, unpretentious Valley farm boy, the Russian Molokan looking in on the world from the outside. "If you met Phillip, got acquainted with him, he was kind of strange," said a Bakersfield friend. "A lot of it was because of the Russian background. He didn't have the same perception of things as someone from an American family would."

Phillip would later be portrayed as having the charisma and warmth of a pit bull. His colleagues on the Santa Barbara freeway project didn't feel that way.

Chris Norton, a burly, jovial foreman with Kasler Corp., the principal contractor on the project, was as close to Phillip as anyone on the job. He recalled him being an absolute stickler about work performance. "If you tried to screw him, you couldn't do it. You couldn't get nothing over on him." But Norton also knew Phillip's more sociable side. "If things got a little tough, I'd say, 'Come on, let's go get a burrito,' " and Phillip would get in Norton's truck, even though it wasn't really kosher for Caltrans engineers to ride around with Kasler foremen. Sometimes they would have a burger at the end of the pier and feed the sea gulls.

Lisa Alviso, another Caltrans engineer, said Phillip had a brusque, sharp manner, which was accentuated by his appearance. With his tousled hair and beard, bronzed skin, and muscular arms, she thought he looked like a mountain man. "He was a very private person," she said. "But after we got to know each other, it was real easy to talk to him. He was fun to joke with."

"He was always in a good mood," Scott Mawhinney said. "Everybody liked him because he always looked 'up' and he was always playing around and joking and having fun."

But after work, when Phillip returned home to Diana at El Capitan, there didn't seem to be much room for fun. The only times Alviso saw Phillip and Diana together were the office Christmas party in 1988 and a trip to a Los Angeles Dodgers baseball game. They didn't fraternize much with other residents of the campground. "The trailer was always closed up, the blinds were always closed," said Selma Gregory, a neighbor. To relax, Phillip was content to open a Coors Light, have a barbecue, and watch a video. "They were creatures of habit," said Jill Brouillard, another neighbor. "They ate the same way, the same thing every night. They cooked steak on the grill, same time every night."

Some of his coworkers thought Phillip had a few too many Coors Lights. Sometimes he would come to work and complain about having a hangover. "I would definitely say he drank too much," said Scott Mawhinney. "He'd come in every so often looking like he had partied hard." But Mawhinney and Chris Norton got the impression that Diana could keep up with him. She told both of them that she only had one drink a night—a ten-ounce tumbler of whiskey.

Brouillard thought Diana was irked by the routine. It wasn't as if she didn't deserve a little fun. After all, she was working, too. But she always had to be there for Phillip, and when she drove past the camp gatehouse on her way home from work, she would ask the attendant anxiously if her husband had made it back before her.

One evening Brouillard heard Phillip and Diana arguing in their trailer about "honky-tonking." "That isn't what I want to do," Phillip exclaimed. "That's not my life. I want to come home and relax. We're not going to honky-tonk."

"That's not what I want to do," Diana countered. "I just want to be able to go out and have a good time and have dinner instead of just coming home day after day."

But Phillip and Diana had something of a secret life in Santa Barbara that was anything but routine, that nobody—neighbor, friend, or relative—really knew about.

The El Capitan Ranch trailer park is picturesquely located just off U.S. 101 at the foot of a canyon of the Santa Ynez Mountains. Its two hundred sites cover terrain varying from open meadows to shady creekside groves. The facilities include three shower blocks, a grocery store, and a swimming pool. There is always a long waiting list for the few sites with a telephone hookup. Those without a hookup make do with pay phones at the showers and at the front entrance.

The park's main selling point beckons across the freeway and the Southern Pacific railroad tracks—a two-mile stretch of unspoiled coastline, anchored by El Capitan State Beach at the south end and Refugio State Beach at the north. The topography of rugged, rocky coves sheltered by steep bluffs is closer to Big Sur than Venice Beach. A *Los Angeles Times* article rhapsodized about the area, describing it as a "cliff-side wonder" and a "Garden of Eden."

Along this Edenic coastline, Phillip and Diana frequented what they considered their secret place, an isolated cove about halfway between El Capitan and Refugio that he knew about from those family trips of bygone years. "That was the only place we ever did go," Diana said.

Getting there from the campground is an adventure in itself. You have to drive north on 101 to the Refugio exit, go underneath the freeway, and then double-back toward Santa Barbara. You drive a quarter of a mile south and slither into a narrow gravel parking area beside the rail tracks. From there, you clamber across the tracks and down a slippery trail to an asphalt bike path. Only then do you see a state park sign and the golden sand of Corral Beach.

The beach, reached from the bike path by another short, steep trail, is only about 150 feet long and, at high tide, 30 feet deep. Rocky promontories seal the beach at each end and jut out into the ocean like bad teeth. Beyond the points are several coves, overhung by cliffs as high as sixty feet and consisting of brittle, oil-bearing shale. In the shale, the capricious action of wind and wave has carved an artist's palette of color. The bike path undulates along the top of the cliffs, fringed by clumps of pampas grass.

Twenty people would be a crowd at Corral Beach and its coves. Most of the time it attracts a few local surfers and surf-fishermen. "People that frequent there like the more wilderness-type beach settings," said Mike Lunsford, a veteran park ranger. "They like it to be remote, they don't like to be around a lot of people."

The Bogdanoffs' special spot was the third cove to the south of Corral Beach. Inaccessible at high tide, it is like a treasure closely guarded by land and sea. The cove is sixty feet long and so deeply recessed into the rock that parts of it are invisible from the top of the thirty-foot bluff. The couple would take any opportunity to go there, particularly during the week when Phillip could get the afternoon off work. "They never didn't go to the beach," Jill Brouillard said. "They didn't do anything else but go to the beach."

What was secret was what Phillip and Diana did once they got there. It wasn't that they sunbathed, snorkeled, swam, or body-surfed; it wasn't even that they did all these things naked. The rangers allowed nudity in the Corral Beach area as long as no one complained. The secret part was that they turned their little cove into a sexual playground.

It was as if Phillip and Diana had opened a cookie jar of sexual possibilities and only had a brief period of time in which to sample them.

Of course, the jar had been tightly sealed during much of their lives, the locks fitted by their church brethren. As the sexual "revolution" raged in the wider world around them, they had been expected to wear the fundamentalist straitjacket. If Phillip did want to prove he was a "real swinger," there was no way he could do so as a member of The Watch Tower Society; similarly, Diana's sexual forays were not what the United Pentecostals would call "conducive to godly living."

After he bought the house in Visalia, Phillip inquired about being reinstated by the Witnesses. To that end, he studied the Bible with a local church official, James Smith, and Diana even studied with his wife. "She was looking into her husband's religion to see if that could help them in their marriage," Gloria Smith testified.

Although they gave up Bible studies, Phillip and Diana both subscribed to Witness publications, including *The Watchtower* and *Awake!*, until his death. But their life-style in Santa Barbara bore no relation to the Witness model.

They rented videotapes of hard-core pornography, some featuring scenes of interracial sex. They copied excerpts onto blank tapes, presumably for repeat viewing. Around the fall of 1988, they bought a camcorder, which allowed them to produce, direct, and star in their own homemade, X-rated tapes. On one of these tapes, Diana penned a note to Phillip: "I Love You. Enjoy."

Even the most innocuous video scenario seemed to have sexual overtones. On one tape, Diana is making tacos in the trailer. Phillip asks to film her sitting at the kitchen table. With her back to a mirror, she puts her hands behind her head and coquettishly ruffles her hair. Then she flutters her tongue at the camera.

"You see my tongue? What's it doing?" Diana says with a chirpy laugh.

"It's just licking out there, honey," replies Phillip in his gruff, staccato tones. "There's a double-lick there."

All that took place behind the trailer door or during weekends in Visalia. The secret cove was also private enough to become another venue for sexual exploration. Using a Polaroid, they shot explicit pictures of each other posing naked on the sand and the rocks like lascivious, middle-aged mermaids. To go with their tapes, they also had snapshots of themselves having sex in the cove.

On one occasion, they were caught in the act by another beach-goer. Steve Lindgren, who, with his long blond hair and well-toned physique, looks like he should be in a chewing gum commercial, walking by with a surfboard, didn't pay them much attention. But five minutes after he settled down in the next cove to the south, Phillip approached him.

He hesitated briefly, then asked, "Excuse me, would you like to join us?"

"No, that's okay," Lindgren assured him.

"Are you absolutely sure?"

"I'm quite sure, thank you."

On either side of Christmas of 1988, Phillip and Diana took several key steps to make their world more permanent.

On December 8 Phillip's marriage to Barbara was finally dissolved, although the settlement was left pending. In a letter dated December 5, his attorney recommended to him that he "go through the process of marriage again with your present wife once I have mailed you a copy of the judgment which should be in 10 days." So on December 20 he duly remarried Diana at the home of retired Judge James Pattillo in nearby Montecito. They were now legally man and wife.

Next came the financial adjustments. On December 23 Phillip removed his parents as beneficiaries of his savings in the California Public Employees Retirement System (PERS) and replaced them with Diana and his three daughters. On December 29 he signed a quitclaim deed to add Diana's name to 1620 Tulare Avenue. Five days later, she wrote the five-dollar check to record the deed at the Visalia courthouse. She could hardly have imagined a better way to start the New Year. Now she had her name on the family house.

Where did Stephanie figure in all this? Where did she fit into her parents' world? Well, Phillip did add Stephanie to his dental insurance plan on December 28. And Diana had also recently started proposing another plan to her seventeen-year-old daughter. Not exactly a health plan. Quite the opposite: She wanted Stephanie to help her kill Phillip.

"Crazy" Tim

Stephanie could not be specific about when her mother started talking to her about killing Phillip. It was definitely while she was living at Nick's. It could have been six months after she moved there—which would be during that very busy month of December 1988.

She also could not recall specific conversations they had at that time. They were generally along the lines of Diana telling her that "things were getting out of hand with Phillip, and that something had to be done, and . . . she wanted me to find somebody to kill Phillip."

How were things getting out of hand with Phillip? Here Stephanie was more specific. Diana said he was getting drunk and beating her and "If I didn't do something, it was either going to be him or her . . . She was really afraid of Phillip and what he was going to do to her if she tried to leave him . . . She just said stuff like, 'Something has to be done or he's going to kill me,' or 'He's going to beat me until I'm black and blue.' "

That was all Stephanie needed to know.

It didn't matter that she and her mother had not been close in any way for the first few months she lived at Nick's. In fact, she had been getting more rebellious.

According to Stephanie, Phillip got reports on her behavior from a neighbor of his father's. Diana would say to her, "Stephanie, that guy's watching you. You're getting me in trouble with Phillip."

"So? I don't live with you," she would snap back. "What do you care? I don't care what you think. Just go back to Phillip; that's who you want anyway."

"Now, stop that," Diana would interrupt. "You don't have to start that."

"Well, it's true! What do you want me to say? That I don't mind your doing your own thing with him? I do!"

"She chose him over me, and that was it," Stephanie told me. "I was hurt, I was real resentful . . . I used to make my mom almost cry just by being that way with her."

It didn't matter that Stephanie had not had another big blowup with Phillip. There was an incident during a brief visit Stephanie made to El Capitan. They were all having dinner at the trailer of Bill and Donna Jarrett, neighbors from Visalia whom the Bogdanoffs had also invited to the camp. Stephanie and Phillip started arguing about whether she could go to another part of the park to watch a movie. He got infuriated and stormed off. Later that evening, Diana came over to the Jarretts'. Stephanie had left, she said, Phillip had locked her out, and he wouldn't let her back in until she found her daughter. Bill Jarrett found Stephanie in another trailer, where she and a boy were smoking dope from a hashish pipe.

But in September, Phillip helped buy her a Yamaha moped for her seventeenth birthday, a seven-hundred-dollar gift that could only give her social life in Bakersfield a boost. A couple of months later, she got to show her wheels off to the whole family, including her sister, Christine, gathered at Nick's for Thanksgiving dinner. As a Witness, Phillip had not observed the holiday. That year he relented, and he and Diana captured highlights on videotape. At one point, Stephanie dances with Nick, looking very frail, in the front yard. As the others plow through their meal, she busily cleans up the kitchen. Everything seems cozy and festive.

That sort of togetherness was either an illusion or it didn't matter. Just as it didn't matter that Stephanie had no firsthand evidence of Phillip being a batterer. What she knew, she knew from her mother. Diana told her about one early incident in Visalia when Phillip got angry over a Christmas present to Stephanie from Steve Allen.

"He said it wasn't a big enough gift, that he should care more about me. And he got drunk and called my dad and called him every name in the book . . . And I guess Phillip— this is what she told me—grabbed her by the hair and threw her outside."

It also didn't matter at the time that Stephanie knew little

about her mother's increased investment in the relationship
with Phillip. She didn't even know they had remarried in
December. Stephanie didn't read much into it when she would
ask her mother why she didn't just leave Phillip and she
would reply "that she wasn't going to be left with nothing
at that age."

There was no discussion of other, less drastic ways of
dealing with Phillip—reporting him to the police, going to
a counselor, seeking a restraining order. It didn't matter that
her mother was asking her to do a lot more than simply fetch
her a glass of water or lie to Gary Wymore.

What mattered was that, after all the rejection she had
suffered from her mother, Diana was reaching out to her. If
she did her that favor, maybe she would get her mother back.
Sometimes, she said, Diana would tell her that with Phillip
gone, "We could be a family again, it would just be us, and
everything would be fine again."

But if she was so rebellious, why didn't she just ignore her
mother's petitions? "She was looking to me for help, so she
needed me at that point . . . She was showing that she needed
me, and that was important to me."

"The problem before was, she didn't seem to need you?" I
asked her.

"Right."

Stephanie said that initially she was confused about what to
do—"I didn't know what was right." But her confusion didn't
last long. On January 15, 1989, she journeyed from Bakersfield
to Santa Barbara with a friend who was supposed to kill her
stepfather. It was less than a month after her parents remarried
and just over two weeks after her mother got joint title to the
Visalia house—and the friend was someone who might just be
unstable enough to kill, a lost soul who might just be willing
to do anything for love or money.

If there was one noticeable thing about Timothy David Gray,
it was his laugh. A stranger might also notice his pale skin,
thick mustache and eyebrows, heavy-lidded brown eyes, and
thin, lanky build—he was five foot eleven and only about 130
pounds. But what stood out was the laugh. "That's what I
remember about him most," Stephanie said. "He had a crazy
laugh. When he would laugh, you would want to hide him

away from whoever you were talking to at the time because you didn't want them to think he was crazy."

The laugh was like an echoing shudder, a whinny from a deep-voiced and somewhat inebriated donkey. Sometimes it erupted for no apparent reason, launched itself into the middle of a conversation, as if responding to an inner joke. But it may not have been crazy. Maybe it was just the sad, despairing laugh of someone who did not have much to laugh about.

Timmy, as he was known, was born July 20, 1968, the oldest of the three children of Tim Gray, Sr., a mechanic and carpenter, and the former Susan Kendrick. When he was about seven, his parents separated and he went to live with his mother in Missouri. In 1978 Tim senior took custody after Susan Gray was arrested for burglary—she would be given a suspended sentence of three years in prison.

The new arrangement didn't work out either. Tim senior was living with his girlfriend, Diane, who had three children of her own. They had another three together, and Diane became his common-law wife. Timmy, a sensitive, hyperactive, and somewhat overbearing kid, now had to compete with eight others for parental attention. That only made him even more of a handful and a constant thorn in his father's side.

"Timmy always had a problem with his dad, always," Diane Gray told me. "Tim [senior] couldn't control him like everybody else. He'd do the opposite of whatever he was told . . . just like to deliberately antagonize him. I think sometimes he'd do it to get even. Deep inside, Timmy was resentful of the other kids."

Tim senior had little time for sympathy. According to Timmy, "I got the fuck beat out of me for hours upon hours, you know, for not doing nothing wrong." Some weeks, he said, his father would beat him "three or four or five times . . . Sometimes I got to go a whole week [without being beaten], and maybe if I really got lucky, I got to go a whole two weeks or a week and a half. But that was home, you know."

One time, when the family was living in Utah, Timmy and one of his stepbrothers were caught defacing a school wall with graffiti. According to Diane, Timmy was so afraid of what his father might do to him that he hitchhiked all the way to California and the refuge of an aunt, Joanne Smith.

Timmy was not the only alleged victim of his father's wrath.

In a legal declaration filed in 1989, Diane Gray, who was then separated from Tim senior and suing for custody of their minor children, said he physically attacked her as early as 1978. She alleged that he "has violently and severly [sic], physically and verbally beaten and abused me and sexually abused me." The abuse was so bad, she was forced to flee to a battered women's shelter.

When I tried to speak to Tim Gray, Sr., at his home in Bakersfield in September 1990, he asked me how I would like to write a book with a "busted nose." He also threatened to kill me if I mentioned his son in a book.

Things deteriorated further after the family moved to Visalia and two of its members—Timmy's twenty-one-year-old step-brother Joe and two-year-old half sister Kristina—were killed in separate accidents in the summer of 1985. The tragedies devastated Timmy. "Out of anybody, Timmy was closest to Joe and the baby," Diane said.

He was soon abusing drugs, including crank and cocaine, and they had a pronounced effect on him. "His whole person-ality changed," Diane said. "He'd beam off walls, say unreal things." Timmy, who was also raised in the United Pentecostal Church, was a fan of heavy rock bands such as AC/DC that had Satanic references in their lyrics, and he would sometimes sound off like a Satanist. "He talked about a person [who sold] his soul to the Devil and now he was a top guitar player," Diane said. "He really believed people sold their souls to the Devil."

Almost inevitably, he got into trouble with the law. In December 1986 he and a friend were arrested for the burglary of a lumber store in the city of Tulare. At the sentencing the following May, his attorney said Timmy may have been induced to commit the crime because his father was upset with him over a traffic accident. "We feel that this particular commission of this act is somewhat due to the fact that he felt he had to come up with . . . three hundred dollars to appease his father and the other party involved in the accident and didn't have any way of doing it," the lawyer said.

No doubt taking account of Timmy's age—he was eighteen and still attending high school—the judge sentenced him to only eight months in county jail.

He didn't get much of a family welcome after he got out.

Diane Gray said his father gave him two black eyes in a January 1988 incident, prompting him to flee to his aunt Joanne in Bakersfield again.

Timmy spent much of the year on the street, oscillating between Visalia and Bakersfield. There was no chance of him completing high school. In September a Bakersfield police officer found him sleeping in a house that was being renovated. He identified himself as "Joe Prawll" and then started to put his boot on. But the boot just wouldn't go on all the way. Eventually the officer told him to empty it. Inside was his wallet with his true ID. He got ten days in jail for giving the false one.

Back in Visalia in October, more trouble. Timmy apparently stepped into an argument between his father and stepsister Michelle. He ended up jumping up and down on the roof of her pickup and kicking in a fender. Police were called, and he would later be charged with vandalism.

At the end of this traumatic year, Tim was in Bakersfield. He got a job at a McDonald's and stayed at Aunt Joanne's. She was living in a house in the 2100 block of South Eye Street, opposite an old Russian man who had this cute, friendly girl living in a trailer in his yard.

Tim and Stephanie had actually met in Visalia in 1987 while she was living with Judy Chojnacki. She and her friend Amy Baca were hanging out on the main strip when Amy spotted a guy she knew. He said he could take them to the Tulare County fair with his friend Tim. They all piled into his pickup and went to the fair.

Tim thought there was something cool about Stephanie right away. Now here she was across the street. He soon started hanging around her. On those rare evenings when she didn't go out, Stephanie said, "Tim would come over and sit in the trailer. We'd watch TV and smoke a bowl [of pot] or something."

To Stephanie, he was just a friend. "We never held hands, we never kissed, we never touched," she said. "I wasn't attracted to him, and he knew about Brandon." But Tim "was always in love with me, always not understanding why I wouldn't go out with him, wanting to hug me and that kind of stuff, and I would never let him."

"Tim said he was in love with Stephanie," Diane Gray told me. "The thing I got out of it was, Stephanie didn't care that much for him."

Tim expressed his frustration a year later. "I just couldn't understand why she had a boyfriend and why we didn't fucking make love because there was no one in the fucking world that was better than I was, you know."

Stephanie tolerated him, partly because she felt sorry for him. After all, she wasn't exactly a novice when it came to domestic turmoil. "He had a lot of problems," she said. " . . . He used to talk to me a lot about [family problems]." Stephanie eventually told him about her big family problem: Phillip.

"It Wasn't Worth Going to Hell"

Exactly how the trip to Santa Barbara on Sunday, January 15, came about, and what happened when Tim and Stephanie got there, may never be clear. Stephanie claims to remember very little about it. The following is derived mostly from an interview given by Tim to police on October 10, 1989, and from testimony at a court hearing three months later. In typical Tim style, the account is full of Valley slang, profanities, and, of course, inappropriate laughing.

According to Tim, he was "kicking back" with Stephanie in her trailer when her parents pulled up to Nick's house in a Ford pickup. She asked him to leave. "My mom and dad are here! They'll get pissed!"

"I don't care," Tim blustered. "I'll kick his ass!"

"All right, go ahead and kick back in here," Stephanie said, stepping out of the trailer.

A few minutes later, Stephanie returned with her mother and introduced her to Tim. They all sat down and started talking. "We were friends when she walked in through the door . . . We felt like friends." So friendly, in fact, that Diana said she would pay him to kill her husband.

"We were just like being there having a conversation between us about killing Phillip," Tim said. "We never really talked about it too much. There was a few words spoken, but we were just being real people, just sitting there talking to each other."

Diana left after ten to fifteen minutes. Phillip, who was in the house with his father, never disturbed them. If he had, Tim said, "I would probably have walked up to him and shook his hand. If he said I was caught with his daughter, I probably would have kicked his ass."

85

He later spotted Phillip in the yard. "Hey, that looks like a pretty decent man," he said to Stephanie.

Diana's offer had two major attractions for Tim: money and Stephanie. Exactly how much money he was offered before he went to Santa Barbara is unclear—Stephanie recalled a figure of three thousand dollars. But it was enough to start him dreaming.

"Earlier, I'd been to the bike shop and I'd seen a brand-new [Suzuki] Kantana and I thought . . . I would have a nice new bike and new outfits and I'd be looking good." With all that money, he might "gain a little bit more out of life that I didn't have and always wanted."

Killing Phillip might also help him get close to Stephanie. "I was all in love and shit. I would have done anything for her . . . I mean, Stephanie's a fine woman, let me tell you." He didn't want to impress her, just make love to her. "I would have went across the world to make love to her."

Neither Diana nor Stephanie gave him much of a reason to kill Phillip. Diana never said "if she loved him or if she didn't" or if he beat her. He thought she said something about insurance money. "She was gonna get a fucking lot of money." As for Stephanie, he knew she "hated the son of a bitch. That was just about it." He also believed Phillip had raped or molested Stephanie. That was like putting a match to the powder keg of his mind.

"I kind of thought . . . the son of a bitch needs to be shot . . . I grew up in the same bullshit in my home, and sometimes I wish I would have had a .45 to blow my dad's head off for what he did to my sister."

Tim became flustered and refused to respond when asked in court what he meant by "the same bullshit." "That ain't even fucking right of you to ask that, man," he objected. "Not even right at all. That's pretty fucked up."

But in her legal declaration, Diane Gray alleged that Tim's sixteen-year-old sister had left home that same month of January 1989 "due to violence and molestation of her" by her father.

A couple of days after Diana's visit to the trailer, Tim said, he and Stephanie "got our shit together" and set off on their mission. He didn't want to take his bike all the way to Santa

Barbara, so they decided to find alternative transportation. They biked over to the huge Valley Plaza mall, where they spotted a blue Toyota in the parking lot beside J. C. Penney. Tim broke into the car, wrenched the ignition block out with a slide hammer, and started the engine with a screwdriver. Leaving the bike in the lot, they drove the car to his house and waited until it got dark.

On their way out of Bakersfield, they stopped outside a church where a service was in progress. There Tim switched the Toyota's plates with those of another car.

They didn't talk about what they were supposed to do. "We never talked about the bullshit. We just like drove down the freeway and kind of was by ourselves." They got lost and started running out of gas, so Tim committed one more crime. In Ventura, about forty-five miles from their destination, he siphoned some gas from a car at a trailer park.

They finally drove into the El Capitan Ranch camp around midnight. Phillip and Diana had recently moved to one of the park's more desirable areas, a group of ten trailer sites shaded by eucalyptus trees and overlooking a creek. Most important, their space (E-16) had a phone hookup.

Stephanie and Tim followed the main camp road from the gatehouse to her parents' trailer—a distance of about a quarter of a mile. "That's where my mom and dad live," Stephanie said, pointing out the trailer. They turned around and made a right into an open, oval camping area called the Lower Loop. At the far end of the Loop, they parked beside a shower block.

To conserve the water in the Jayco's holding tank, Phillip often took his early morning shower in that block, which could be reached from the trailer by a footpath. The plan was to wait for "him to get out of his trailer to walk to the damn shower so from there I could take his damn life and go on."

Tim wasn't sure how to take his life. "How in the hell am I going to do this?" he asked Stephanie as they waited in the car. "You know, what do I use to kill the son of a bitch with when he comes out?" He had brought a knife with him, but no gun. "Maybe I can hit him in the back of the head or stab him or something, or I could get a crowbar or something," he mused. He elected to "fucking take a crowbar and beat him to death."

But as the hours dragged by on a chilly winter's night, Tim started getting frustrated. "Shit, I need a break," he said. "I need some fresh air."

Tim got out, took a walk up a steep embankment, along the main road, and then back through the Loop to the car. As he walked, he thought, "Why aren't we making love instead of fucking being here, instead of doing something stupid?"

After another fruitless spell of waiting in the car, Tim called it quits. Around 4:00 A.M. he said: "Hey, you know, forget it, Stephanie. Let's go."

Tim said there was more to his decision to give up on killing Phillip than simple boredom. Whatever his need for money or passion for Stephanie, he wasn't ready to suffer the eternal consequences of murder. "I knew I'd go to hell if I killed him," he said. "I figured it wasn't worth going to hell. I had too much going, too much of my life to take away."

"Isn't it true that back when you considered Stephanie your woman, you would have done anything for her?" he was asked.

"Yeah, except go to hell . . . It's like I never done anything wrong in my life, okay. So why should I do fuckin' that much wrong when I ain't done none before just to send myself to hell?"

He added: "No matter what I do, as long as I don't teach wrong or do wrong, when I die, if I take a gun and blow my head off, I'm going to Heaven . . . I could die right now and I'd go to Heaven, man. I ain't done nothing wrong."

Tim got a second chance to "gain a little bit more out of life" after he and Stephanie returned to Bakersfield. In one, maybe two phone conversations, he said Diana solicited him to come back to Santa Barbara and kill her husband. And she was ready to sweeten the pot for him.

According to Tim, "Right after we came back to Bakersfield . . . I went home and took a shower and came back over to Stephanie's, and as soon as I got there, boom, the phone rang and it's her mom saying, 'Get your ass back up here, I'll give you the gun and shoot him.' "

Diana was angry that he had brought Stephanie with him to Santa Barbara. "She wanted me to come back up there alone by myself without Stephanie." She was ready to raise her offer to ten thousand dollars cash, half to be paid up front, and the rest after he executed his commission. In addition, Tim and Stephanie would get the house next door to Nick's, the one Phillip rented out.

Diana gave Tim detailed instructions on what to do when he came back. He should call her when he got to Santa Barbara, and she would meet him at a motel and give him the up-front money. Then she would take Phillip to the beach and "they would be kicking back, you know, by theirselves, and I would walk up and . . . shoot her husband, and she would, you know, act scared or cry or whatever and call the cops and I'd be gone . . . [After] I shot him, then I was supposed to go back to the motel and collect the other half" of the fee.

They also discussed the gun. "I was supposed to come up with one of my own, but she was supposed to provide one maybe if I couldn't." If she provided the gun, she would give it to him at the motel. It would be a .45 pistol.

This time Tim didn't need to consider the afterlife in order to back out of Diana's offer. Apparently the main stumbling block was that he simply would not go back to Santa Barbara without Stephanie. "We got into a big fight because he wouldn't go, and I wouldn't go with him," Stephanie told me. "I told him no, that I was going to Brandon's. That made a bigger fight because he doesn't like Brandon. That's the last time that I saw him for a while."

Or, as Tim put it: "Me and Stephanie got in a fight, and fucking she went her way and I went my way."

Tim forgot to mention an unexpected encounter with Stephanie two weeks later. On January 30 she tried to commit suicide. Around midnight she went to Nick's house and, searching through some medication belonging to his late wife, found a bottle of painkillers. She swallowed fifteen of them.

Stephanie staggered into Nick's room and woke him up. "Pop, I'm scared," she said. "You've got to help me. I don't want to die."

She showed him the bottle of pills. He immediately called 911 for an ambulance. After treating her in a hospital emergency room, a doctor noted in his report that Stephanie "feels unwanted and abandoned by her parents" and that she was having problems with her boyfriend.

"I was in a way [trying to kill myself], but in a way I wasn't," she told me. "I wanted to die, that's for sure. It had a lot to do with my mom and her pressuring me to do the thing about Phillip, and I just couldn't handle it anymore. To top it all off, I had gotten in a fight with Brandon . . . It was like everything came to a head."

Tim was by Stephanie's side that night. He saw the commotion from his aunt Joanne's house across the street and rode with Stephanie in the ambulance to the hospital. He gave the paramedics a false name: David Smith.

Much of Tim's account of the Santa Barbara trip can be corroborated. A blue Toyota was reported stolen from Valley Plaza at 6:20 P.M. on January 15. On the way home from Santa Barbara, Tim said he took items including a driver's registration from the glove compartment and threw them out the window. The registration was found in the Ventura area. The car was recovered in the Valley Plaza lot on January 19. Tim had washed it "to be cool to them for letting me use the car and to get rid of fingerprints" and, as a further token of his gratitude, removed the stereo. Records show four calls from Nick's phone to the Bogdanoff trailer on January 16, the day Tim and Stephanie got home.

What cannot be confirmed is how Tim was solicited. Stephanie said he did meet her mother in her trailer. It was over a weekend, and Diana showed up before Phillip, who was traveling in another vehicle. But according to Stephanie, nobody discussed killing Phillip that day. Diana simply wanted to get Tim off the property. "My mom was telling me, 'Get him out of here. Phillip's coming' . . . She did ask him and offered him money, but it wasn't in the trailer, it was on the phone . . . Maybe he was just confused."

Or Tim had good reason to embellish his account of the trailer meeting. Maybe out of loyalty to Stephanie, he was trying to show that the plot was all Diana's creation, that her daughter had little to do with it. Wouldn't it have made more sense for Stephanie to have made the initial approach to Tim about helping her mother and then for Diana to seal the deal?

Stephanie herself was vague on this issue. "Specifically, did you ask Tim Gray to kill Phillip Bogdanoff?" she was asked in court.

"I don't think I came out and asked him, but I might have," she replied. "I won't deny it. It's very possible."

Along the same line, she was asked, "Did you tell Tim Gray that your mother would pay him money, or did she tell him that she would pay him money?"

"Well, I know for a fact that on the phone she offered him money, but I don't know if I told him first or if it was her that told him first."

In an interview with Stephanie, she conceded that the Tim Gray solicitation "came about through me in the beginning, but she directly asked him also."

No matter how the deal was made, Stephanie insisted that neither she nor Tim was really serious about holding up their end. "I think it was more he was just excited to steal a car and drive down there . . . We did come down to kill Phillip, I won't deny that fact, but I'm saying it wasn't like that. It wasn't serious as you would think somebody would be serious if they were going to kill someone. We weren't serious."

There wasn't any real plan, she said. If Phillip had walked into the shower block while they were there, "I'd have fell on the floor and told Tim to drive . . . He wouldn't have done it."

Stephanie understates the case. Phillip's life does seem to have been in considerable danger on the night of January 15 and the early morning of January 16.

For one thing, the idea of attacking him in the shower had a diabolical aptness. Phillip, returning to his injury-prone ways, was then incapacitated by a severely separated shoulder. He first suffered the injury body-surfing at Corral Beach on November 12 and was taken by ambulance to a hospital emergency room. He aggravated the injury on December 6 and again on January 1. On January 18 he was scheduled for surgery to repair the shoulder.

Stephanie was well aware of the injury. During the Thanksgiving visit captured on videotape, Phillip wore his arm in a sling. She said her mother told her before she and Tim went to Santa Barbara that Phillip "would be weaker if Tim was to jump him in the shower and beat him up that way."

Stephanie and Diana also knew there was a good chance of catching Phillip in the shower block in the early morning. Tim, shielding Stephanie again, tried gamely to take the credit for that idea. "How did you know that his shower was not in the trailer where he lived?" he was asked.

"I didn't know that," Tim said.

"Stephanie told you that Phillip would always go from his trailer to a shower to take a shower, isn't that right?"

"No. I don't remember that at all."

"You just guessed that?"

"I kind of figured he got up in the morning to take a shower at the showers, you know. Didn't know if he uses the one in the trailer, if it worked at all, you know."

"How did you know that Phillip didn't take a shower at night before he went to bed?"

"Maybe he did. But, you know, everyone needs a good shower in the morning before they go to work. You take one when you get up."

Tim might go to nonsensical lengths to fudge the issue, but Stephanie and Diana had come up with a plan that might just have worked.

Still, how serious could anybody be about a murder if she expected Tim Gray to do it? Who in her right mind would hire someone as criminally unsophisticated as he, someone who most people thought was crazy?

Again, there could have been a twisted logic to it. Tim might be crazy enough to kill someone he didn't even know. Wind him up the right way, put the right weapon in his hand at the right time—anything could happen. If he did do it and got caught, it wouldn't matter if he implicated Stephanie and Diana. He would be too crazy to be believed. His own family probably wouldn't believe him. What chance of the police or a jury buying his story?

On that winter's night in Santa Barbara, Tim Gray, however scrambled his thinking, turned out to be a lot saner than many people gave him credit for. He still had his place in Heaven, and Phillip Bogdanoff, for the time being, still had his on earth.

"He Is Going to Pay-Pay-Pay"

As another long southern California summer approached, Phillip and his new wife were full of plans for their life together. A future of prosperity and financial security seemed within their grasp.

His battle with his second wife over their divorce settlement was still dragging on, but he had just played a potential trump card. He had filed a motion to disqualify Barbara's lawyer, Bill Cook of Chico, California, from the case on the grounds that he had met with Cook before she hired him. Only two family lawyers were practicing in Chico at the time, so how could Phillip be mistaken? If the motion was granted, Barbara would surely give up the fight, rather than incur the expense of hiring a new lawyer. A hearing on the motion was scheduled in Oroville for May 26, 1989.

On May 24 he got an unexpected windfall when the tenant on one of the five-acre lots in Shingle Springs paid off the promissory note for the property in full. The amount was $11,863.80. Phillip talked about investing it in another real estate venture, and he and Diana took a trip with their neighbors, the Jarretts, to scout possibilities near Kings Canyon National Park.

His daughter Christy recalled seeing Phillip in Sacramento over the Memorial Day holiday. "He said the relationship [with Diana] was great, but sometimes he made her jealous by saying something about some girl's boobs. I asked if he cheated on her. He said, 'I'm too old.' "

But by that time, Diana had revived her efforts to dispose of Phillip, a campaign apparently triggered by a bizarre incident on the 101 freeway.

*   *   *

Rumors used to fly around the worksite about the rather dumpy, florid-faced woman who was that engineer Phil's wife and who, in pumpkin jacket and hard hat and brandishing her STOP and SLOW sign, worked as a flagger.

One was that she had made it to the top of the list of flaggers on call at the union by accusing the local's business agent of sexually harassing her. Another rumor was that she had something going with a foreman. Connie Jarvis, a Kasler mechanic, couldn't help noticing how she sat in the foreman's lap during one lunch break. He thought it was just "a joke-type thing," but added: "I goddamn wouldn't want my wife sitting on somebody's lap, not even my own brother's."

Still, as far as Kasler management was concerned, she was diligent and reliable in performing her duties, and they had no problem involving her—until that business with the water truck operator flared up.

Frank Dominguez, then sixty years old and divorced, was a partner in White Line Water, a firm hired by Kasler to compact earth before asphalt was poured on it. In the rough-and-ready man's world of construction, behaving crudely toward women is as common as wearing hard hats. But Dominguez allegedly went beyond even construction norms.

In an interview with police on September 26, 1989, Diana alleged that Dominguez verbally harassed her while she was working on the freeway. It got so bad, she said, that "I was almost feeling guilty to come home and not say something to Phillip." On May 3, 1989, Dominguez allegedly grabbed her, putting his arm between her legs. She said this took place in plain view of a California highway patrolman giving a ticket to a trucker on the other side of the freeway.

The following day, Diana said, she was flagging again when Dominguez exposed himself to her. "He said, 'I know you want some of this. When are you going to come and get some? I know you want this.' And I said, 'That's it. You have overstepped your lines.' "

Diana did not immediately inform her foreman "because it was right at the end of the day. All I wanted to do was get home and tell Phillip. I knew I had to tell him then. That's all there was to it."

After Diana duly told her husband that evening about the incident with Dominguez, Phillip did not hesitate to act. He called Kasler's office and relayed everything to a manager. The next morning, Kasler dismissed the truck driver.

On May 6 Dominguez allegedly yelled at Diana as he drove by the construction site, telling her that he had friends associated with drug rings who could do whatever they liked to anybody. That prompted Kasler to call in the police. Diana was interviewed that day but said she was not sure if she wanted Dominguez prosecuted. On May 15 she agreed to press charges for battery and indecent exposure.

When Dominguez was interviewed by police, he denied ever exposing himself to Diana, touching her, or threatening her. The Santa Barbara district attorney decided not to prosecute, citing "the victim's initial reluctance, the one-on-one nature of the contact and lack of corroboration, and the fact that defendant was willing to submit to a polygraph."

More important than Diana's allegations against Dominguez is their effect on Phillip. On the one hand, he was extremely concerned. He arranged to meet the CHP officer Diana had seen at the time of the alleged May 3 incident. Officer John Runjavac told Phillip that he noticed nothing unusual other than the water truck driver yelling something inaudible at him across the freeway. "Mr. Bogdanoff seemed quite concerned for the welfare of his wife," Runjavac reported.

On the other hand, Phillip allegedly beat Diana on the night of May 15, the day she agreed to press charges against Dominguez. The Bogdanoffs' neighbor at the trailer park, Rogena Nutt, was sufficiently alarmed to call the park manager, Al Clarke, and suggest he do something about all the screaming and bawling.

Clarke knocked on the trailer door around 7:00 P.M. Phillip stood in the doorway, but Al could see past him to Diana. "Her left eye was black and blue, all puffed up," he recalled. "Her lip was puffed up and . . . her sides of her face was [sic] swelled up." Al asked Phillip to quiet down because the neighbors were complaining about the arguments and yelling. Phillip, appearing embarrassed, agreed.

The next day, Al asked Diana about her injuries, and she told him Phillip had hit her.

*   *   *

Maybe that beating put Diana back on a course for murder.
Maybe she didn't even need that excuse. What is certain is
that on May 24 she mailed a letter to Stephanie. Written in
her loopy, cursive hand on lined paper, it read:

> Dear Steph,
>   I'm so sorry that it did not work out for me to be with you
> for a day. One of these days he is going to pay-pay-pay
> and I don't mean mabey [sic]. Here is a little money to
> tide you over until I can see you. We will be coming
> through Bakersfield mabey sometime before Tues. I will
> be at Aunt Martha's off an [sic] on Fri night & Sat . . .
>   I love you very much
>   Mom

The note is ambiguous. It does not say what Phillip was
supposed to pay for or how he was supposed to pay for it.
According to Stephanie, her mother was supposed to visit her,
but it somehow didn't happen because of Phillip. Presumably
they were going to stop over in Bakersfield on the way up to
northern California for the May 26 hearing in Phillip's divorce
case. "I was mad, and so I guess she said he would pay for it,"
Stephanie recalled. "Not financially, I mean literally."

This time, however, Diana did not enlist Stephanie to help
her make him pay. Maybe the memory of Stephanie's behavior
after the Tim Gray trip was still fresh—the attempted suicide
of a daughter wasn't something a mother could easily forget.
But there may have been another reason Stephanie was off the
hook. Diana had someone else to turn to for help, a knight in
shining denim—Al Clarke.

The Pencil-Tree Man

By the time he got embroiled in the world of Diana Bogdanoff, Alfred Clarke was a fifty-four-year-old former truck driver whose recent relationships were like rest stops on an interstate highway. His gray hair, Popeye-like jaw, deeply furrowed brow, wiry build, and bowlegged gait suggested many hard miles and many hard knocks.

The trailer park manager, who still dressed in plaid shirt, boots, and blue jeans, had been married an uncertain number of times. A marriage in 1982 to Karin Price was listed as his first, but the next one, to Barbara Harvey in 1987, was listed as his fourth. The marriage to Karin lasted only three years, and about a month after the Bogdanoffs moved to El Capitan, Barbara left him.

"When I used to get totally aggravated with him, people used to say, 'He's kind of sad because his wife left him and he's got problems,'" recalled Jill Brouillard.

But Brouillard and other El Capitan residents found it difficult to feel sympathy for Al. They complained he was despotic and deceitful, arbitrarily deciding who would get the best trailer sites or unnecessarily harassing late rent payers. It got so bad for Brouillard that she bypassed Al and took her requests to the camp's owner. "He had no power. He'd do whatever he could [to] impress people that he did," she said.

"He liked to be in control, liked being put on a pedestal," echoed Selma Gregory.

What made Al particularly notorious was his inveterate womanizing. "He was always chasing skirts," said Gregory. Few women, married or single, appeared safe. One story had Al pursuing a married woman in the most remote section of the camp. She eventually told her husband, who waited for

Al to come over one day. When he did, the husband came
out and beat him up.

Al seemed to have a preference for younger women, even
those less than half his age. Karin Price was twenty when
he married her, and Barbara Harvey was twenty-six. "Every
time they [girls] came through the gate in the summer, he'd
be hanging on the door. He broke his neck trying to get over
to register them," said Gregory.

Another of his younger conquests was Christine Allen,
Diana's oldest daughter. During a visit to El Capitan with
her year-old son in late 1988, Christine, then twenty-one,
had an affair with Al. Despite the huge age difference, Diana
encouraged the liaison. "Looks like Christine has fallen madly
in love with Al!" she wrote Stephanie at the end of November
1988. "Personality-wise they are perfect for each other."

Christine and the baby moved in with Al in December, but
they left the park on Christmas Eve—just as well since the new
woman in Al's life, a thirty-eight-year-old called Sylvia whom
he had met on vacation in Mexico, arrived two days later.
Al said he married Sylvia right after Christmas. That seems
unlikely since his divorce from Barbara wasn't final until
February 1989. Whatever his relationship with Sylvia was,
it didn't stop him having an affair with Diana Bogdanoff.

Exactly how deeply Al became involved with Diana in the
summer of 1989 is unclear. The key issue is, who did the
manipulating—Al or Diana?

Al said the flames of passion were kindled as early as
a week after he went to the Bogdanoff trailer in mid-May
to quiet Phillip down. By chance, he ran into Diana outside the camp store and started talking to her. Then they
drove to a secluded spot and had sex. The next time was
just as impulsive. "I stop by to see Dianne [sic] and she
ask me in," he wrote in a statement. "Then she got real
friendly and close and we had sex standing in the kitch-
en area."

The El Capitan trailer park, where privacy is at a premium,
is a hive of gossip. But at the time, nobody suspected the
quiet woman from E-16 was carrying on with the sinewy
park manager. Selma Gregory, who lived two spaces from the
Bogdanoffs, always thought Al was after Rogena Nutt. "She

[Rogena] said he wanted to, but she didn't want anything to do with him," Gregory said.

Al recalled having, at most, four trysts with Diana. The affair was over, he said, at least a month before Phillip was killed. No big deal except that Diana expected more from him than sexual gratification: She wanted him to help her murder her husband.

A week or so after the first tryst, Al said, Diana asked him if he could get some cocaine for her. "She was wanting to put it in Phil's food . . . She told me she wanted to do away with him." Al said he had no way of getting any dope.

According to Al, this was the first of seven or eight conversations during which Diana spoke of finding a means to kill her husband. The means always involved lacing Phillip's food with a supposedly lethal ingredient. Al asked Diana why she didn't leave or divorce him. She replied that "she was scared that Phil would have her done away with . . . that Phil had friends in higher places that could have her killed."

Diana also spoke of the Visalia house in the context of why she wanted Phillip dead. "She stated . . . that it was her house and she wanted to keep her house, and if she got a divorce, she thought that Phil would take it away from her."

Despite all this, Al didn't take Diana that seriously. "She was pretty mad at him, and I figured it was just a normal revenge thing for her being hit," he said. "It didn't really make sense that she would really want to do something like that." He did nothing to advance any murder plan, and eventually Diana stopped talking about it. "I guess she knew I couldn't get it [dope] at all or have anything to do with her anymore other than talking out front at the store."

Al's story has its bizarre elements. The plan to doctor Phillip's food with cocaine, for example, would have had little chance of success. But the core of the story is convincing. Al had no reason to make it up, and when it became public, he suffered agonizing consequences.

The problem area is his vagueness about key details—a vagueness that suggests he was not such a benign player as he tried to make out. Could he have led on a vulnerable Diana in order to prolong their affair?

Certainly he offered Diana some protection, a shoulder to cry on. He gave her his beeper number to call if she had any more problems with Phillip. "I would do the best I could" to protect her, he said. It might not have taken much for Al the womanizer to exploit Diana's gratitude.

It's unlikely that he instigated any scheme to kill Phillip. But it is possible that once Diana broached the subject, he helped keep it alive. In fact, after the cocaine option was rejected, he volunteered another murder weapon—the pencil tree.

The plant is so obscure that few botanical textbooks list it. A cactuslike native of Ethiopia, its name comes from the pencillike, rubbery branchlets and twigs. When a branch is broken, a stream of milky sap spurts out, which can cause temporary blindness if it enters the eyes. There have been cases of acute vomiting if the sap is ingested. But according to the textbooks, no fatal poisoning of humans has been documented.

Al said he discovered the pencil tree on a visit to a nursery in Morro Bay, one hundred miles north of Santa Barbara. He mentioned the plant to Diana in a casual aside. After telling her he had not been able to obtain any dope, he added that he had heard of something called a pencil tree. "I had told her it was poison and that's what I had heard, and I told her that I did not know if it was or not." Diana wanted him to get some of the poison, "but I told her . . . 'No way I am going to do something like that, and I wouldn't go to Morro Bay either.' " Al assumed she wanted to do the same with the pencil tree "as she did with the rest of the dope."

The obvious question then is, why even bother mentioning it in the first place? If Diana was serious about killing Phillip, it was like dangling a carrot in front of a horse.

Moreover, Al's statements that he didn't think Diana was serious about killing Phillip seem hollow in light of a confession he said Christine Allen made to him. During his affair with Christine, she allegedly told him that "Diana had wanted Phillip dead and was trying to 'do away' with him." This plan actually predated the Bogdanoffs moving to El Capitan. Christine denied any such conversation. If Al's version is true, then it must have occurred to him that Diana was serious, that she could be the type of woman to follow through on a plan to kill her husband.

A final problem area for Al is, just what was in it for him, what reward did Diana offer for his help? In an October 1989 interview with police, he said Diana told him that if he did anything about the cocaine or poison, she would "make it worth his while." But when he was asked if he was sure he did not lead Diana on to get sexual favors, he admitted that he may have, because he wanted the relationship to continue.

If Al Clarke helped keep the fire burning, it appears certain that Diana lit it. In doing so, maybe she calculated that here was a possible ally, a man weak enough to be seduced into extramarital sex and murder. After all, she had to know of his reputation—since the Bogdanoffs arrived at El Capitan a year previously, he had been involved with at least three women, including her own daughter. And she seems to have done her best to entice him. Al said they once made love after Diana showed him some sexual paraphernalia.

But Al did not turn out to be any better an ally for Diana than he was a mate for her daughter Christine. He may have been willing to humor her for sex, but he wasn't going to do anything useful. Indeed, it seems that she gave up on him pretty quickly. Al Clarke was a detour that became a dead end. Possibly in early July 1989, Diana returned to the main road—Stephanie and her friends in Bakersfield.

Call to the "Cosbys"

Kristy Yeich got to know Stephanie in the first quarter of 1989. They would race around town on Stephanie's moped and party and drink beer with some guys at the local campus of California State University.

For a while they planned to rent an apartment together. Diana told them she would cosign any lease for the two teenagers. But when they found something suitable, she backed out. She said "her husband wouldn't let her sign for it, that she couldn't do it," Kristy recalled.

Kristy, who was another West High dropout, could hardly have been surprised at this outcome. She had been well briefed by Stephanie on her volatile family situation. "I know she didn't like her stepdad at all . . . [She said] her stepdad used to beat her mom all the time. Her mom hated him . . . He used to not do anything for Stephanie; he wouldn't help her out. She said her mom used to want to help her out all the time, do things for her, but her stepdad wouldn't let her." Divorce was not an option because "her stepdad would end up killing her mom . . . and she was scared to death of him."

Kristy could see how unhappy Stephanie was. "I think she felt abandoned . . . She was kind of hurt her mom chose that way of life, that she wasn't helping her out. I think she probably took a lot of anger out on Phillip." She also felt guilty—that it was her fault Phillip was beating her mother. Stephanie would say that "every time she needed something from her mother, she would get hurt because she tried to do something for Stephanie."

What Stephanie seemed to want most was a normal family life. "I could just tell that's where a lot of her hurt was at. She didn't have to say anything to see it."

In the summer of 1989, Stephanie moved in with Brandon McLeod and his parents and finally sampled a normal family life—or at least the nearest thing to it since her early childhood in Washington.

She had left Nick's yard around April, apparently because Phillip had tired of her irresponsible behavior. "He wanted me out," she told me. "I told you, man, they were spying on me. They knew I was doing what I wasn't supposed to be doing, so he wanted me out of there." But Bertha McLeod said Stephanie told her she had to move because Phillip "wanted to put Grandpa in a nursing home down in L.A., and he knew Grandpa wouldn't leave as long as she was there."

Initially Stephanie lived with a friend called Christine Ferman in a complex behind the McLeods' residence. By then she had dropped out of continuation school. As Christine's parents paid for everything, including rent and food, there was no need for either of the girls to work. "We were partying twenty-four hours a day," Stephanie recalled.

The pure self-indulgence ended when Christine moved back to her parents in northern California, leaving Stephanie facing virtual homelessness. The McLeods looked around in vain for somewhere to house her. As a last resort, Bertha pleaded with her husband to let Stephanie stay with them. Lonnie wasn't keen on the idea. He was worried about his son's life-style and poor study habits, and feared things would only get worse if Stephanie moved in. But his wife talked him into it. "Stephanie's just a kid; I hate to see her in the street," she told him.

Both Brandon's brothers had left home, so Stephanie got her own room. She settled in right away, and it is easy to see why. Bertha and her husband have a warm informality, a no-nonsense bluntness, and their home is a hub of sometimes chaotic activity. The three-bedroom tract house in southwest Bakersfield is a far cry from the crumbling frame houses of the city's ghetto neighborhoods. An aquarium and Brandon's sports trophies adorn their living room, and an American flag guards the fireplace.

"Brandon's family is like Cosby's," said Jodie Davis.

Stephanie was now so attuned to being around black people that, if you spoke to her on the phone, you might think she was black herself from her mastery of black slang. She liked the culture, the music—she and Bertha were both fans of Anita Baker and Luther Vandross.

"When I lived with Brandon and his parents, I was real comfortable . . . with the way they lived. I fit in there," she said. "I loved living there, I really did."

Bertha, whose silken voice is as calming as a cooling breeze from her native Mississippi Gulf Coast, became another substitute mom. "I got used to her being around me," she said. "I never had a daughter. So I guess that's what made me so close to her. If she needed to talk, she could always talk to me, and she would talk to me."

But being part of the McLeod family couldn't completely fill the void in Stephanie's life. Bertha would find poems that Stephanie had written and left around the house. "They always had to do with, why doesn't somebody love me? They all had to do with somebody loving her or caring for her."

Bertha did not need to be a psychoanalyst to pinpoint the root of Stephanie's sadness—her relationship with her mother. The phone conversations were a big clue. If Stephanie got a call from Diana, she would immediately brighten up. By the end of the conversation, she would be crying, screaming at her mother that she didn't care about her, that she had discarded her.

But Stephanie was quick to defend Diana if Bertha dared criticize her mother. "Why do you continue to put so much into this relationship with your mother when you know she doesn't care anything about you?" she would ask.

"She's my mom and I love her."

Bertha would press her, ask why her mother didn't do more for her, why she had allowed Phillip to kick her out of the Visalia house. She would respond that Diana was scared of Phillip, that he drank all the time, and that when he was drunk, he would beat her up.

If Bertha asked why Diana didn't leave Phillip, Stephanie would usually reply that he would hunt her down and kill her. But one time she said: "She doesn't want to give up all the things that he gives her. She never had those things before, and she wants them."

"What do you feel is more important?" Bertha asked. "Material things or you?"

"Me."

"Now you understand what I'm saying."

Bertha didn't have much sympathy for Diana. "I don't feel sorry for her," she would tell Stephanie. "She can get out of that situation. What does she want to do? Stay there until he beats her to death just for material things?"

The tension with her mother rubbed off on Stephanie's relationship with Brandon. Sometimes when she got off the phone with Diana in tears, he would rip into her mother for upsetting her, and they would start arguing. Brandon noticed a pattern in her communications with her mother. Diana wouldn't call for a while, then she would call to say, " 'I love you, this and that, do you want some money?' Then she'd give her some money. Then she'd call back a little while later and say, 'Phillip just beat me up for giving you that money; I just came from the hospital'—shit like that."

The McLeods never heard anything about Diana wanting Stephanie to help her kill Phillip. According to Stephanie, she wasn't under that sort of pressure while she was living with the family. From the May 24 letter, she knew Diana was plotting again. But it didn't involve her.

She said her mother told her "she was looking for a hit man in Santa Barbara to kill Phillip" and that "she had found somebody there in the park to help her, and she told me it was Al [Clarke]. I asked her what he was going to do, and she said he was going to find some kind of poison or something to put in Phillip's food that would kill him."

Diana also asked Stephanie "if I knew a way that she could do it by shooting a needle with air in his veins, or doing it with cocaine or something."

But she didn't seem to have much use anymore for Stephanie and her Bakersfield friends. Then she allegedly made this strange call to the McLeod residence.

Neither Brandon nor his mother can remember exactly when the call took place. Their best guess is it was toward the end of Stephanie's stay with them, maybe around early July.

Brandon picked up the wall phone in the kitchen, which opens out into the living room. It was Diana, and she wanted to speak to her daughter. They talked for a while, then Stephanie broke off and said to Brandon, "My mom wants to speak to you."

That in itself was strange. Bertha, who was cooking in the kitchen, was puzzled, because Stephanie had always maintained her parents were prejudiced. "I wanted to know what she wanted to talk to Brandon about. Stephanie hadn't wanted him to talk to her mom before."

Brandon took the phone from Stephanie. Diana had a simple question for him: "Do you know of anyone that would kill somebody for money?"

The seventeen-year-old was stunned. "No, I don't know anybody like that," he muttered. He hurled the phone back at Stephanie. "See, I told you!" he said, glaring at her. "She's crazy! She don't care nothing about you."

As soon as Stephanie got off the phone, Brandon started yelling at her about her mother. "Just leave her alone," interceded Bertha. "Don't talk about her mother, man; that's her mother."

After Brandon stormed out of the house, Bertha tried to calm Stephanie down. Although she heard her son's side of the conversation with Diana, she had no idea about the request that had sparked his temper.

This incident only added to the tension between Stephanie and her boyfriend. After going steady for most of the past two years, they were wearying of the demands of a close relationship. They still loved each other, but they were kids, and here they were behaving like man and wife.

"He treated me like a wife or something a lot of the time," Stephanie said. "I did his laundry. He wanted me to go somewhere with him, and I'd go. I couldn't go anywhere with my friends if I wanted to . . . We were kids trying to be grown-ups."

Brandon's parents were relieved to see the two of them grow apart. Lonnie's worst fears about what might happen if Stephanie moved in seemed to have been realized. He had barred them from sleeping together in his house, but he knew they did so with impunity behind his back. They were using drugs more heavily than at any other time in their relationship, often staying up all night snorting crank. In this atmosphere, they had no time for Lonnie's lectures about finding a decent job and finishing school.

"Brandon was acting like he was possessed or something,"

Lonnie said. "I had to punch him to get him to listen to me . . . To me, he was making a fool out of himself . . . It was sickening to me. I knew Stephanie was the reason why he was doing all of this."

Lonnie was so concerned, he called her mother. When he had agreed to Stephanie moving in, it was with the understanding that Diana would soon get her an apartment of her own. Now he wanted to know what progress Diana had made.

He got straight to the point: "Stephanie has to leave, because I'm fed up with what's going on. You have to find her somewhere to stay."

"You don't know my situation," Diana replied.

Lonnie drove over her excuse as if it were a pothole beneath his truck. "Your situation is your choice. You have to do something for your daughter, you have to get her out of here because it is disrupting everything I stand for."

In the end, Stephanie jumped before she was pushed. She and Brandon had another major fight after she came back early from a wedding in Los Angeles and he wasn't home. By the time he showed up the next day, Stephanie was packed and moving out. She returned to Nick's to live in the trailer until she found her own place.

Faces of Death

In late July, over a year after she left Visalia, Stephanie finally got that place. It was almost ideal, part of a tidy complex of seven beige stucco cottages where persimmon trees cast shade over manicured lawns.

Unit B, 107 North Eye Street, was one of two apartments in the northernmost cottage and consisted of a bedroom, bathroom, and combination kitchen-living room. The back door gave onto a yard separated by a wooden fence from the parking lots of businesses on the parallel H Street. Nothing fancy, but certainly enough for a seventeen-year-old's first apartment.

The location was a big plus. It was only a block from the busy intersection of Chester Avenue and Brundage Lane in central Bakersfield. Crowded around the intersection were fast-food restaurants—a Taco Bell, a Pioneer Chicken, and Andre's Giant Burger with its neon burger sign—as well as AM-PM and 7-Eleven minimarts. The apartment was also just over a mile from Grandpa Bogdanoff's, if Stephanie wanted to drop by and check up on the old man.

The rent was not cheap, $415 a month, but her mother cosigned the lease and got her going by paying the deposit and the first month. The deposit was Diana's way—nine years later—of compensating Stephanie for selling her horse when she divorced Steve Allen. Phillip and Diana came from Santa Barbara to help her move in and give her some necessities, including food and a vacuum cleaner.

Phillip also bought her some new transportation—a 1980 Ford Fairmont sedan with cream-colored exterior and black top. But it wasn't what she wanted. It looked like a cop car to her. "I just didn't like the way it looked, because if I drove it in the ghetto, people would look at it," she said. One of the back doors wouldn't even open.

Also, Phillip had promised her a 1979 Chevrolet El Camino, which he bought in early 1988. At first he said she could have the somewhat battered car, which had over one hundred thousand miles on the clock. But according to Stephanie, he later turned around and told her, "I'm not going to give it to you, because I can get a lot of money for it. I'm going to fix it up and sell it instead."

At least the Ford was an upgrade on the moped. Stephanie seemed on her way. Phillip and Diana had finally come through for her. But the apartment and the car turned out to be catalysts for the final disintegration of her relationship with her parents. They provided Phillip with a constant source of frustration— a frustration that Diana, in turn, was able to use to inflame Stephanie.

Precisely what Phillip thought of his family life in the summer of 1989 is impossible to tell. He had no confidants, having even lost contact with his old Bakersfield friends. Tommy Byford couldn't recall speaking to Phillip after he bought the house in Visalia. Nobody at work got close to him. He didn't keep a diary or write letters.

"It was like he really didn't want people to know the real Phil," his first wife told me. "I don't think Phil liked Phil. He thought other people wouldn't like Phil if they got to know him well."

Everything seemed to revolve around Diana. "We were very superdependent on each other," Diana said later.

His daughter Christy could see why he was fond of his third wife. During a visit she made to Santa Barbara in July, Diana "was really sweet. She'd always ask, 'Is there anything I can do for you?' She bought me a T-shirt. She seemed like a real giving person."

One afternoon Diana took her to Corral Beach and pointed out the secluded cove. "This is the special spot where me and your dad always go," she said. As they walked on the beach, Christy questioned Diana about what seemed to her a very claustrophobic marriage. "Doesn't it bug you being here without friends or family? What do you do for entertainment?"

Diana replied that everything was fine, that things were just

the way she wanted them, that she had never had the things she
had with Phillip. "She finally felt they had met the right people.
He was the right person for her, she was the right person for
him." They didn't even argue.

By the time the visit ended, Christy was convinced "she and
Dad were real happy together."

During the summer, Phillip and Diana kept busy planning
improvements on the Visalia house and working on a new
common interest, something they could do without having
to worry about Phillip getting hurt. They were taking golf
lessons at a Santa Barbara course. Phillip was looking forward
to buying clubs and playing a game.

The divorce proceeding with Barbara was stalled again—
the motion to dismiss her lawyer was denied. But that didn't
bother Phillip, who proceeded with other financial projects. In
July he opened an IRA with a balance of over five thousand
dollars and made Diana its primary beneficiary. He talked
about buying property in Big Bear, and he and Diana made a
trip to the San Bernardino Mountains ski resort with her sister
Kathy and brother-in-law.

But beneath the apparent contentment, some of his colleagues could detect a frustration in Phillip. Scott Mawhinney
of Caltrans remembered him talking about what would happen
if Diana gave him too many problems. "It was like, 'She gives
it to me too bad, I'll just look for my fourth wife.' He never
specifically talked about 'Hey, I'm getting ready to split.' But
he said, 'Shit, I did it twice, I can do it three times.' It wasn't
like, 'I finally found the perfect one and I'm positive I'll never
leave her.' "

According to Rogena Nutt, the Bogdanoffs' neighbor, Phillip
even told his wife that she was welcome to leave. A few weeks
before his death, they were arguing loudly in their trailer, and
Nutt heard him "tell her if she wanted to leave, she could
leave and go live with her daughter, if that's the way that she
wanted it."

There was no doubt about the main source of frustration.
Phillip had not had to deal with teenagers like Stephanie
before—as for his own children, Diana said, "He put them
on a pedestal . . . They did things right. There just wasn't any
wrong with his kids." But now, whenever he tried to deal with
Stephanie, he would get nowhere fast.

"He always used to tell me, 'Stephanie, she's a worthless bitch,' " said Chris Norton, the Kasler foreman. " 'She don't got a job, she don't know what she's gonna do with her life.' It used to piss him off."

"He talked about . . . what a no-good bitch she was," recalled Connie Jarvis, the Kasler mechanic. "He said, 'She's fucking every nigger in Bakersfield.' "

What made matters worse was the same phenomenon that exasperated Gary Wymore: Diana seemed to subvert his efforts to guide Stephanie. According to Scott Mawhinney, Phillip believed that Stephanie should be left to her own devices without material support; then when she hit rock bottom, they could come in and put her back on her feet, hoping she had learned her lesson. Diana preferred to make excuses and keep propping Stephanie up.

"Ninety-five percent of the problems he seemed to talk about with his wife was the fact that Diana kept wanting to bail her out. He kept saying, 'Let her go and do her own thing, and then we'll pick the pieces up later.' "

Phillip summed up his frustration in a comment he made to Lisa Alviso, his Caltrans colleague: "Never get married where there are other children involved, because they cause a lot of problems."

Helping Stephanie with the car and the apartment put their relationship on the line. As her part of the deal, he expected her to settle down, get a job or finish school. He had that extra leverage over Stephanie, and so, indirectly, did her mother.

The refrain began as soon as Stephanie had a phone installed in her new apartment. It was the same refrain she had been hearing since the winter—Phillip was abusing Diana, terrifying her so systematically that she couldn't leave him because he would hunt her down and kill her. "She used to tell me that he was always mean to her, always—verbally, mentally, physically, every way possible, he was awful to her." The only way out was for Stephanie to find someone to kill him.

As before, Diana would sometimes say that she would be left with nothing if she left Phillip, and in particular, would lose the house in Visalia. "She said that it was rightfully hers because her parents had that house built, and she was raised in it, and that she wasn't going to lose it to him," Stephanie recalled. As before, Stephanie didn't read too much into those statements.

The refrain was now as insistent as a case of tinnitus. It wasn't an obsession but "something like that." Almost every time Diana called the apartment, and she called almost daily, she would bring up the problem with Phillip.

Again, Stephanie, not a marriage counselor, a social worker, or even the operator of a domestic abuse hot line, was her only hope of resolution. "She would just ask me, 'What's going on? Why isn't anything happening?' or 'When is something going to happen?' . . . She just kept bugging me about it, telling me all the stuff he was doing."

Diana continued to make Stephanie feel that she was to blame for her agony. "She said that the reason Phillip was beating her was because of me, because either I didn't have a job, or I wasn't doing what he wanted me to do. I wasn't acceptable for one reason or another."

The threads of tension—Phillip's frustration, Stephanie's rebelliousness, and Diana's manipulation—intertwined during the only visit Stephanie made to her parents in the summer of 1989.

It was the last week in August, and Stephanie had still not got a job in Bakersfield. So Phillip arranged for her to work as a flag person on a highway project some sixty miles up the coast from Santa Barbara. She stayed at her parents' trailer and commuted to the job site. The idea was that she earn enough to pay the next month's rent on her apartment. As a nonunion laborer, Stephanie was paid twenty-four dollars an hour, a gold mine compared to what she had been used to earning at fast-food restaurants. A week's work would easily cover the rent.

Whenever she was around the trailer, however, there seemed to be a problem. Her smoking was one issue. Phillip told Norton she "used to want to borrow a dollar from him to buy a packet of cigarettes, and he says [to her], 'What are you going to get out of life? All you want to do is smoke your cigarettes. You got to get your shit together.' "

One night sitting around the trailer, Phillip told his stepdaughter it was time they had a talk. "You're not here to play games," he lectured her. "You're not here to go running around town. You're here to work. You're not a guest in this house, you're an employee."

"Don't talk to me like that," Stephanie yelled back at him. "I'm leaving now."

She stormed out of the trailer and got into her car. Diana came running after her. "I'm not going to sit there and take all that from him when I didn't do anything to him," Stephanie told her.

Diana implored her, "No, don't go. He'll take it out on me. He'll beat me if you leave because you're supposed to be here to work and he set it up for you and everything, and he would just take it out on me."

Then she added: "Hopefully it won't be much longer and we won't have to put up with this."

Stephanie was still angry the next day when she encountered Al Clarke in the trailer park. She thought he was somebody she could talk to—she knew her mother had asked the park manager to help in disposing of Phillip, and she had heard about him from her sister, Christine. She was a little put out when Al introduced himself by grabbing the back of her leg as she was using one of the camp pay phones. After she got off the phone, he followed that up by kissing her on the mouth. Still, that didn't stop her from venting her anger toward Phillip.

Al asked how her parents were doing. Stephanie waded into Phillip, saying how she hated him, how he had taken her paycheck, barred her from talking to anyone at the park, and even told her which shower block to use. According to Stephanie, Al indicated that he was still available to help her mother. He said Diana had asked him to "help her find something to poison Phillip with"—specifically, the pencil tree—and that "he was looking around."

Stephanie didn't need to turn to Al Clarke to help her mother. She already had a suitable candidate back home in Bakersfield. He was her new boyfriend and roommate. Her parents had almost met him when they delivered the Ford, but she hurried him out of the apartment before they arrived. She wasn't even supposed to have a roommate, and he was not the type to have a cordial visit with them. He was a black drug dealer and convicted felon called Brian Stafford.

Their first meeting was back in April when Brian spotted Stephanie on her moped as he drove around southwest Bakersfield with some friends. He thought she was so cute that he made a U-turn, followed her, and, when she stopped, invited her to a party. She declined the invitation.

Then one day in July, Jodie Davis suggested to Stephanie that they go on a weed-shopping expedition. After a long hiatus, the two former West High friends had gotten back in touch and had been spending a lot of time together as Stephanie and Brandon drifted apart.

Jodie's family life had almost completely collapsed since she first met Stephanie. When she was sixteen, she ran away from home after an argument with her stepfather and lived with an aunt. Then she shared a place with her older sister that was paid for with welfare checks. She gave up on high school in her junior year and was now majoring in the dropout culture at the university of the street. She could discourse on crank as if testifying as an expert before Congress.

Stephanie was game for Jodie's suggestion. They drove to an apartment complex near West High called Village Lane and walked over to a dingy ground-floor apartment backing onto one of the parking lots. Brandon McLeod was already there with Jodie's boyfriend, a twenty-four-year-old black ex-convict named Calvin Monigan. A crowd of people were crammed into the living room, some watching a videotape called *Faces of Death*. One video guide describes the film as "the ultimate in tasteless exploitation," featuring "graphic, uncensored footage of death autopsies, suicides, executions, and the brutal slaughter of animals."

Brian was living in the apartment with his girlfriend, Rosalyn, and her three-year-old daughter, Kerisha. He recognized Stephanie and invited her to accompany him to the bedroom. At five foot nine and about 150 pounds, he was a little undersized compared with most black guys she knew. He wore a fashionable hairstyle—a flattop like a fuzzy strip of carpet and "fades" at the back, ending in a tuft or "shag" at the nape of the neck. He had deep-set, intense eyes and a widely splayed nose. A bristly mustache hovered above a full-lipped mouth. A pronounced gap divided his front teeth. Most distinctive of all, his fingernails were so long that his hands looked like talons.

He certainly wasn't as good-looking as Brandon. But she hadn't gone into the bedroom to have sex with him, just sample some of his drug wares. He gave her an eighth of an ounce of weed on the house. Then he asked if she did crank. "Sometimes," she answered. So he lined up some of the coarse, brownish powder on the dresser for her to snort.

"You're going to be mine," he told her.

She started coming around to the apartment almost every day after that. Brian gladly doled out more free dope to her. She slept with him for the first time at a fancy motel in a Jacuzzi-equipped suite he paid for and to which Calvin and Jodie were also invited. They spent several other nights at motels.

When Stephanie got her own place, she suggested an alternative arrangement. "It bothered me that he would go stay the night with [Rosalyn] and then come back and stay the night with me. So I told him, 'Why don't you just move into my apartment?' "

Bertha McLeod recalled seeing Brian at Eye Street only a few days after Stephanie got the apartment. He was wearing khaki trousers, a white undershirt, and a pager. She thought he looked like a gang member. He was sitting on the couch in the living room with a white guy. When Stephanie took Bertha outside to show off her car, she wanted to know who he was. Stephanie just said he was a friend called Brian.

"What's he do for a living?" Bertha persisted, wondering about his pager.

"He sells drugs."

"You better be careful," Bertha warned. "Don't get yourself in nothing over here with this guy."

"It's okay, I won't," Stephanie assured her.

If Bertha had had even an inkling of Brian Stafford's character and background, she would have had a lot more cause for concern.

Boy and a Pig

Brian has a way with a story. In two interviews for this book in 1991, he was articulate and compelling. Under close scrutiny, much of what he says turns out to be dubious, if not false. But the fabrications and embellishments often provide the keenest insights into his character.

Brian Keith Stafford was born August 4, 1968, in Bakersfield. He was the third of five children of Billy Stafford, a construction laborer, and his wife, Nellie. According to Brian, his father disowned him at birth because "I had gray eyes and blond hair." His two older brothers "are what we call 'Daddy's boys.'" He favored those because he said they looked more like him. Me, my younger sister and brother, he kind of disowned. He didn't accept me because of the way I came out."

These days, Brian does not even acknowledge having a father. He calls him his "father figure," and the very mention of his name seems to give him acute indigestion. "My mother is my father," he says. He even abjures using his last name, preferring to call himself Brian K.

He recalled Billy walking out on the family when he was an infant. The public record shows his parents separating in 1971 and Billy moving to Denver, Colorado. But he returned to have two more children with Nellie in June 1972 and February 1974. There was another separation in July 1974, and a divorce petition was filed in September 1975. It became final in 1977, two weeks after Brian's ninth birthday.

Billy returned to Denver, where he started a cement contracting business. Brian said he visited him when he was ten "to see what it would be like to have a father." But the experiment was a failure. He said Billy would call him a spoiled brat and continually put his mother down. Brian went back to Bakersfield after seven months.

Again, the record tells a different story. According to a court filing, Billy had legal custody of Brian as well as his older brothers at the time.

In Bakersfield Brian settled down with his mother, sister Twylla, and younger brother, Shawn. Home was a series of rented apartments in low-income, mostly black neighborhoods in the central part of town. To make ends meet, Brian said, his mother worked long hours as a "diet technician" at local hospitals. According to a 1988 police report, Nellie was a "food service worker."

It was a struggle for survival. They were part of a huge slice of Bakersfield's black population living in poverty. In 1979 28 percent of black families were living below the poverty line, and of those, two thirds were headed by women. Brian said his family got by because "we had each other. That was all that was important." He took over the role of father, taking care of his younger siblings while his mother was at work. "He was the man of the house," recalled Patrick Brown, a longtime friend.

In addition to the strong family bond, Nellie and her children had their faith. They belonged to a mainly black church, the "Apostolic" Pentecostal Church of Jesus Christ, located in east Bakersfield. Like the United Pentecostal Church, it preached an ecstatic form of religion, with members commonly speaking in tongues during its raucously emotional services. It also had a full menu of moral taboos to divert members from the evils of the outside world.

"You couldn't wear long hair; you couldn't listen to what they call the music of the world, like pop and rap; you can't watch TV because it's of the world," Brian said.

His family and church responsibilities made Brian something of an outsider at school. He wasn't able to play football after class because he always had to hurry home to take care of his siblings. Dressed in pants that came at least to his knees and short-sleeved shirts, he was a sartorial eyesore to his more fashionable schoolmates. One time he got in a fight at school with some boys who wanted "to change my clothes by force."

Brian was content to shoulder the burden. He didn't regret it "because of the simple fact I helped my family." Patrick Brown said his friend would always try to get him to go to church with him. He had no interest in the temptations of street gangs, of drink and drugs. "He wanted to be with people that were doing something for themselves, [getting] a good education," Patrick said. He was an above-average student who took college prep classes and talked about a career as an architect.

Brian also wrote poems to express his feelings, and enjoyed being around animals. One summer he took a job at the Kern County Animal Shelter. "I liked it because we got to connect people back with their lost animals," he said. The only thing he didn't like was the euthanasia. "You would hold the animals while they put them to sleep. It made me cry."

Even more traumatic was the affair of the pig.

Brian was then a student at South High in Bakersfield, and as part of a project for Future Farmers of America, he raised a pig. His teachers told him the animal would have to be slaughtered at the end of the project. But he refused to believe them. "The pig was my best friend at the time . . . This pig would follow me by the sound of my voice. It was like the only thing that could understand me."

His sister, Twylla, recalled he would sit for hours talking to the pig, even reading the animal poems he had written. The only things you couldn't mention around the pig were death or dying. "If the pig heard those words, he would destroy things, he would kick, scream, and holler. The pig would act like he was going to be killed."

Brian prayed with all his might that the pig would be spared—"I felt my prayers would save this pig's life." But the pig was eventually taken from him and slaughtered. Brian couldn't understand why they did that, why God had let him down. Why did they have to kill it after he had gone to all that trouble to raise it?

Things were never the same after that, he said. He was no longer the dutiful son, a churchgoing, overachieving kid who was on track to rise above the obstacles of race and poverty and make a positive mark in the world. He was now a loose cannon just waiting for an opportunity to go off.

According to Brian, this rebelliousness began when he was about fifteen years old. Court records show he was charged with petty theft in December 1981 and with receiving stolen property and forgery the following month. He was sentenced to a work program and two years probation on the theft charge. Brian was then thirteen.

Certainly it was a different Brian who transferred to Bakersfield High as a junior in 1984. He looked innocent enough in the yearbook photo, with his timid smile and Afro hairstyle, but he was no valedictorian. He was "seeing the things I hadn't been able to see, going to dances, going skating, talking to girls, all kinds of stuff." The "stuff" included drugs.

His family was then living in a small housing project on Cannon Avenue in a Hispanic-black neighborhood on the southeastern edge of town. The area, known as Cottonwood, is a barren ghetto-scape of seedy street-corner liquor stores, abandoned buildings covered in gang graffiti, rickety frame cottages, and front yards filled with junk. In the mid-1980s, it was an open-air crack cocaine market.

When he was fifteen, Brian ran away from Cannon Avenue after an argument with his mother and went to stay with an older cousin, Francine McCoy. According to Brian, McCoy left one day with one hundred dollars and came back with a white, rocklike substance. "You going to sell this to somebody?" he asked.

"Yeah, we're going to make money off of it."

He tried the cocaine for himself and helped McCoy sell it. "It felt good. I always had money in my pocket."

McCoy would be convicted of crack cocaine possession three times between 1988 and 1990.

At Bakersfield High, Brian sold weed to students and helped start "Players Inc.," a group of friends dedicated to ditching classes and getting high on weed, beer, and fortified wine. He was such a successful "player" that he was sent to the Vista East continuation school.

These outlets for rebellion were nothing original for teenagers in Bakersfield. But Brian did venture into unusual territory by "trying to break the color barrier." His steady girlfriend was a button-nosed, dimple-chinned white girl called Rosalyn "Sissy" Bookout, whom he had met at South High. He crossed into the all-white stronghold of Oildale, where he briefly attended a Baptist church. He went there "because I was trying to break away from my mom and establish me."

In the summer of 1985, Mom reined him in enough to get
him to enlist in the National Guard. "This is your option," she
told him. "You either do this or you get yourself together in
school."

"Forget it. I'm going in the army," Brian replied.

He went to Fort Benning, Georgia, for basic training, which
included the use of handguns and rifles and self-defense. Mostly
he performed occasional weekend duty and maneuvers with the
Guard in Bakersfield. Brian enjoyed the regimen enough to
consider joining the regular army, but decided he wasn't ready
yet to leave Bakersfield. "I was still skeptical about leaving my
family and friends, because that was all I knew," he said.

Brian would soon make a move—not to an army barracks,
but to the Kern County jail.

It was January 1987. According to Brian, he was just trying
to rescue a damsel in distress. The damsel wasn't Rosalyn,
who had moved to Los Angeles; it wasn't Gloria Rodriguez,
an older Hispanic woman who was estranged from her husband
and who had been living with Brian; it was "this girl I knew,"
Helen Caithness.

He said Helen needed some money, so he called a cousin
and told him, "Look, I need a way to make some money
real quick." A few hours later, the cousin showed up with
a microwave, a VCR, and a TV in his truck. He offered to
sell them for sixty dollars. Brian knew a good deal when he
saw one.

After he had taken the items over to Helen's house to store
them temporarily, she called him in a panic. The police were
over and threatening to arrest her and take her baby daughter
away from her. "They say the stuff you gave me was stolen,"
she wailed.

Brian called the police switchboard operator from a pay
phone to find out what was going on. The operator got his
location and kept him on the phone long enough for officers
to speed over and arrest him for burglary.

"I've always become a victim for some reason," he said
ruefully, concluding his account of the crime.

But Brian told the arresting officers that he did commit a
burglary. According to the police report, he stole the items on
January 23 from an apartment in the same complex where

he was living with Rodriguez. He called a cab to transport himself and the loot to Caithness's apartment. From a number of leads, including information from the cab driver, police arrested Brian on January 26 after Caithness confirmed he had brought her the items.

Helen told me she had been dating Brian for a month when he appeared on her doorstep with the items. It was nothing to do with her needing any money. He simply offered them as a token of his love. "He used to tell me a lot that he loved me," she said.

Brian pleaded guilty to first-degree burglary, which normally carries a sentence of from two to six years in state prison. At his sentencing on August 26, 1987, there was no mention of having been duped by a cousin or having failed in an act of gallantry. He told the judge he had made a "mistake" and asked for leniency because it was a very quick mistake.

Haltingly he said: "I've learned a great lesson. It has affected one life with the mistake that I did. If I do go to jail, I'll lose my . . . years that I have invested into the [National] Guard . . . [With] one mistake that was less than an hour, I could lose all that time that I have invested into that. I would just like to say that I did it, I have had problems." Brian also said he was under the influence of marijuana and alcohol at the time of the offense.

Kern County Judge Roger Randall responded prophetically: "Even one hour can be a long time. Very few seconds is required, for example, to take someone's life. [It] might result in your imprisonment or a defendant's imprisonment for the rest of his life or possible execution."

But taking into account Brian's age and lack of an adult criminal record, the judge gave him a "substantial break." He sentenced him to a year in jail and placed him on three years probation. Now a convicted felon, Brian was also discharged from the National Guard.

If his conduct had been affected by substance abuse, Randall told Brian in conclusion, "I would certainly seriously recommend that you examine that as a potential problem and avoid that situation again."

Brian didn't act as if he had examined anything. In jail he was accused of throwing his weight around. According to a jail report, guards and inmates complained that he was "causing friction and animosity among other inmates" and "trying to be a 'tank boss.' "

He also allegedly used friends on the outside to keep his drug business going. One of them was Shalamar Fields, Stephanie's old boyfriend, who was now pursuing an active career in small-time crime. "I was selling for him while he was in jail," Shalamar told me. "He still had a substantial amount of drugs that needed to be distributed." The drugs included weed, acid, and cocaine, and were sold in Patriots Park, across the street from West High. "The proceeds went to Brian while he was in."

Brian claimed that jail was a form of higher education in drug dealing. "Jail totally changed me, because I got a lot of knowledge from the people in there as far as mistakes they made and how they got caught. I had knowledge from books on how to balance and finance. Then I gathered more knowledge in there on what people use to make their money, how they package and sell [drugs]."

After he was released in March 1988, he said he made a bid for legitimacy, getting hired to work as a stock clerk at a grocery store. He enjoyed the job, but the owner's son started harassing him and had him fired for showing up fifteen minutes late for work.

Brian resumed full-time drug dealing and, around August, began selling from a new location, an apartment in the Village Lane complex. The apartment wasn't even his. The tenant was his old girlfriend Rosalyn, who had returned from Los Angeles after giving birth to a girl called Kerisha. The father was allegedly her own stepfather, whom she accused of raping her. Brian moved in after "persuading" her current boyfriend, who he said was a cocaine abuser, to move out. "I didn't think it was right that the child was submitted to that."

When he and Rosalyn were kids, they always talked about getting married and having a family. They weren't married, but with Kerisha, they had a family. Brian "was a very good father," Rosalyn said. "I didn't really have a daddy. I had men who were staying with my mom. It made me feel good."

Brian's own family was going through another upheaval. His father was back in town and trying to reconcile with his mother. According to Brian and Rosalyn, Billy was at the same time dating Rosalyn's mother. "I felt torn because I didn't know whether or not to tell my mom," Brian said. He eventually did tell her.

Now Brian was the man around another house. It was his duty to make sure Rosalyn and Kerisha "had everything they wanted." Dealing drugs, including cocaine and marijuana, was a means to that end. That would obviously submit Kerisha to more of the drug culture. But if that was a contradiction, he didn't see it.

He could make some easy money with little effort in Village Lane, a sprawling mass of grimy brown stucco. All he had to do was serve a fraction of the complex's two hundred apartments. Whereas some apartments are buried so deep in the complex that a visitor would need navigational tools to find them, Rosalyn's backed onto a parking lot off the street. Even better, the rear had a sliding door hidden from the lot by a fence. To make a sale, Brian would ease the door open and pass the dope over the fence.

But Brian wasn't exactly breaking into the big time. According to James Oliver, a Village Lane resident and friend of Brian's, he was selling mostly weed in quantities of an eighth of an ounce. "It was nothing serious." There were scores of black guys like him in Bakersfield doing the same thing, getting by on nickel-and-dime sales. The only thing that made him stand out was that he managed to get busted—in court.

On December 19, 1988, Brian appeared before Judge Randall to explain why he was behind in paying a fine levied for his burglary conviction. Stepping up to the bench, he fumbled in his overcoat pocket for some paperwork. Out came the papers, and so—onto the floor—did a bag of marijuana. Before Brian could grab it, the bailiff was upon him.

"Man gives judge straight dope in court," headlined the *Bakersfield Californian* on its front page the next day, giving Brian his first taste of notoriety. "Every time I think I've seen it all in this business, as a lawyer and a judge, something else comes along to prove me wrong," it quoted Randall as saying.

Two weeks later, the judge dispatched Brian back to jail for sixty days for violating his probation. He also ordered him to take regular drug tests as part of his probation.

After Brian was released again, he found a way to stand out for something other than stupidity. It was a drug that black people rarely used, let alone sold; it was a drug that was on the cutting edge of fashion in Bakersfield; above all, it was a drug that might make Brian somebody people looked up to, even feared.

The Eighth Deadly Sin

Methamphetamine is like an evil Cinderella. The ugly sisters Cocaine and Heroin go to the ball, seducing the attention of law enforcement, the drug warriors of the White House, and the media. In recent years, synthetic drugs such as PCP and Ecstasy have grabbed some headlines. Meanwhile, Cinderella "Speed" stays quietly at home, wreaking just as much social havoc as her high-profile sisters.

Speed has generally been portrayed as the "poor man's cocaine," the drug of cramming students, long-haul truckers, bikers, and blue-collar workers. It's not associated, like cocaine, with glamorous Hollywood stars and jet-setting smugglers or, like crack cocaine, with the urban poor; it's not associated, like heroin or other opiates, with rock musicians or even Romantic poets.

During the late 1970s, as TV commercials warned that "speed kills" and as cocaine became more available, use of amphetamines declined sharply. But from Bakersfield to Baltimore, speed is staging a comeback. Where once it was most popular in the form of amphetamine pills—the famous "pink hearts" or "black beauties"—it is now pouring out of clandestine labs as powdered methamphetamine.

According to a recent study, meth use in some parts of the country is up 500 percent compared with the mid-1980s. "Domestically produced methamphetamine looms as a potential national drug crisis for the 1990s," the National Institute for Drug Abuse warned in 1988.

From the supply standpoint, there is no need to bother with Colombian kingpins, Mexican airstrips, or poppy growers in the Burmese Triangle. Speed can be made with commonly available chemicals and lab equipment. Meth labs dot the countryside of rural California like cacti. For consumers, the drug is a cost saving compared with competing products. They also get just as potent—and at least as addictive—a narcotic bang for their buck.

Aldous Huxley, author and drug connoisseur, said speed was the only addition to the seven deadly sins. Writer Gail Sheehy called it a "Christmas package with a time bomb inside." One study, *The Speed Culture*, compared speed with opiates: "The taste for heroin or morphine is an acquired one . . . It is like a taste for olives and oysters. The taste for amphetamine is more like a taste for chocolate layer cake—easier to come by and possibly more dangerous . . . The fact is that amphetamines are much more likely to produce damaging drug dependency than opiates."

The physical effects of speed dependency are bad enough—loss of sleep, appetite, and weight, acute stomach cramps, facial sores, and tics. Users may feel so exhausted, they cannot even stand up. The mental toll of abuse reads like a laundry list of modern-day horrors. Indeed, Lester Grinspoon and Peter Hedlom, the authors of *The Speed Culture*, wrote, the amphetamine abuser "is a gross caricature of many of the pathological, ultimately destructive features of the society that produced him."

The distinctive features of behavior on speed include endlessly repeating the same action. The central nervous system is so stimulated that users have to keep busy at all times, even if it means compulsively cleaning house or fixing electronic gadgets. More destructive still is a tendency toward paranoia, particularly during withdrawal. Users can experience hallucinations, both visual and auditory. They are incapable of maintaining stable emotional and sexual relationships. And it also takes very little provocation—an imagined slight, a shadow on the wall—to turn speed abusers extremely violent.

Dr. Ronald Siegel, a UCLA drug expert and author, argues that methamphetamine "might prove to be more violent-associated than cocaine because . . . the meth user tends to be more of a working person, drivers, people that are in situations where they can become violent on the highway or at work."

Others believe that antisocial, schizophrenic-type personalities are predisposed to use speed. One study looked at the histories of fourteen people admitted to hospitals after psychotic episodes that were related to amphetamines. It found that twelve of them "had a clear history of overt or covert rejection by one or both parents."

In Bakersfield, methamphetamine is "crank," its users "cranksters." When users are high, they are "tweaking" or "amped up." They inhale the drug through the nose, eat it, or "slam" (inject) it directly into the bloodstream. Crank has the consistency and texture of Parmesan cheese, and varies in color from white to peanut butter brown, depending on how thoroughly it is cleansed of impurities. Its noxious smell is like that of stale urine or dirty socks. It is cut with everything from vitamin B-12 to talc.

According to one dealer, an eight ball (one eighth of an ounce or 3.5 grams) of crank now fetches a top retail price of $200 in Bakersfield, compared with $250 for the same quantity of cocaine. As for potency, "coke fiends have to snort the whole eight ball to get high," the dealer said. "With crank, you only have to do one line." Depending on how much it is cut, an eight ball can yield as many as fifty lines.

Some users gave me graphic descriptions of crank's effects. Here is Jodie Davis, Stephanie's friend: "Once it hits your stomach and there's nothing in your stomach, it makes the acid in your stomach more disturbing. So you get severe cramps. Your stomach kind of goes, 'Oh my God,' because there's nothing in your stomach."

Or on a "tweaker" she knew from Oildale: "She had cranker sores. You get them when you touch crank and touch your face. They're not like zits, they're dry spots, like cold sores. This lady had very bad skin. She was very skinny, extremely bony. Her mouth constantly did this," she said, twitching her jaw from side to side.

Here is James Oliver on the mental toll: "When you start coming down, your body starts feeling ran [sic] down. You start feeling tired and groggy. You can't sleep because you're still amped up. When people come in with problems and stuff and start nagging at you, it gets on your nerves and you start getting frustrated. Then before you know it, you're trying to do something to end it so you don't have to listen to the problem."

Detectives Steve Ramsey, Jim Bennett, and Bill Bailey of the Bakersfield police are on the crank front lines. The city's large blue-collar oil-field-worker population and proximity to the meth labs of southern California make it prime territory for the drug. "There's a huge market for crank up here," Ramsey said.

The detectives are familiar with all the attributes of the crank culture. They can spot a "crank dude" by his garage. Junked cars fester outside, and inside, car stereos in various stages of disrepair are stacked from floor to ceiling. "You drive by the house at three or four in the morning, the garage door's open, he's running back and forth," Bennett said.

They know that all cranksters care about is the next high. "It becomes a life-style to them," said Bailey. "Personal hygiene is nothing—they don't brush their teeth, they smell. Their family doesn't make any difference to them anymore."

The "narcs" also know of cranksters so paranoid that they install listening devices on their front porch to alert them to approaching visitors. Bennett estimated that 90 percent are armed, and "it's not uncommon to find tons of guns in their houses . . . It's one hundred percent accurate to assume these people are more violent than people on any other drug except perhaps PCP."

Bailey agreed: "As far as the people I've gone up against in law enforcement, they are the scariest because they're so unpredictable. They have guns, and you can't tell what they're thinking."

One thing, however, that all three veteran cops had never encountered was a black dealer. It was an all-white drug in Bakersfield, they said. The city's blacks were too busy messing with crack to move into meth.

When I told them that not only was Brian Stafford a black crank dealer, but he also sold exclusively to whites—some even from Oildale—they reacted as if cocaine cartel boss Pablo Escobar had decided to start pushing Quaaludes. "All-white customers going to a black guy to buy it is real weird," Bennett said. "I can't think of any dealer in this area that's been black."

Brian told me he heard about crank for the first time in jail, but he didn't try it until the late spring of 1989 when he, Rosalyn, and Kerisha went to see some friends, Kevin and Teresa. The two couples played cards while Kerisha played with Teresa's daughter in the bedroom.

As the evening wore on, Brian started to get tired. "Check this out," Kevin said. "I know something that will keep you awake. Let me fix it." He poured two glasses of orange juice for Brian and Rosalyn. "Just drink it."

Fifteen minutes later, Brian couldn't sit still. At three-thirty in the morning, he and Rosalyn went home because Kerisha was falling asleep. But they couldn't sleep at all. A couple of days later, Kevin told Brian what it was he had served them— an orange and crank cocktail. "I'll make you a deal," Kevin said. "I'll buy some if you think you can sell it."

So Brian sounded out some people at Village Lane and discovered that many of them used crank and were looking for a reliable supplier. At the time, he had dropped out of the cocaine business and was only selling the occasional marijuana joint. But after this informal poll, he told Kevin, "Go ahead and get some. I know people who are going to buy it."

Crank is a potent enough substance in anybody's hands. In Brian's, it became positively explosive, a means of acting out his ultimate fantasy. "He wanted to be the God everybody looked up to," said Rosalyn. "He always thought of himself as Al Capone. We were watching [the movie] *Scarface*. He said, 'That guy right there, I'm Al Capone. I'm the black Al Capone.' "

Joker and the Bitches

With crank, Brian started making enough money to edge up the drug-dealing charts. He said he quickly progressed from buying small quantities such as eight balls to quarter ounces. He would spend from $325 to $425 a quarter, depending on quality. "I wanted the best quality, so I spent three hundred seventy-five. Off of that quarter ounce, I'm going to make close to fifteen hundred dollars ... I'm moving up the ladder."

James Oliver, who said he was "more or less Brian's right-hand man" at the time, said Brian was making as much as twenty-five hundred to thirty-five hundred dollars a week. "One day I had his beeper when he was at his mom's house. I made fifteen hundred dollars in seven or eight hours ... Before I got back [from making a delivery], somebody else was paging me."

Rosalyn Bookout came up with similar figures. "The business was ninety percent crank. Once he started doing crank, he left weed alone ... He'd make five hundred to seven hundred dollars a day."

Brian's market for crank expanded beyond Village Lane to neighboring apartment complexes, as far afield of the Bakersfield city limits as Oildale to the north and Old River to the south. He also had no trouble with supply. One early wholesale supplier was a fifteen-year-old called Tommy whose father stored vast quantities of crank in the family garage. "His father had a freezer full of cubes that looked like sugar," Rosalyn marveled.

Brian recalled Tommy coming over with a pound of crank in a Ziploc bag that he had stolen from his father. He wanted only three hundred dollars for it when it was probably worth at least thirteen hundred. "This is what I want to get," Tommy said, showing Brian a photograph of an Uzi assault rifle.

Despite the healthy profits, Brian did not act the part of the flashy drug dealer. He didn't buy a car or wear gold jewelry. A lot of his product, he distributed free to friends and prized customers. The free samples "didn't bother me," he said. "Money wasn't an issue."

The real issue involved in dealing crank was something less tangible than money but equally seductive—power. "For Brian, drug dealing was more of an ego trip, more of a power thing," said Jodie Davis. "He'd give you a line, ten people a line. That's twenty-five dollars you've given away. It was like, 'Hey, I'm a dope dealer.' It was like a big game . . . more of an 'impress you' kind of thing. You know, Mr. Badass, don't burn me."

Brian found there was almost no limit to what people would do for him in exchange for a free line of crank—even white people. All his customers were white, and he developed a hard-core group of about half a dozen who became more than just customers. They found him new customers, delivered crank for him, ran errands for him. They called him "Joker," a name coined by a Village Lane customer with whom he saw the *Batman* movie several times. Other people called them "Brian's bitches."

The first connection with this group was through James Oliver. He took Brian to an apartment complex near Village Lane to meet Steve Emmons, a crank user who worked at a gas station. "We sat there all night getting wired and stoned," James recalled.

He continued: "Two or three days later, Steve dropped by Brian's house and said he had some friends he wanted to introduce Brian to and he thought would make a lot more money for him. Brian was all game for it . . . About two days later after that, Steve came by and said, 'Okay, they're on their way over now to meet you.' So they came over, and we got introduced to them. Things just went from there."

(Emmons declined to be interviewed for this book.)

Brian's sister, Twylla, started noticing these new friends at Village Lane whenever she visited. When she asked him what they were there for, he replied: "We're in a Bible-study group."

They were a motley-looking crew. They included brown-haired, blue-eyed Steve, who was twenty years old; burly, bearded Charles Bohlinger, twenty-two, known as "Gator" since childhood, when he used to eat like one; Mike Bohlinger, twenty-five, Gator's brother and physical opposite with his tall, skinny build; and finally lanky Rickey Rodgers, twenty-four, with the shoulder-length, dark hair.

You wouldn't expect to see any of them hanging around with a black guy. Some of them looked like heavy-metal rock fans, some would never set foot in a black neighborhood such as Cottonwood, and some had spent time in all-white Kern County oil towns such as Taft.

In Brian's favor was that he didn't conform to the stereotypical Bakersfield view of blacks. Compared with Jodie's boyfriend, Calvin, who talked in a heavy southern drawl, his words eliding into one another and his language laced with slang, Brian sounded like an elocution teacher. He even conversed more articulately than many of his white friends who had pronounced "Okie"-style accents and never met a double negative they didn't like.

Calvin would complain to him about it. "I would use words another black person would know. Brian wouldn't know what it mean. I'd say something like, 'Dude, there ain't no ups with dude.' He'd say, 'What do you mean, "no ups with"?' 'It mean nothing is happening, Brian.' "

He also didn't have the black "attitude," said James Oliver. "Brian wasn't what you would really call black . . . Most black guys you meet have this attitude when they get around a bunch of white people because they feel uncomfortable. Because Brian was going out with a white chick, it never bothered him. He was just like one of us."

Rosalyn sometimes wondered if Brian wanted to be white. "I always teased him about being a white preppy rich dude. It was the way he talked and carried himself. I used to call him 'Whitey,' and he used to get real mad at me."

"Brian acted white," said Stephanie. "I acted more black than him . . . You know how a lot of black people think white people are better, and in order to be somebody, you have to talk properly? Maybe that's what he strived for, because Brian's the kind of person who liked to demand respect."

His "whiteness" could only win Brian so much respect from whites. Largess with crank was his main weapon. "They were his friends because of drugs," Jodie Davis said. "If my friend asked me to do something for them, I wouldn't expect anything in return. They expected Brian to give them a line . . . If it wasn't for dope, I don't even think those people would be around together."

Whatever he wanted them to do—fetch him a Pepsi from the store, collect money from a customer, do his laundry—they would do for a free line. "You could say he was the boss," James said. "What he said, everybody did."

Calvin recalled that Brian, who didn't even have a driver's license, always found a willing chauffeur. "It was, 'I'll give you a little bit of crank to take me here, I'll give you a little bit of weed to take me here.'"

It wasn't any old crank he was dishing out as payment. You could get heavily cut junk all over town. But according to Jodie, "Good stuff is hard to find. It's not like you can buy it at a grocery store and take it back." Brian offered only premium merchandise. "He was giving off excellent stuff," said James. "You couldn't find any better."

Like all drug dealers, however, Brian faced the daily threat of being burned or ripped off. With crank, you couldn't even trust your friends. Moreover, if you had a lot of users around you, they weren't likely to be mellow and passive but hyperactive and aggressive. They could undermine you at any moment. Brian was able to cement his power by using, or threatening to use, violence.

Other members of the group—for example, Gator Bohlinger—weren't exactly pacifists. Gator, who sports a tattoo of a pit bull on his arm, was another Bakersfield High School dropout. He stayed there until he was eighteen, but only completed his sophomore year. During his last semester, he failed almost every course he took, including gym and "Family Living."

He had only been out of school a few months when he was convicted of assault after a bizarre confrontation with a bicyclist in Bakersfield. He was riding in his friend Chuck Oliver's pickup. The truck's windshield water jets were modified to squirt water away from the truck rather than on the windshield. As they passed "this huge dude on a bicycle riding down the street," Oliver sprayed him with the jets. The cyclist chased them and starting pounding the truck with his pump. Gator reached for his slingshot. Using a lug nut as a projectile, he fired—and missed. He and Oliver then drove off.

The first to be arrested two hours later was a friend of Gator's, a victim of mistaken identity because he had the misfortune to have extremely bad teeth like Gator's. Four hours after that, Gator turned himself in. Although accused of felony assault with a deadly weapon, he plea-bargained to a misdemeanor and got off with sixty days in jail and three years probation.

"Probably wouldn't be a good idea to mess with me," he boasted at a court hearing several years later. When I asked him for an interview outside the courtroom, he responded, "I'll knock you down if you come near me again."

But Brian was a veteran of violence compared with Gator. He had grown up on the rough streets of black neighborhoods and had thrown his weight around in jail. He would later insist that it was not until he met Stephanie in the summer of 1989 and started using large quantities of crank himself that he became unusually violent. But there is evidence that— long before Brian even discovered crank—he used violence to solve problems or vent his wrath.

"Yeah, he had the meanness in him before he started doing [crank]," James Oliver said. "But as he started doing it, it started bringing it out more."

To Rosalyn he was always two different people. "He had a temper that scared me. He could be real nice one minute, then real mean. Since I've known him, he's always had a double personality. It came out worse when he did drugs. The third day in a week would be his fucked day. He'd be mad at everybody. I'd stay away from him."

She added: "He was always violent . . . He liked to hurt people, he liked to see people in pain."

Rosalyn recalled an incident after Brian's father returned to town. One day he asked Billy to lend him a VCR. "Do you really think I'm going to trust you with something that's mine?" Billy said. "You'll probably go out and hawk it." A few days later, he let an older son borrow it.

"Brian got very upset," Rosalyn told me. "That night he and

[a friend] went out in his mom's Pinto with a BB gun and shot at his dad's house."

On August 15, 1988, Brian allegedly assaulted Felipe Garcia, a fourteen-year-old neighbor at Cannon Avenue. According to police, Garcia wanted to talk to Brian's brother Shawn about problems he was having with several neighborhood kids. "Brian Stafford came instead, and Garcia said Stafford argued with him, then hit him in the face," the report said. Charges were not, however, pressed against Brian.

He was charged in the case of Tadeusz Osinski, a fifty-eight-year-old Polish immigrant who was attacked and robbed in his apartment in a complex near Village Lane on the night of May 19, 1988. Police found him so badly beaten about the eyes that they were barely open. Blood covered his shirt. In police photographs, he looks like he got hit by a bus.

He told police in broken English that he answered a knock on his door, and two black women entered the apartment. They were immediately followed by a black male and a white male. The black male knocked him to the ground, beat him, and stole his wallet while the women stole items including stereo equipment, a TV, and a VCR from the living room.

The commotion awoke Osinski's twenty-seven-year-old son, Peter, in his bedroom. Peter said that when he tried to come to his father's rescue, he was confronted in the hallway by a white male brandishing a knife.

The Osinskis only gave vague descriptions of the suspects, and the initial investigation harvested no leads. Then, in December 1988, state parole agents found credit cards belonging to Tadeusz at a home where Rose Marie Shoemake, a cousin of Brian's, was living with her ex-con boyfriend. The following February, she pleaded no contest to robbery in the Osinski case, and implicated four others—Brian, Gwendolyn McCoy (sister of Francine), and two guys called James and Jason.

McCoy and Brian were charged with robbery and assault on March 6. Brian was arrested at Village Lane on March 22 in nothing but his underwear. But the charges against him were dismissed in mid-April after Tadeusz Osinski was unable to identify him in a lineup. "As far as Mr. Stafford, we had no case," said Bud Starr, a Kern County prosecutor.

It turned out they didn't have much of a case against Brian's cousin McCoy either. Defense witnesses at a preliminary hearing gave McCoy a strong alibi and impeached Shoemake by testifying that she had a grudge against McCoy. "She came off as credible, and her witnesses came off as credible," Starr told me. He decided to drop the charges.

In my interview with Brian, he said the whole thing was a setup by Shoemake, "one of my crazy cousins."

But in researching this book, I was given another account of what happened at the Osinski apartment, in which the "James" identified by Shoemake was James Oliver, and in which the beating was Brian's handiwork.

The account was that of James himself. A muscular youth, six feet tall with brownish blond hair, mustache, and jagged teeth, James avoids drugs these days and maintains a full-time job. But James, who ran away from home at age fourteen, admits that when he knew Brian, he was a full-time teen-age delinquent. At the time of the Osinski beating, he was seventeen.

According to James, McCoy and Shoemake were already at the Osinskis' when he and Brian knocked on the door. Brian, who believed his cousins were being held there against their will for sexual purposes, asked to see McCoy.

"The Russian [sic] guy said, 'Who are you?' . . . [Brian] started beating the crap out of this Russian dude." When Osinski tried to grab a knife, "I kicked the guy in the face full force . . . That more or less took the fight out of him . . . I even got blood on my shoe . . . But Brian continued to pound him . . . The old man's laying there, he ain't getting up by any means, but Brian's still sitting there beating the crap out of him."

James said he was responsible for confronting the younger Osinski. "I turned around and looked up the hallway and saw this big, huge Russian dude . . . I knew I was going to get my ass creamed if I didn't do something fast, so I got my knife, chased his son down the hallway . . . I ended up chasing him into the bedroom, and he barricaded the door."

As for the robbery, "We ended up taking his microwave, his color TV, his stereo, the money he had."

It is possible that James has an ax to grind with Brian. In the late summer of 1989, they became enemies. But the details in his account closely match those in the police report. James accurately pointed out to me the location of the Osinski apartment. I also showed him a copy of the photos of the battered Tadeusz Osinski and asked if he had ever seen the man before. "Yeah, that's the Russian dude Brian beat up," James replied, without hesitating.

If Brian had been tried and convicted in the case, he could have been sentenced to a maximum of fourteen years in prison, five alone because of his prior burglary conviction. Starr said he could have easily got a dozen years.

After making his new friends in the summer of 1989, Brian beefed up his potential for violence by accumulating an arsenal of guns. The days of fists and BB guns were past—now he was interested in real artillery. "He got really obsessed with guns," said Rosalyn Bookout. "He loved to show them off. It was so people would be afraid of him."

One time, Rosalyn recalled, a drug customer came around to the apartment, claiming that Brian had cheated him on a dope deal and demanding his money back. Brian pulled out a shotgun and pointed it at the customer. "Leave before I kill you!" he yelled.

Rosalyn said that Brian mostly got his guns through Steve Emmons and Gator Bohlinger. Around July, he made a particularly good deal with Gator, trading him a .44 Magnum for two shotguns. Brian had acquired the .44 in a crank deal. Gator had paid fifty dollars to a drug user for one of the shotguns, a twelve-gauge. He took the other, a twenty-gauge, from a guy he said "burned" a friend of his. "I told him that I was going to take it, and if he didn't like it, that was just his problem . . . I just knocked him down and took it."

The twenty-gauge shotgun was already sawed off. Brian wanted a matching pair, so he went with the Bohlingers to their parents' comfortable home in a new subdivision of southwest Bakersfield. Mike sawed off the barrel of the twelve-gauge in the garage. Brian now had what he would call his "toys."

It was a good deal for Brian—"I don't like handguns . . . They're easier for children to play with," he said—but not for his friend. Gator sold the .44 magnum to the boyfriend of a woman named Linda Swanson, whose teenage sons, Chad and Travis, were also customers of Brian's. According to Gator, Swanson, whom he called "a conniving old lady," told him it was stolen and she was going to the police. He took the gun back and destroyed it with a blowtorch.

However, Gator never confronted Brian to discuss how the deal turned out. "Did you say, 'Hey, I gave you two guns and now you gave me a stolen .44 Magnum?' " he was asked in court.

"No," he replied, as if the question were ridiculous.

"Did you talk to Brian at all about making it square, [that] you had to torch this gun that you got, but he still had the two shotguns?"

"No."

Such was the loyalty—or perhaps fear—that Brian Stafford then inspired.

By July 1989, Rosalyn Bookout wasn't feeling much more for Brian than fear. Despite the money he was making for her and Kerisha, she was finding that life with Joker was no joke.

She was caught in a catch-22. She didn't like Brian dealing crank around the apartment, especially in the presence of her daughter; but if he carried on business elsewhere, she hardly saw him. She would ask him to stop dealing altogether, suggest he get a job and settle down. But he would just say, "Why should I when I'm making twice as much money in one day?"

Most worrying was that Brian would now hit her during their arguments. If Rosalyn tried to hit him back, "he'd choke me to where I'd pass out . . . He said he knocked me out so he wouldn't have to beat up on me."

The tension peaked on August 4, Brian's twenty-first birthday. According to Rosalyn, he came home with Calvin while she was wrapping some Nintendo games as his present. He found the front door bolted and apparently presumed she was with another man. When she let him in, he started packing.

"What's wrong?" she asked.

He threw her against the wall and stuck a loaded shotgun in her face. "I'm going to kill you," he screamed. "If I can't have you, nobody can." At that moment, the doorbell rang. It was Brian's mother, who had come over to take Kerisha to church. Brian hid the shotgun under the bed and eventually left with Calvin.

"The gun was what scared me," Rosalyn recalled. "I knew

that wasn't the same Brian. He hadn't pulled a gun on me before. I really think he would have killed me if his mother hadn't come in. When I looked in his eyes, it was like nobody was there. I thought I was gonna die."

"I didn't see the gun," Calvin said. "I just heard the conversation. There was a lot of cuss words. It was like, 'I'll blow your head off.' "

After this blowup, Brian moved the two miles east to Stephanie's place. With him came his drug business, his "bitches," and his "toys." He had not known Stephanie for even a month. But that did not matter to him. According to Brian, he had a genuine rapport with his new live-in lover. "No one's ever been there for her, and that's the one thing we share in common because my parents were divorced," he theorized. "Maybe that's why we hit it off so well, because we both knew how it felt."

Stephanie said later that Brian was "real nice" to her. He listened patiently to her problems, even told her he was planning to become a child psychologist. But she insisted the basis of the relationship was convenience, that Brian was a convenient way of getting back at Brandon.

"I wanted [Brandon], but I wanted to show him I could make it without him," she told me. Brian "just happened to be in the right place at the right time, and he had money and drugs, and I just got involved."

One thing she didn't say was that Brian was in the right place at the right time to do something about Phillip.

Simple Morals

According to Brian, they were more than just friends. He, Stephanie, Jodie, Calvin, and the white guys he had met at Village Lane had become a family. He didn't feel they were all together because of drugs. "Everybody was trying to watch out for each other. All my friends were like a family. Nobody wants to see anyone get in trouble because we're all like family, because all we've got . . . are each other."

James Oliver saw it the same way. "If one of us had a problem, then everybody had a problem," he said. "All of us would get together and solve it. If somebody was threatening to kick somebody's ass, we'd go over and take care of it."

He added: "It was friendship that brought us as close together as we were. The drugs and the money and everything were just something else added. Even without the drugs and the money, we would still have gotten along as we did."

It didn't have to be a prospective "ass kicking" to mobilize the family forces. They could point, for example, to what they did for Gator Bohlinger.

Gator, who, with his balding pate, blond beard, and bulging stomach, now reminded people of a bartender or a corpulent Moses, was arrested in Pismo Beach, a San Luis Obispo County resort, on August 4. He was charged with being in possession of a stolen all-terrain cycle and with giving a false ID to a police officer. After hearing of Gator's plight, Brian drove the 140 miles from Bakersfield with Mike Bohlinger to bail him out of jail. Their mission turned out to be fruitless—they didn't have enough money to post a cash bond, and besides, Gator was going to be released the next day. On August 8 Gator pleaded no contest to the false ID charge and was put on three years probation.

What mattered about the whole episode was that even though he bungled it, Brian had tried to come through for Gator in the clutch. What would he do about the much more serious problem Stephanie was having with Phillip?

Brian was aware of the problem even before he moved into the Eye Street apartment. One day he, Jodie, and Stephanie were sitting in Jodie's car, smoking weed. According to Jodie, Stephanie was saying that "Phillip had been harassing her mother for quite a long time, and she felt that it was either her mother or Phillip. At that time, she said that she wished or she wanted Phillip to be dead."

Jodie continued: "Phillip would kill her mother if she left. [Stephanie] felt the sooner Phillip was dead, the better off her mother would be. She said her mother did want Phillip killed."

Brian recalled some talk about Stephanie's mother being abused and "wanting someone to help her with a problem she had." Stephanie said "she was worried about her mom getting beat up by this guy and stuff. And the question came up, 'Why wouldn't her mom leave this dude?' It was more or less . . . that the dude would find her mom no matter where she went because he had friends."

Brian also said the subject of Phillip molesting Stephanie came up in this conversation. "Jodie had brought that up, and Stephanie never denied the allegation." She just looked at the floor. Brian was inclined to believe it, just as Tim Gray had.

Stephanie vehemently denies that Phillip ever molested her or that she ever told anyone he did. But as far as Brian was concerned, Phillip already had two major black marks against him in his moral grade book—he beat women and he molested children.

"My morals are simple," Brian told me. "One, don't hit women; two, don't molest children; three, your word is your life. Your word is nothing, you're nothing." But Brian hadn't given his word he would do anything yet. "It wasn't at the point of just coming out and taking somebody out."

He started edging toward that point after he moved in with Stephanie. Brian was usually around when Diana called the apartment, and Stephanie would tell him what they talked about. "She was just telling me how she was worried about her mom getting beat up by this guy." Then, as things got "more and more out of hand, the question came up about the killing. Diana was asking Stephanie, did she know anybody that could help her?"

Not surprisingly, Stephanie turned to Brian. She knew of his reputation for violence and of his access to guns. When he was living at Village Lane, she saw how he dealt with customers. "This guy came over, and Brian wanted his money from him. I guess he didn't have his money, so Brian socked him, gave him a black eye." But she only asked him at this time for his help finding someone else to kill Phillip. "The question came up, did I know anyone?" Brian said.

Stephanie told her mother she had asked Brian for help. Despite Diana's reputed prejudice toward blacks, she also told her that her new boyfriend was black. Because Brian often answered the phone when Diana called, Stephanie presumed her mother knew she was living with him.

Brian recalled one time when Stephanie got off the phone with her mother and "she tells me, 'My mom wants to know if you've heard anything about anyone helping her with her problem.' The problem was the murder—if there was anyone that we could find information out about doing it . . . More or less like every time she would get a phone call, she would ask me, do I know anything?"

During another call, Diana asked her daughter, "Does Brian have a car?"

"No, he doesn't."

"Well, tell Brian when all this is over, he can have the El Camino."

The car that Stephanie had wanted was now being offered to Brian. He thought it was "cool." "It was more or less like you do this for me, I'll do this for you . . . and you guys can live happily ever after and everything is gonna be all right, because I'm gonna take care of you."

It is not clear whether Diana directly solicited Brian for his help. In an interview with police on October 6, 1989, Brian said she asked him directly over the phone five to ten times. "She was asking me on the phone, do I know anyone who would be interested in this?" But in later court testimony, he contradicted himself, saying that all inquiries filtered through Stephanie.

Stephanie was adamant when I interviewed her. "She talked to him about it . . . I don't care what he denies. I was there . . . She would talk to me about it, and I would have to relay it to Brian, and then I'd say, 'You know what? You talk to him,' and hand him the phone. That's pretty obvious what they're talking about." She added: "It was my phone, in my apartment. I know they talked."

Brian had no trouble empathizing with Stephanie. He could see for himself how unhappy Phillip made her. The week she was at El Capitan, she called him and complained about how her stepfather was treating her—it was this call that Al Clarke interrupted. "She was saying Phillip wouldn't allow her to smoke and he was just on her ass all the time."

He decided to embark on a "comfort" mission and recruited Mike Bohlinger to drive him to Santa Barbara so he could give his girlfriend a hug. Like the Gator trip, it was futile—the gatekeeper would not allow them into the park. When Stephanie got back to Bakersfield, she was still "pissed off" at Phillip.

Brian could also see how Stephanie blamed herself for her mother's plight, how she felt pressured to do things so Phillip wouldn't beat her mother. Two issues were particularly aggravating.

There was the September rent that Stephanie was supposed to pay from her flagging wages. The money soon disappeared, some of it literally when she and Brian went to a fast-food restaurant. Stephanie took out her wallet, but her boyfriend "didn't feel it was right" for the woman to pay. He put the wallet on the roof of the car. By the time they drove off, they had forgotten about the wallet and it was lost. Stephanie said she gave the rest of the money to Brian, who spent it on drug supplies.

Diana paid the rent, and Stephanie started complaining to Brian that Phillip wanted it paid back immediately. She would say that Phillip was going to beat up her mother again because of the rent, and that "her mom was telling her that Phillip was going to kick her out of the apartment and not help her anymore."

Another issue was something Phillip didn't even know about yet—the telephone. He had told Stephanie she could not have a phone in the apartment until she got a job and proved she was responsible. She had one installed behind his back. When Diana called her, it was usually in the afternoon before Phillip got home from work. But Diana kept telling Stephanie that the subterfuge would be over as soon as he saw the August phone bill.

According to Stephanie, "She would just start saying he couldn't find out I had a phone because I wasn't supposed to have a phone. And when the phone bill comes in, he was going to beat her up for it. And she was afraid, and we had to do something fast."

James Oliver recalled some talk within the "family" about going to Santa Barbara to beat Phillip up. They had heard "all those stories" from Stephanie about how her mother "was always being beat on and mistreated. So Brian said, 'Okay, we'll just go over there and beat the crap out of him and show him what it's like.' "

Another plan Brian supposedly floated involved Danny Taylor, a thirty-year-old, tattoo-covered, long-haired biker from Oildale. Taylor, who had recently served jail time for raping his ex-wife, would later claim to be Brian's "enforcer," but nobody associated with Brian's business could recall him doing any enforcing. They do recall him being a crank customer.

Taylor testified that he went to a barbecue at Eye Street and had this conversation with the host:

"Danny, you know what? I can trust you and I need a favor done," Brian said. "I need somebody put away."

"Like who?"

"Stephanie's stepdad."

Taylor wasn't interested. "Man, no way. I've had enough trouble, I don't need no more."

Brian denied ever soliciting Taylor, but Jodie Davis confirmed some of the biker's story. She remembered him coming to the barbecue in Harley-Davidson T-shirt, jeans, and cowboy boots—"not somebody you'd see talking to a black dude." But she overheard him talking to Brian.

Brian "was telling him that Phillip was a real asshole and that he was beating up Stephanie's mom and . . . he mentioned to him something about killing Phillip. It was like, 'Would you kill him?' " She said Taylor replied jokingly: "Even if I got caught, they wouldn't put me in jail because I'm crazy anyway. I'd get out."

Nothing materialized with the beating plan or with Danny Taylor. Brian really didn't do much about Phillip during the first few weeks he knew Stephanie. The obstacle was not empathy or incentive, but concentration. He was just so busy. "I had so many other things that I had to think about," he explained. "I had obligations that I had to fulfill . . . I had people that I was helping out."

Obligations

Just look at a typical day in Brian's life as he organized himself and his friends at the Eye Street apartment. It would be so hectic that he and his new right-hand man Gator would have to plan it the night before.

"It was just like going to school," he said. "We set up a daily plan. Okay, today we're going to do this. We're going to go over here, we're going to buy some clothes, we're going to come back, we're going to get high; then we're going to go buy some weed and come back and get high; then we're going to go pick up the crank, come back, and get high. Package it up, go sell some, come back. By then, it should be dark. Then we'll go out."

The dope business seemed only to have prospered since Brian moved to Eye Street. A procession of buyers filed up the flagstone path leading from the street to the stucco cottage. "There was foot traffic from seven A. M. to five the next morning," said Linda Good, a neighbor. "We used to sit out and watch people come and go."

When Brian wasn't at the apartment, he could conduct business with a pager which Gator had obtained for him. This wasn't the primitive kind that only provides the caller's phone number; on this pager, the caller could leave a voice message, drug request included.

Stephanie also helped out. "I did [crank] for him when he wasn't there. I'd wait for people and they'd come and get it, but he was the one who went and picked it up." She said Brian was dealing mostly in quarter ounces and eight balls of crank. Sometimes she would mind hundreds of dollars in cash for him.

Brian and his freeloading friends were as busy using as they were selling. As their tolerance to the drug grew, they had to use more to achieve the desired effect.

Brian said his personal use, which had begun at only a couple of lines a day, was now approaching a quarter ounce. That seems very unlikely—if each line was a quarter gram, he would have had to be a human vacuum cleaner, snorting nearly thirty lines a day. More likely, he was doing about a couple of grams. At any rate, Calvin Monigan said, "Every time I look at him, he was partying. He was snorting, sniffing everything in sight."

The "family" was equally voracious. Gator tried to pass himself off as a "moderate" user. "There's times I won't touch it for a week," he said. "Then there's times I will do more in a day than I would have done in a week . . . It's not an addiction. It's just that sometimes I want it so, you know, I can either do it or I can't."

Brian was a cordial host. "I just put it on the mirror," he said. The house policy was: "Take what you want."

Sometimes they would challenge one another to crank-snorting competitions to see who could stay up the longest without sleep. Two- or three-day sleepless binges were common among the group; one or two of them could even make it to a week. "It's a challenge," Brian explained. Stephanie also joined in. Three days was her limit.

Despite all this activity, some who dealt with Brian when he lived at Eye Street contend the scale of his drug enterprise was actually quite puny. "He was a piddler," said Sean Stanphill. Another associate, Derrick Oliver (no relation to James), said Brian was still a low-level, "nickel and dime" dealer.

Brian obtained most of his supplies through "fronts." In such deals, the retailer does not pay his wholesaler with up-front cash, but with the proceeds from his sales. As the retail price is higher than the wholesale, there should be some profit left over for the retailer. But according to Stanphill, Brian used so much of his "front" for himself and his friends that he struggled to pay back his wholesaler, let alone make a profit. As a result, his wholesaler would only trust him with small quantities such as eight balls.

"We wouldn't consider somebody picking up eight balls as that big a deal," said Sgt. Mark Grimm of the Bakersfield police narcotics squad.

"He wasn't really dealing crank," Stanphill said. "The guy who was selling it to him was the one dealing."

The point may be not that Brian was a major dealer, but that he was trying desperately to act like one. "He was always trying to be something he wasn't yet," said Shalamar Fields. "Like, he's the biggest dope dealer around this side of town . . . He always thought he was bigger than what he was . . . His life was based around fantasies."

The fantasy meant taking care of his obligations as "Mr. Badass," meting out violence whenever he needed to maintain his reputation. He seemed to be involved in enough fights during the summer of 1989 to fill a top rank boxing card, and he usually made sure other "family" members were around to serve as seconds or spectators.

One opponent was eighteen-year-old Chuck Blankenship, who was a friend of the Bohlinger brothers and Rickey Rodgers and had met Brian at the same time they did. Apparently Chuck committed the sin of describing Rosalyn Bookout, Twylla Stafford, and Steve Emmons's wife as bitches. "Brian was on drugs and he just had enough," James Oliver said.

After Gator and another friend brought Chuck to a Village Lane parking lot, Brian went up to the car and "started socking him through the window. Then he dragged him out and slammed his head on the car. I guess Chuck went out, because his whole body just went limp."

James himself was another opponent. The former "right-hand man" said he had become disillusioned with Brian and the crank life-style. "As he started doing more drugs, his attitude started changing. It was, fuck everybody. He was just out for himself . . . I was tired seeing him get worse into it. I didn't want to end up like that." When James tried to break out of the circle, Brian interpreted that as disloyalty. "He was feeling like I was a traitor to him . . . You just got your ass whupped if you weren't all the way one-hundred percent loyal to him."

Brian told me that James did betray him but in a different manner. He said James was hanging around with someone who had become his worst enemy—Shalamar Fields. "He was thinking Shalamar was the thing."

Attempted "whuppings" soon materialized. According to James, Steve Emmons and Gator in one car and two strangers in another tried to run him down. Then Brian cornered him one day at Village Lane. "Brian started egging me on to fight him. I wasn't too keen. I'd seen him beat up people pretty good." Each later claimed he kicked the other's ass, but according to Shalamar, "It wasn't really a fight . . . It was a disrespect, power-trip type of thing. Brian thought he had all the power."

The most bitter and violent of Brian's feuds involved Fields. "Shalamar was my arch rival, my enemy of enemies," Brian told me.

It was as if Shalamar were his mirror image, trying to muscle in on his territory. He also sold drugs, hung out with white guys, and was an alumnus of the Kern County jail—his record included convictions for battery, receiving stolen property, and theft. He looked a lot like Brian, with his toothy smile, ebony skin, flattop hairdo, and stocky, burly build. He even spoke as articulately as Brian.

"They were always competing," Rosalyn Bookout said. "Shalamar didn't bow down to Brian as easily as other people did. Shalamar let that be seen, that he was not afraid of him."

"It was getting to be a gang type of thing," Shalamar told me in an interview. "I got this side of the road, you got that side of the road, don't fuck with my side of the road. It got to the point where we hated each other."

Shalamar admitted to being somewhat intimidated by his rival. "It was the way he talked to people. He talks a gang of shit . . . He talks enough shit to make a person intimidated . . . When you're sitting down talking to him, it's a trip, because he's got a fucked-up evil look and he can talk sensible as hell if he wants to. I guess that's what makes it so much more intimidating, because someone that's evil-looking and sensible at the same time, you don't too much want to fuck with anyway."

What caused most of the trouble between them was women. Brian suspected Shalamar of going out with his then girlfriend Gloria Rodriguez while he was in jail on the burglary charge. All hell broke loose when Shalamar went to stay with Rosalyn after Brian left her.

Although Brian had found himself a new girlfriend, he still visited Village Lane regularly. Rosalyn let him see Kerisha, who now called him "Daddy," whenever he wanted. According to Rosalyn, she and Brian would sometimes sleep together. But more often, it was more physical abuse, not love, that he dished out. On September 5 Rosalyn went to the hospital with a severely sprained wrist and hand. She later testified that Brian had rammed her fist into a cement wall. Brian denied ever assaulting Rosalyn. Such behavior would obviously conflict with the second plank of his moral credo. But several sources said they saw him abuse her. James recalled seeing him slam her into a closet door and slap her in a parking lot near Village Lane.

Rosalyn said she had no romantic interest in Shalamar—"I told him he could move in because he didn't have a place to stay." She also wanted him around to protect her when Brian visited.

Brian was having none of it. "The first time Brian came around after moving out, he came in through the back door, saw Shalamar, and hit him," she said.

"Me and Brian had probably five fights," Shalamar estimated.

One fight featured the two of them trading blows in a Village Lane parking lot arena. Brian was "talking all that shit—you were with Gloria and this and that, and fucked me around, whatever," Shalamar said. "I said, 'Fuck it, since you feel that way, we might as well just do it.' "

"They pounded on each other pretty good," said James Oliver, who was at ringside. "Everybody we knew was out there in the parking lot watching this fight."

Brian didn't just rely on his fists. When Shalamar knocked on Rosalyn's door one day, Brian burst out, sawed-off shotgun at the ready. How Shalamar escaped with his life is unclear. According to Rosalyn, she grabbed the gun away from Brian before he could fire it, allowing Shalamar to make his getaway. Brian claimed the gun wasn't loaded and that he wasn't really serious about killing his rival. "If I was going to smoke Shalamar, I could have smoked him then."

Amid all this mayhem, Brian also had to keep thinking up "fun" things for the Eye Street circle to do, capers that would provide an exciting outlet for cranker aggression and energy. That was the original intent of cow shooting.

Cow Shooting

Brian—who, as a kid, cried over the slaughter of his pig and euthanasia at the animal shelter—was nonchalant: "We had to go out and do something. That's why we invented cow shooting . . . We went cow shooting because we were high. We didn't have nothing else to do, so we decided to have a barbecue. We needed the meat."

Gator Bohlinger had a similar attitude: "You just drive up there and have a good time and shoot some guns . . . That's about it."

"Did that strike you as being cruel?" he was asked at a court hearing.

"Not really," he replied, looking perplexed.

"Why not?"

"Well, it did . . . I was high. It didn't really matter."

"Now do you think it is?"

"A little bit . . . It is pretty cruel. I wouldn't like people shooting at me."

Stephanie was embarrassed: "The cow shooting is crazy. I mean, who do you know that would do stuff like that? Nobody. But they did it and they were comfortable with it, to top it all off. I can't say 'they,' I should say 'we.' I was there . . . We all accepted it."

Cow shooting was "something [Brian] enjoyed doing," Rosalyn Bookout said. "He just said he liked to shoot cows. The cows became a target."

According to Brian, he had the idea after he and Mike Bohlinger returned to Bakersfield from their failed mission to see Stephanie at El Capitan. They headed for a dairy just southeast of town, but "it was depressing. There's not a cow out there. So we drive to this other dairy. We see a cow right by the fence. We see security. Like, man, we're getting no luck." They tried Old River, they tried along the Kern River—still no luck. "Then we hit the spot on Round Mountain Road."

The Eye Street "family" launched at least three cow-shooting expeditions to that area over the next couple of weeks, driving past the pump jack forests of Oildale, the willow-lined banks of the Kern River, and on into the foothills of the Greenhorn Mountains. Close to the summit of Round Mountain, on land leased for free-ranging cattle, they would find their prey.

Brian recalled only one hit. It was just him and Mike in Mike's Celica. Their weapon was a .30-30 rifle which belonged to Mike's father and which Mike had "snuck" out of the house. As they approached a cow standing in the middle of the road, Brian stood up through the sunroof and fired.

"I hit it right here," he said, indicating a spot between his eyes. "It fell down. But it didn't hurt the cow. There was no blood, nothing . . . I shoot it again, I don't know if I hit it or missed it. The cow just shook his head and walked on down in the ravine . . . It may just have stunned him."

"It was the only time we actually hit a steer, and no one was there," he added, ruing the irony.

The largest expedition was the one described in the prologue to this book when ten people in three cars, armed with sawed-off shotguns and a small-caliber pistol, traveled up Round Mountain. According to Brian, they were seriously planning to butcher any cow they killed. "We had it planned. We had saws and everything. We were going to cut this cow to our specifications and then barbecue it in a deep pit."

None of them had any butchering experience. Rickey said he pointed out to Brian, "You can't do that. You have to cure the meat."

But Stephanie, who drove the car in which Brian, Calvin, and Jodie were passengers, recalled nothing about any barbecue. "I don't believe it," she said. "I surely was not going to barbecue a cow." Apart from "fun," the only purpose of the trip she knew of had to do with Sean Stanphill. "They were going to shoot him. This is what they said. I didn't believe they would have done it, because we were high."

Brian's memory was hazy: "If something like that might have come out of my mouth, it might have come out because of the influence of drugs. But I don't recall saying anything about me trying to take out Sean."

A customer of Brian's, Stanphill had apparently antagonized him by failing to pay a debt of $100 to $250. "Brian was real mad about it," Jodie testified. "He wanted to kill him for it or said that he [did]. He wanted Sean to see that he wasn't playing with him and that he couldn't just take his dope and not pay him his money for it."

Linda Swanson said Brian, driving Stephanie's car and accompanied by Rickey Rodgers, stopped by her house one day in September and asked if she knew where Sean was. She told him Sean was out with her sons, Chad and Travis. When she asked Brian why he wanted to find Sean, he replied that Sean "burned him, and he was going to cut him up and feed him to the pigs when he caught him." Swanson testified that Brian seemed "really amped up. He looked like he was crazy."

On the night of the big cow shoot, Gator drove Sean up Round Mountain Road in his Dodge compact, along with Chad and Travis. The idea, Jodie said, was to get Sean out of the car once they reached their destination, and then Brian would deal with him. But Sean "never once got out of the car. I guess Gator had told him that he shouldn't get out of the car, because Brian was real mad about him."

After Gator drove Sean back to Bakersfield unharmed, Brian was "real pissed off," Jodie said. "He didn't think Gator was his friend anymore . . . He was bitching and yelling and screaming about Sean not getting out of the car, and he wanted to know why, and if anybody told Sean anything."

In an interview for this book, Stanphill said he never owed Brian any money. The problem between them flared up after he "fronted" Brian an ounce of weed. The next day, Brian asked for another two ounces. Sean refused because he hadn't even been paid yet for the first ounce. That enraged Brian because "he didn't like it when a person wouldn't do what he wanted. That's the kind of person he is . . . He wanted to be like a gangster, like an Al Capone."

Sean said Gator talked him into going cow shooting that night. He thought it was a stupid idea—"You can't kill cows with a sawed-off. All you can do is wound them." But he went along anyway, just to "goof off." While they were on Round Mountain, nobody warned him to beware of Brian or to stay put in the car. In fact, he did step outside for a while as the others chased cows. He finally left with Gator and the Swansons because they were all getting tired.

It was only on their way home, Sean said, that Gator informed him of Brian's intentions. "Brian really wanted to kill you up there," he quoted Gator as saying.

Sean said he didn't see Brian again after that night. He wasn't avoiding him—"I was just off in my own world."

As for Brian, he was soon preoccupied with what had become another "obligation," one that Stephanie mentioned during the cow hunt. According to Jodie, her friend told her: "Brian's gonna go sometime this week and have it done."

Brian didn't wait long. It may even have been the next day that he organized a shooting party to Santa Barbara to kill Phillip. Stephanie later figured that day as Wednesday, September 13. Maybe it was just coincidence coming so soon after the cow hunt. Maybe Brian now loved Stephanie enough to help her. Or maybe he was now angry enough—after all the fights and the Sean fiasco—to concentrate on doing something about Phillip.

The Shotgun Trip

They smoked some weed and set off for Santa Barbara in the early evening. Stephanie drove the Ford, with Brian in the front passenger seat and Jodie and Calvin in the back. It was the same foursome who went cow shooting. They even had the same weapons, the sawed-off shotguns.

Climbing the treacherously steep stretch of Interstate 5 across the Tehachapi Mountains known as the Grapevine, the Ford made a pinging noise, so they had to pull into a truck stop at the summit of Tejon Pass. It looked as if a wheel assembly had been damaged, probably as the car was bouncing around the cow pasture on Round Mountain. They borrowed a tool at the truck stop and bent the part back into shape. But it took a while, and Calvin suggested they just turn around and go home.

"Yeah, by the time we get there, it will be too late anyway," said Stephanie, seconding the motion.

But Brian was game for continuing, and he was, after all, the guy in charge.

Before the freeway reached the northernmost Los Angeles suburbs, they turned onto Route 126, a largely two-lane highway lined with oak trees and fruit orchards that reaches the coast at Ventura. After another stop at a McDonald's, they arrived at El Capitan around 10:00 P.M.

According to Stephanie, the idea was to ambush Phillip on his way home from work. They would make it look like one of those freeway shootings, the sort of thing that was all the rage in L.A. those days. Brian and Calvin would roll down the car windows and blast him with the shotguns.

"It would be just like somebody drives by and would shoot him while he was driving his car and kill him, and that would be that," Jodie recalled.

By the time they got to Santa Barbara, it was too late for that. But all was not lost. They had brought sleeping bags in case they had to stay overnight. They could camp out at the state park across the freeway from the trailer park and then greet Phillip in the morning on his way to work.

Stephanie and Jodie dropped their boyfriends off at the state park and went in search of a convenience store. They came back with chips, bean dip, and soda. As the four of them sat around a fire, they discussed ways of killing Phillip. "We'll have to get up early to catch him," Stephanie said.

They spent an uncomfortable night. It was a lot colder by the ocean than they were used to in Bakersfield, and they were squashed like sardines into the Ford. Calvin and Jodie tried sleeping outside but soon gave up.

Around 6:30 A.M., Stephanie sounded reveille on the horn. Barely awake, they drove under the freeway and stopped where they could see cars exiting from the trailer park. But then Stephanie said, "I think we missed him." To make sure, they drove into the camp and cruised past the Bogdanoffs' trailer. Both their vehicles, the state car and the pickup Diana used to go to work, were gone.

Foiled again, they headed for Santa Barbara. Stephanie suggested they check out various places downtown where her stepfather might be working. But all they found at the job sites were "people in orange vestlike things with orange hats on." No Phillip. There was one last possibility—the Caltrans district office.

At that time, it was housed in a two-story structure on Gutierrez Street just off the 101 freeway. Next door was the local United Way headquarters; across the street, a lumber yard and a warren of auto body shops. Phillip worked on the second floor in an open-plan area accessible from the parking lot by an outside staircase.

When Stephanie and her friends got there, she pointed out his state car in the parking lot. She recognized another vehicle, the El Camino that Phillip was storing there. According to Jodie, she said, "If Brian kills Phillip, then that El Camino is going to be Brian's El Camino."

They had found Phillip. The problem was how to get to him. They were still thinking about a freeway shooting. Maybe he would leave the office to go to a job site, and they could just follow him. They would just have to wait and see, conduct surveillance like they do in those cop movies. They parked on a side street, Garden Street, a block away from the office. From that location, they could watch the front entrance and the parking lot.

So there they were, sitting in the car waiting. By now, the shotguns were out of the trunk. Brian, in the front passenger seat, had one between his right leg and the door; Calvin, in the back, had the other in a similar position.

A passerby that morning might have been suspicious even without seeing the shotguns. For one thing, black people stood out in Santa Barbara a lot more than in Bakersfield—they were sighted about as often around town as rain clouds. In fact, fewer than two thousand of them lived there, about 2 percent of the population. These two black guys in the Ford stood out even more because they were with two white girls. They certainly didn't look like tourists, and the industrial neighborhood wasn't on the sight-seeing map.

Jodie started thinking the whole thing was "pretty stupid." She figured that "if a cop came by, we'd be arrested."

But neither a cop nor Phillip appeared, and after half an hour or so, they felt hungry. So Stephanie drove them a few blocks to Milpas Street, a busy thoroughfare on the east side of town, where they found a doughnut shop. Fortified on doughnuts, they returned to the lookout spot on Garden Street. Phillip's car was still in the parking lot.

What happened next is unclear. The following account draws mostly from court testimony of Jodie and Calvin.

According to Jodie, they resumed their vigil and then Brian blurted out, "I'm tired of waiting out here. I just want to get this over with." He suggested that he and Calvin walk into the office and "flat-blast" Phillip there and then.

"That's really stupid," Jodie warned. "People would see you. You're not going to kill somebody in a room full of people."

But Calvin and Brian proceeded to load the guns anyway. "I was having trouble with mine, so I got Brian to help me,"

Calvin recalled. Then, he said, it dawned on him that Brian might just be serious.

Despite all the talk he had heard about killing Phillip, Calvin had never thought any of it was serious. He scoffed when Brian used to say he wanted to do something to show Stephanie how much he loved her. After all, Brian had only known her a few weeks.

"Things are that good in the bed?" he asked Brian once.

"Yeah, man."

"Then if she that good in the bed to make you go out and kill a man, why don't you let me get some of that and maybe it'll make me do something?"

He thought it was more about money than love. He had heard Stephanie and Brian discussing the El Camino and boasting about how much property her parents had, how they could go off to Jamaica and gorge themselves on weed once it was all over. He couldn't understand how, if Diana was so loaded, she didn't just leave her abusive husband. "If a woman is getting beat that bad, she got that much money, she can get away from that man," he theorized.

Calvin even wondered if Stephanie was stringing Brian along a bit. He was friendly with Brandon McLeod, and he knew Stephanie and Brandon had slept together since she went off with Brian. The whole thing just didn't make sense to him. Yes, Brian told him they were going to Santa Barbara to "kill this dude," but he just thought Brian was "running his mouth off," taking off on one of his ego trips.

Jodie felt the same way. Stephanie, her best friend whom she even likened to a "sister," had told her all about the problem with Phillip, about her mother wanting her help in killing him. But she thought the trip to Santa Barbara was a joke, a game, a charade, to soothe Brian's ego and keep Stephanie's mom off her back. "It was more like we were bored. We didn't have nothing to do. Why not? Calvin didn't think one bit and I didn't think one bit that we were going over there to kill Phillip Bogdanoff."

But something—literally and figuratively—clicked when Brian and Calvin loaded the shotguns.

According to Calvin, he told Brian at that moment, "If Stephanie want him dead, let her go in and do it. Maybe if it was just me and you, we might have a chance of going in there and doing it. But I got Jodie here with me. I could care less what happens to you and Stephanie, but Jodie ain't getting involved in this. I'll tell you what you're gonna do. You're gonna turn around and take me and Jodie home."

"Calvin, what's going on?" Brian remonstrated. "You tripping or something?"

"Tripping, my ass. Take me and her home."

Jodie recalled Calvin saying something like, "I ain't gonna be around when you kill somebody. I want to go home. Take me back to Bakersfield. I'm tired of being here. I'm tired of being in this car sitting around the corner from this guy's office thinking you guys are gonna kill him."

Calvin got his way. They drove away from the office and headed home, their mission unaccomplished.

How seriously was Phillip's life threatened that day? Stephanie and Brian also claimed that nobody was really serious. "We went with the intent of killing Phillip Bogdanoff, but I did not think it was really going to happen," Stephanie testified. " . . . Jodie didn't think it was going to happen, and neither did Calvin.

"It was just like a big joke, is what it was," she added. "A big joke."

"In reality, I didn't have it set in my mind to just go out and smoke this dude with a sawed-off shotgun," Brian chimed in. Going to Santa Barbara was "just something you up and do. Like a road trip."

They apparently didn't even bother to forewarn Diana they were coming to Santa Barbara, and they were so casual that they didn't get up in time to ambush Phillip. On the other hand, they did remember such necessities as sleeping bags. And— just as the shower idea on the Tim Gray trip did not come out of thin air—their plan to shoot Phillip on the freeway reflected some serious thinking.

Stephanie knew from her mother that Phillip had special insurance through his job that kicked in if he was killed in his state-issued car. "That's where we came up with the freeway shooting thing," Brian testified.

More revealing still, Brian told police that he spoke directly to Diana about the advantages of killing Phillip on Caltrans time. "She said if Phillip was killed on the job, she would get

some type of benefits that the state have for their employees
or something."

So what saved Phillip this time? Was it just circumstances—
that they woke up too late and he stayed inside the Caltrans
office? Or did Calvin Monigan really come to his rescue?

Ironically, neither Brian nor Stephanie were very keen on
having Calvin come along in the first place. A few months
before meeting Brian, Stephanie had bought some weed from
Calvin in Patriots Park. Even though he was dating Jodie, he
asked for her phone number. While Stephanie was breaking
up with Brandon, Calvin thought he was in line to be her next
boyfriend. Both Brian and Stephanie suspected he might still
be hot for her.

He also made himself unpopular because of the way he
treated Jodie, hardly letting her out of his sight, always fighting with her, sometimes hitting her. "Brian and Stephanie . . .
didn't want Calvin over at the house, because every time [we]
were at the house, we would normally get in an argument or
some kind of fight," Jodie said. They only tolerated him so
Stephanie could see Jodie.

At one point, Brian decided to teach Calvin a lesson. He got
a piece of tape and stuck it to a shotgun shell. On the tape he
had written "Calvin." "If he ever raises his hand to you again,
I'm gonna take him out," he told Jodie.

She just laughed and said, "No, you're not."

According to Jodie, Stephanie distrusted Calvin enough to
ask her not to tell her boyfriend about any plans to kill Phillip.
But Jodie told her that was out of the question.

"He's my boyfriend and he knows just about everything I do
and everywhere I go," she explained. "I can't keep this secret
from him. I have to let him know what's going on. If you're
telling me this, then I'm telling Calvin this."

"Is he going to start any problems?"

Jodie assured her that he wouldn't.

By the time they went cow shooting, diplomatic relations
between Brian and Calvin had been restored. They spent that
whole evening around each other, they used the shotguns
around each other, without any hassles. Maybe he really could
be a loyal member of the "family."

Maybe Calvin could even be a killer. Of all the people who
hung out at Stephanie's apartment, he certainly seemed the best

qualified, at least on paper. He was one of nine children his mother had with three different men; his father died when he was seven, and he started getting into trouble with police at fifteen. Four years later, his criminal record included battery on a police officer, fighting in a public place, and assault with a deadly weapon—his kick-boxing feet. On the assault charge, he was sentenced in March 1986 to four years in state prison.

When he was released in late 1987, he had few legitimate skills to market. Unlike Brian and Gator, he managed to graduate from Bakersfield High, Class of '84, a dubious honor since he could not even read or write. What skills he did have were illicit. While still in school, he sold drugs, including crack cocaine and marijuana. After his release, he went back to selling weed in Patriots Park. That was where he met Jodie, then a sophomore at West High.

Jodie was the first person he met who could help him control himself. "When I came out of prison, I was mad at the world," Calvin said. "Jodie showed me I don't have to be that way. In many ways, I owe a lot to that girl . . . Through loving Jodie, I learned how to love my family, too."

But his insecurity could still make him fly off the handle. In March 1989, he went on a bizarre rampage after a fight with Jodie that culminated in him taking a drive with her and her mother. Nothing unusual about that except he was clinging to the hood at the time. After they stopped, he tried to smash in the car window. Jodie sought refuge in the freezer of a nearby convenience store. Arrested as he drove the car away, Calvin received sixty days in jail.

According to Brian, Calvin played an active role during the shotgun trip. When they were waiting outside Phillip's office, it was Calvin who "came up with the theory 'Let's go in and flat-blast him.' " Brian then told him: "That's stupid. Too many people will see you."

Stephanie said they went home only because "everybody was tired."

Certainly there is something miscreant about Calvin, something untrustworthy behind his habitual sly grin. But if anyone in the Eye Street family was going to stand up to Brian and prevent this murder, it was Calvin.

Labeling it a "conscience" might be going too far. But he had less reason than the others to be afraid of Brian. He alone came from the same tough ghetto neighborhoods of Bakersfield as Brian. He alone knew what state prison, a much harsher world than a county jail, was like.

He also wasn't attached to Brian by the methamphetamine membrane. "Calvin didn't do crank," Jodie said. "He didn't like the feeling of not being able to sleep when you want to. He didn't like your heart beating twenty times faster than [it's] supposed to." He tried to stop Jodie from using it. Calvin's pleasure was weed, and though he got plenty of free weed from Brian, it did not create the same dependency as crank.

There was something else important about Calvin: He had seen someone get shot to death. It happened on October 15, 1972, when he was seven and his family was living in East St. Louis, Illinois. The victim was Lewis Calvin Monigan, Sr., his father, and the culprit was his mother.

Lewis was shot after he came home with a gun and confronted his wife, who was also armed. Twenty years later, Calvin choked up when he recalled the scene: "He said, 'I know you're with another man. At least let me have one of the kids.' My mama said, 'Which one you want?' 'I'll take my oldest boy [Calvin].' Mama started hollering, 'Nah, I ain't giving you either one of them.' "

Lewis picked Calvin up and headed for the door. He stopped and put the boy down when his wife brandished her gun at him. "She shot one time, the bullet went into the ceiling. She shot again, the bullet hit the door. He was kind of laughing at her—'You kind of missing me, ain't you? You kind of misaimed, didn't you?' "

The third time, Lewis wasn't so lucky. The bullet entered his abdomen. He died in the hospital five days later. He was forty-four. The death certificate recorded: "Shot with .38-caliber weapon by wife in home during argument."

His mother was not prosecuted, apparently because she acted in self-defense. She collected on the insurance and remarried. But rebuilding for Calvin wasn't so easy. "When his father was killed, his whole life was shattered," his sister Lena told me.

Maybe alarm bells really did ring for Calvin when it seemed as if Brian was poised to kill Phillip. Maybe he did have limits.

"[Calvin] had no intentions of killing Phillip Bogdanoff, a man he didn't even know," Jodie testified.

"You're saying that Calvin is a peaceable person?" she was asked.

"No. I'm saying Calvin would never kill anyone."

Two Meetings

Whatever saved him during the shotgun trip, Phillip only enjoyed a reprieve of about a week. It was a frantic week for him—filled with frustration on the one hand, and hope on the other.

The frustration involved his new family, the most jangling variation on a theme that had been haunting him all summer. The saga of Stephanie and her apartment had turned into a crown of thorns, and now, to top it all off, Phillip found out she was being evicted.

Norman Church, Stephanie's landlord, started receiving complaints about her soon after she moved in. They mostly concerned drug traffic at the apartment. He warned Stephanie a couple of times, and she said she would take care of it.

Linda Good, who lived opposite Stephanie, complained after her cat went missing. "My roommate told me she saw it in Stephanie's window," she said. "I knocked on her door, and she told me she had let the cat go." Good didn't believe her and took her case to the landlord. "The same day, she released the cat. It came back higher than a kite."

Church also spoke to Diana, the cosigner of the lease. "I asked her if she suspected her daughter of being on drugs. She said no, that she didn't know about that at all . . . I said, 'There's a helluva lot of foot traffic in that place. I can't tolerate that; the neighbors are complaining.' She said she'd try to straighten it out."

Stephanie asked Brian to conduct business elsewhere. It was becoming impossible for her to keep the apartment clean and tidy, and things used to go missing all the time. For a while, Brian dealt from a nearby car wash, but he continued using the apartment for business, too. On September 8, Church ran out of patience and sent one month's notice of eviction to Stephanie and her mother.

Diana did not pass the bad news on to her husband. Chris Norton, the Kasler foreman, recalled running into an irate Phillip at a construction site. His friend was brandishing a letter he had just received at his office. "They're evicting Stephanie, and I'm going to have a talk with Diane, and I'm going to throw her out of that goddamn trailer if she knows anything about this letter," Phillip threatened.

According to Norton, Phillip went looking for her where she was flagging that day for a company called Lash Construction. When he came back, he said, "Diane don't know nothing about it." But he was going to Bakersfield that weekend to "kick Stephanie out, clean up the place, and get the cleaning deposit back."

Norton couldn't be exact about the date of his encounter with Phillip. But he was sure it was just before Phillip was killed. Diana only worked for Lash for four days around that time—September 15 and September 18–20.

As he was planning this showdown in Bakersfield, Phillip also seized an opportunity for a much more hopeful meeting. That involved his old family, the one he had deserted nearly eight years previously.

Because of his disfellowshipment, reconciling with his children was as laborious a process as climbing Mount Everest. There had been some progress over the past two years. In December 1987 his stepdaughter Cindy Cook invited him to attend a talk given by her husband to a Witness group near Visalia. He surprised her by showing up. A year later, he made his daughters cobeneficiaries of his retirement fund. He also asked for their Social Security numbers so he could include them in a will he was planning to draft.

The major breakthrough occurred in the summer of 1989 when his daughter Christy was going through a divorce and disfellowshipment of her own. With other family members sidelined by financial and religious constraints, she called her father for help. "When she called, he cried, because he thought, they're finally coming to me and not their mother," Diana said later. Phillip bought Christy a car, which she picked up when she saw him in Santa Barbara in July.

Christy recalled discussing the family breakup at length with her father during that visit. "He always felt everybody took my mom's side when they split up and we hated him. I was trying to tell him that's not the way it was, and we all really cared and loved him and missed him." She felt that "just me being down there made him start thinking about seeing us all again."

He even talked about it at work. "About a week prior to his death, he mentioned he was going to have some type of reconciliation with his daughters," Lisa Alviso said. "He was pretty excited about getting back together with them." Who would make the first move?

His stepdaughter Cindy gave him the opening when she called him at the trailer around 7:30 P.M. on Wednesday, September 20. She wanted to talk about Christy, who was still wrestling with her personal problems. Initially Phillip wasn't very forthcoming. "She's an adult, Cindy," he said. "What do you want me to do?"

"I just want you to kick in as a father," she answered.

Phillip paused. "I think it's about time all of us got together," he suggested. "A lot of things have been said about what happened with me and your mother. I want to get together with all five of you and clear the air."

Cindy could hardly have been more shocked if he had announced he was remarrying her mother. This wasn't the old Phillip—the one who, when he called, introduced himself as "Phillip Bogdanoff," talked only about family business matters, and hung up as quickly as possible. He also told Cindy, "I love you," something he hadn't said to her in years.

Phillip didn't want to wait around for the reunion either. He discussed having it that very weekend, and he was willing to drive over four-hundred miles to Sacramento, where most of the family lived, to be there. Cindy said she would talk it over with her siblings and get back to him the next day.

Diana said she was for the reunion. "I had worked with him very hard to get this communication going between him and his children," she told police. But just before Phillip spoke to Cindy, Diana had set the final wheels in motion that would prevent him from dealing with one family in Bakersfield or reuniting with the other in Sacramento.

Diana and Phil in happier days at the Santa Barbara Marina
(Santa Barbara Sheriff's Office)

Stephanie Allen
(Santa Barbara Sheriff's Office)

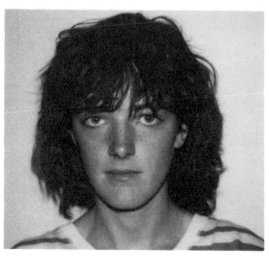

Stephanie's booking photo
(Santa Barbara Sheriff's Office)

The house in Colfax (Matthew Heller)

The Visalia house with Stephanie's Ford
(Matthew Heller)

The murder scene   (Matthew Heller)

Diana poses on the murder scene beach
(Santa Barbara Sheriff's Office)

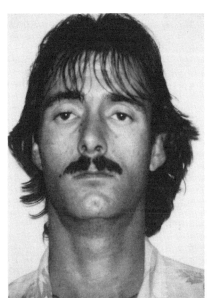

Rickey Rodgers in custody
(Santa Barbara Sheriff's Office)

Tim Gray in custody
(Santa Barbara Sheriff's Office)

Diana outside the trailer
(Santa Barbara Sheriff's Office)

Diana at her preliminary hearing
(Matthew Heller)

Stephanie and Brian at
their preliminary hearing
(Matthew Heller)

Diana and Rickey at
their preliminary hearing
(Matthew Heller)

Brian at Village Lane
(Santa Barbara Sheriff's Office)

Brian at his preliminary hearing
(Matthew Heller)

The Alibi and the Shadow

When Diana found out Stephanie had been on another abortive
jaunt to Santa Barbara—possibly in a call made from the trailer
on Thursday evening, September 14—her reaction was Tim
Gray revisited. "Her mom was mad at her because she had
came on the shotgun trip with us," Brian testified. "Her mom
didn't want her involved in it or around it when the incident
occurred."

According to Brian, Diana was as committed as ever to
having someone finish the job. "After the shotgun trip . . .
things became more or less persistent," he said. "The phone
calls started increasing from Diane to Stephanie. And it was
like in a tone where 'You've got to do this.'" When Stephanie
got off the phone with her mother, "She would be like, 'My
mom really wants to get this done.'"

Brian returned to Santa Barbara on September 21. Stephanie
would say later that the decision to go back so soon was "just
on the spur of the moment . . . It just happened." But if that
was the case, the moment lasted well over twenty-four hours—
long enough to arrange an alibi and recruit Brian's "shadow"
to go to the coast with him.

Tuesday, September 19, was an average day at the Eye Street
apartment. The tenants were busy "tweaking" on crank. For
Stephanie, that usually meant cleaning the house endlessly.
"Sometimes I'd go over there, that house be so clean, I
wanted to throw some dirt on the floor," Calvin recalled.
They had been tweaking since at least the day before, which
was Stephanie's eighteenth birthday and which she later could
remember nothing about.

On Tuesday, the tweaking was interrupted by a call at 4:30

P.M. It was Christine Allen, phoning from Tacoma, Washington, to wish her sister a belated happy birthday. They had not seen each other since Thanksgiving at Nick Bogdanoff's, and they had not spoken for two months. Their relationship, never close, had not been helped by Stephanie's preference for black boyfriends—a reminder to Christine of her rape trauma.

Nevertheless, Stephanie felt free to unburden herself to her sister about Phillip. "I can't take it anymore," she said. "I'm really pissed off with him. I'm going to kill him, and Mom knows about it."

Christine knew about the animus between her sister and her stepfather. Stephanie had told her that Phillip was beating their mother. But she said later that she did not take Stephanie's threat seriously. It sounded to her as if Stephanie was stoned on marijuana at the time.

One hour after that call, Diana phoned Stephanie. Their conversation lasted fourteen minutes, but Stephanie was unable to recall the content. Brian vaguely recalled Stephanie telling him something afterward "about the golf course or the beach . . . That's where her mom said they might be."

On Wednesday, September 20, things started taking shape. Stephanie called Jodie around midafternoon at the home of Calvin's sister Ernestine, where the couple were then living. She wanted her best friend to come over to her apartment. Jodie relayed the request to Calvin.

Since the shotgun trip, Calvin hadn't been too keen on hanging around Stephanie and Brian. The day after they got back, he said he took Brian outside Stephanie's apartment and tried to talk some sense into him.

"Why do you want to kill this man?" he demanded.

"I want to prove to Stephanie that I love her."

"She don't love you." Searching for more ammunition, Calvin added: "You don't know that man. That man did nothing to you. If the bitch want him dead so bad, let her pull the trigger."

"I want to show her that I love her," Brian insisted.

"Man, don't show her that way. Nobody made you God, nobody told you, you should decide when that man die and when he should live."

"If I kill him, they're going to give me half of the money,

and me and Stephanie are going to go away to Jamaica."

"You do it, you'll get caught."

"I won't get caught."

"You'll fuck up some kind of way. You're so stupid. Who do you think everybody going to put it off on? Think about it. You got two white people and one black. Who they going to put it on? They're going to put it all on you."

"Stephanie wouldn't do that," Brian objected again.

"When it comes down to it, Stephanie going to drop the bomb on your ass and you'll have to ride this out alone, by yourself."

Calvin was still leery of them when Stephanie asked Jodie to come over. "No, you can't go," he told his girlfriend.

After breaking the bad news to Stephanie, Jodie handed Calvin the phone. "Calvin, can Jodie come over here?" Stephanie pleaded.

"What do you want Jodie over there for?"

"Just to answer the phone."

"Answer your own phone. Jodie ain't going nowhere."

Stephanie put Brian on the line. "Why don't you come over with Jodie, man?"

"Why do you want me over there now?"

"We're going to smoke some weed and rent us some videos."

That offer did the trick. "Then tell Stephanie to come and get us," Calvin said.

After Stephanie picked them up and drove them the mile and a half back to her apartment, the small living room was Party Central as usual. There was plenty of weed, which they smoked from a selection of bongs. They watched a video called *Leonard, Part 6*, starring Bill Cosby as a secret agent out to save the world from homicidal domestic animals.

But weed smoking and video watching weren't the only reasons that Stephanie and Brian had asked their friends over that afternoon. This time Calvin and Jodie weren't supposed to go on a trip to Santa Barbara; this time they were supposed to provide an alibi for the people who were going.

It is unclear what Calvin knew. But Jodie testified: "Later on that evening, she [Stephanie] told me Brian was planning to take a trip over to Santa Barbara. She said, 'Brian and Rickey are going to take a trip over to Santa Barbara to kill Phillip.' "

Jodie and her boyfriend were supposed to man the drug switchboard while Brian and Rickey, who were planning to leave around three in the morning, got some sleep. If anyone came around to see Brian while he was gone, they were to be told he was still in bed. "No one was supposed to know if I left town or not," Brian said later.

The alibi in place, so was the "shadow." When Jodie and Calvin arrived at the apartment, he was in his customary place on the small living room sofa. He joined in the weed smoking and he watched the video. Over the kitchen stove, he and Brian also hollowed out .22-caliber bullets.

A family friend described Rickey Lee Rodgers as "typical all-American." If that was so, it may be time for a new definition of "typical all-American."

Rickey was born in Bakersfield on March 4, 1965, the first of two children of Donald and Cleta Sue Rodgers, both Oklahoma natives. His mother was only fifteen years old when she married and when she gave birth to Rickey six months later.

As a child, he was so hyperactive that he was briefly medicated with a drug commonly prescribed for "attention deficit disorders." He was also sensitive. After he shot a rabbit at the age of six, his father said, "He couldn't eat, he couldn't sleep, he couldn't do nothing for a year later."

A poor student at school, he was put in learning-handicapped classes. At home, his father, an oil field worker, had an alcohol problem and verbally abused him, calling him "stupid and dumb." Sometimes his parents would start fighting after his mother stepped in to protect him from Donald Rodgers's vitriol. Every few months, she said, her husband would physically abuse her.

At Bakersfield High, Rickey was another to distinguish himself by smoking marijuana and cutting classes. But he didn't get in any serious trouble until around the time his parents separated in late 1982—they would divorce two years later. Then seventeen years old, he was arrested twice in six months on theft and burglary charges. He was sent to a juvenile detention facility for about three months.

After dropping out of high school in his twelfth-grade year—having attained fourth-grade academic skills—he found work in the oil fields of Taft and at a pizza parlor in Bakersfield. He shared an apartment in Taft with an old friend, Mike Bohlinger. There he experimented with a variety of drugs, including crank and cocaine. He also sold cocaine to support his habit.

When he met Brian Stafford in the early summer of 1989, Rickey was living with a girlfriend in an apartment complex near the Valley Plaza mall called Royal Palms. At first he was something of an outsider within the group. In fact, he almost made an enemy of its "leader."

According to Brian, Rickey had been tardy paying him for a forty-dollar front of crank. He sent his scouts out looking for him, and eventually Gator brought him over. Rickey explained he had gone halves on the deal with Chuck Blankenship and only had fifteen dollars of the money on him. A few days later, Rickey coughed up another ten dollars and suggested they go see Chuck for the rest of the money. When they found Chuck, Brian said, "Rick and him almost get into a fight because Rick is thinking I'm going to take him out. So Chuck comes up with the money right there on the spot."

There were no hard feelings. After that, "he started hanging around and kind of grew on everybody."

He grew into perhaps Brian's most reliable "bitch." "If Brian asked him to do something, he would do it," Stephanie said. "It could be the middle of the night; Brian asked him to do something, and he'd do it. It was probably because he got his drugs from Brian . . . It was 'Go pick up something, go to the store!' "

"He was like a puppet," Calvin said.

Brian preferred to describe him as his "shadow." Tall—six foot one—slim, and pale, Rickey even looked the part, as if he could just fade into the white-hot Bakersfield sun. He had thick eyebrows, thin lips and mustache, but the only thing that really made him stand out from the crowd was his wavy, brown hair down to his shoulders.

According to a psychiatric report, Rickey "desperately wanted to be liked and accepted by Brian and went to great lengths to accommodate Brian." He wanted free marijuana from him, but not crank, the report said, and he was also afraid of him. The Bohlingers counseled him, "You don't want to piss Brian off," and Rickey was present when Brian taped Calvin's name to a shotgun shell.

However, others painted a portrait of Rickey that suggests he was not a complete wimp. "Whenever he came around, for some reason it just gave me an uneasy feeling," James Oliver said. It was partly because Rickey "talked like he was some kind of macho badass with a real deep, hard voice, like he was somebody to be feared."

Rickey also had an unnerving habit of popping up with guns, James recalled. "He was always carrying guns and stuff in his trunk . . . Rickey always had a gun to bring over." One gun that popped up was a chrome-handled, .22-caliber semiautomatic with an ammunition clip holding six rounds. It was probably a Jennings, a snub-nosed Saturday night special that is one of the cheapest handguns on the market. Mike Bohlinger recalled Rickey showing it off at a friend's house and saying, "Look what I got."

Brian figured his "shadow" obtained access to artillery through a half sister working at the Kern County sheriff's office. "He's got access to damn near anything he wants," he told police. Rickey said he got the .22 from an uncle in exchange for stereo speakers. "Bakersfield is a dangerous place," he explained. "I was noticing lots of people having guns. I wanted one for my own protection." Asked which people he knew had guns, he replied: "Mike and Gator—probably everybody in Bakersfield."

Gator, who knew Rickey better than most, certainly did not think his friend was a wimp. "I seen him talk some mean shit, get in somebody's face," he said. "It could have been my brother Mark."

"He's kind of a wimp, isn't he?" Mike was asked.

"Not really," he replied. "He can hold his own."

After he was evicted from his apartment in July for not paying his rent, Rickey was homeless. He slept either in his mother's beauty salon on Chester Avenue or in his car, and spent most of his waking hours at Eye Street. Stephanie tired of his interminable presence. "I hated it, man, I hated seeing him every day, every night," she said as if recalling a skin rash. "I'd say, 'Go home! Don't you have a home? Get out of my apartment!' You can only see somebody so much. It wasn't like he was my buddy or nothing . . . Brrr! It would just drive me crazy."

On the afternoon of September 20, it was okay for Rickey

to be hanging around the apartment. According to Brian, he told Rickey they were taking a "road trip" the next day to Santa Barbara. And the "typical all-American" was supposed to do the shooting. "Rick was going to do it because I didn't want to get my hands dirty," Brian said. "I think I told Rick I would get him some crank for it or 'Just do it for me as a friend,' you know. It wasn't no big thing. We all watched out for each other."

"Rickey was supposed to do the damn thing in the first place," Stephanie told me. " . . . It was the plan. Rickey was going to do it."

He certainly looked as if he was preparing in advance for his role. Hollowing out the points of his bullets wasn't just a way of passing the time. Hollow-points do a lot more damage when they hit their target. Or, as Calvin put it: "When you shoot somebody, it make a bigger hole."

One other important thing had to be resolved on Wednesday, September 20—time and place. Despite the call from Diana the day before, things were still apparently unclear.

Diana had spent Wednesday working for Lash at the site of a new shopping mall in downtown Santa Barbara. At 3:30 P.M. she saw her supervisor, who told her she would not be needed to work the rest of the week. An hour later, she picked up her paychecks at the Lash office. By 5:17 she was home at the trailer.

That was when she called Stephanie in Bakersfield. It was almost exactly the same time she called the previous day, and the call even lasted the same time, fourteen minutes. It was two hours before Phillip spoke to Cindy Cook.

Jodie said she heard bits of Stephanie's side of the conversation over the noise of the video. "I remember her saying, 'I used to lay out there' . . . and 'What time did you say?' " When Stephanie got off the phone, she took Brian into the bedroom but left the door open. "She was telling Brian, 'Remember where we were when we went over to the beach, over to El Capitan'—something about down by the water, down in some cove or whatever, and what time to be there—and 'It should just be my mom and Phillip at the beach. They should be laying out.' " According to Jodie, they also called Rickey into the bedroom.

Stephanie recalled only fragments herself. "She was telling me that they would either be at the beach or the golf course that they went to, and she told me where the golf course was." From her visits to El Capitan, she knew where her parents' favorite sun spot was.

So, apparently, did Brian: Stephanie pointed it out to him during the shotgun trip. "He'd been there with me," she told me. "He knew the way. I showed him when I was there the first time . . . I told him, 'Go down that road and you'll be where they go all the time.' "

Stephanie hadn't slept since she started a crank "run" on her birthday. Possibly around ten o'clock, she retired with Brian to the bedroom. Jodie heard Stephanie tell him, "It's getting late, you need to go to sleep."

Jodie settled down on the large sofa in the living room, her head nestled in Calvin's lap. By then she certainly knew something was going on and that they were supposed to provide alibis. But she said she still didn't think it was serious. She thought "maybe it was one of his [Brian's] ego trips."

Calvin said he had been too busy watching the video to pay anything else much attention. "I wasn't really putting the pieces together," he told me. He had plenty of weed to smoke, and besides, he thought he had got through to Brian when he lectured him after the shotgun trip.

Rickey was the last to go to sleep. For one night at least, he wasn't homeless. He had the small couch.

Murder at Corral Beach

The alarm clock Rickey had put on the living room floor went off around 3:00 A.M. Calvin and Jodie, asleep on the sofa, barely stirred. Rickey knocked on the bedroom door. "It's time to go, Brian." Getting no acknowledgment, he retrieved the ringing alarm clock and put it next to the door.

Finally awakened, Brian dressed quickly. He put on Levi's 501 jeans, white Boys Club boxing tournament T-shirt, and L.A. Gear shoes. In the living room, he told Rickey to get the shotguns and put them in the car.

They were ready to leave at 3:15. Like Brian, Rickey wasn't exactly dressed for the beach. He had on jeans, a floral print shirt, and Nikes. He also took with him a bag containing some of his other clothes and the .22 semiautomatic. Their drug provisions included an eighth of an ounce of marijuana and a quarter gram of crank. Brian got the car keys from Stephanie, kissed her, and gave her a hug. "Love you," he said.

As they left the apartment, the sun was still far below the Tehachapis. The air was cool and clean before the day's heat and pollution—the temperature would reach eighty-eight degrees in Bakersfield that day. They drove off in Stephanie's Ford, stopping off at a minimart to buy gas before they reached the freeway. Brian also got a cup of coffee. He didn't need Coffee-Mate: he dumped most of the crank into the cup.

With Brian driving, they retraced the route taken the previous week—over the Grapevine to Highway 126, through the Ventura County farm country, finally hitting the coast at Ventura. This time the Ford didn't have any mechanical problems, and they reached the Santa Barbara area around six o'clock. Along the way, they smoked most of the weed and talked briefly about their mission. "I think I was telling

[Rickey] something along the lines of, the dude is Stephanie's stepfather, he molested her, he's beating up on her mom, and her mom needs help," Brian said later.

When Brian and Rickey got to Santa Barbara, they headed for the El Capitan Ranch trailer park. After exiting northbound U.S. 101, they parked near the entrance to the camp. From there they could spot Phillip as he left for work in the state car Brian had seen during the shotgun trip.

The plan was another freeway ambush. They would catch him on the freeway underpass or, as Brian called it later, the "dead spot." They would drive alongside him, and Rickey would roll down the passenger window and blast him with one of the shotguns. At that hour, "we would have caught him right there, and there would have been no evidence, no witnesses, no nothing."

Once again, however, they had missed Phillip. Brian and Rickey sat in the car for about an hour, telling each other jokes, smoking joints and cigarettes. The shotguns, loaded, sat in the backseat. Eventually Brian looked at his watch and realized it was past the time that Stephanie had told him Phillip went to work. In that case, there was only one thing for it—pay another visit to where Phillip worked.

At the Caltrans office in downtown Santa Barbara, Brian spotted Phillip's car. The problem, again, was how to get to him. "It's in public and people see you. You don't want things like that to happen if you're going to be serious about something," Brian explained later.

It was becoming an inaction replay of the shotgun trip. Drive all the way to Santa Barbara, hang out at the trailer park but miss Phillip. Find him at Caltrans, but doing it there would be too risky. This time Brian didn't have Stephanie with him to help, but he could call her.

They drove the few blocks east from the office to Milpas Street. Where Milpas intersects with Montecito Street is a Thrifty gas station. Brian gave Rickey ten dollars for gas and walked over to a bank of three pay phones. He called Stephanie's number collect. The time was 7:38 A.M. Jodie, awoken by the ringing, answered the phone. "Where's Stephanie?" Brian asked immediately.

"She's in bed asleep."

"Go wake her up right now."

Dragging herself off the couch, Jodie went into the bedroom and woke Stephanie up. This is Brian's recollection of the subsequent conversation—Stephanie would later remember nothing about it:

"I'm in Santa Barbara. We missed Phillip on the freeway," Brian told Stephanie when she picked up the phone. "Call your mom and find out what's happening."

"No, you call my mom. You're down there."

"What am I supposed to say to your mom?"

"Just tell her you're there."

"I don't know the number."

By this point in the conversation, Rickey had finished pumping the gas and rejoined Brian. He was holding a large soda in a paper cup with a garish red, orange, and yellow pattern. As Stephanie gave Brian the number at her mother's El Capitan trailer, he relayed it to Rickey so they could remember it. The call finished at 7:43.

Now Brian was supposed to call some woman he had never met to talk about how to kill some man he had never met. He may have seen a snapshot of them, but that was all. Stephanie had one in her purse that showed them standing on a wharf at the Santa Barbara marina. She looked happy enough in her Santa Barbara warm-up top; so did he in his Santa Barbara T-shirt. Brian had only spoken to this woman on the phone maybe half a dozen times. But if this thing was finally going to happen, he had to call her.

The exact time of this key call is unknown. Because it was just a local pay phone call, there was no phone company record. Brian said he called the trailer right after hanging up with Stephanie. The call was over by 8:19 when Diana called her mother, then living east of Los Angeles.

According to Brian, they didn't waste much time on small talk. Diana told him that she and Phillip would be at Corral Beach at noon and gave Brian directions on how to get there from Santa Barbara. He relayed the directions to Rickey.

How would they recognize each other? Brian told her what they were wearing and that Rickey was white. Diana described Phillip and the vehicle (a brown pickup) they would be driving.

She said she would be wearing a green sun visor. "The key was the sun visor," Brian recalled.

They did not go into detail about what was supposed to happen on the beach. "They were going to go over there and be sunbathing, I guess, and me and Rick were supposed to be creative enough to come up and just handle it." Brian did not want Diana to see the actual shooting. "When this gets ready to happen, all you got to do is get up and walk away," he told her. "Go to the bathroom or something."

There was one other thing. After buying the Thrifty gas, Brian and Rickey were down to their last few dollars. They might need some more to get home. "Don't worry about it," Diana assured Brian. "I'll give you guys some money when this is over for gas to get back to Bakersfield."

Brian said later that the call lasted five to seven minutes.

Now they had a new problem—what to do with the next four hours. The only places Brian knew in Santa Barbara, they had already been to. Their drug supplies were almost exhausted. Why not check out the beach? According to Brian, the idea was "to look to see who was there, to see if there was people there, see if there wasn't. See if there was a way in, see if there was a way out." That may have made sense in theory, but it turned out to be an advertisement for evil.

On the morning of September 21, most of the visitors to the Corral Beach area were regulars. They came from all over northern Santa Barbara County to enjoy the perfect late-summer weather and peaceful setting. That morning they all noticed something that would be strange anywhere in the Santa Barbara area, let alone a remote beach—a white guy with a black guy. "It was the first time I ever saw a black guy there," said Victor Brecht, a fisherman.

The strangest thing was that the black guy and the white guy made no effort to make themselves inconspicuous. Just the opposite. They could hardly have advertised themselves more if they had landed in a balloon and set off land mines.

Brian and Rickey arrived about 9:00 A.M. After they clambered down to the bike path, they urinated against the railroad embankment. Rickey finished his Thrifty soda and threw the cup on the path. Then they headed along the water's edge to the coves north of the main Corral Beach. The shotguns, too cumbersome to take with them, were left in the car, but Rickey had the .22 tucked away in the back pocket of his jeans. His shirt hung loose over the pocket.

They had plenty of time to check out the coves and seashells, paddle in the water. They didn't get much chance to do that in Bakersfield. No beaches there, just dust and fields. Brian had never seen the ocean before. They chased sand crabs and wrote their names in the sand. Brian didn't pay attention to a fisherman on top of the bluffs. "I was more amused by the sand crabs," he said later.

After about an hour and a half of such amusement, they were getting tired and bored. They had been up since 3:00 A.M., and neither had slept much the past few days while tripping on crank. Rickey, who was still supposedly the designated shooter, was beginning to express some tentative doubts about the mission.

"Look, man, this isn't a show or anything," he said.

"Yeah, but this thing keeps Stephanie's mom off her ass, and she's telling us everything's going to be okay."

They retraced their steps to the car, pulled onto the freeway, and took the first exit, the El Capitan exit. Then they went under the freeway, past the "dead spot" and the trailer park, and back along the frontage road (Calle Real) toward Refugio. At the turnoff for Refugio State Park, they went in the opposite direction toward the mountains. A mile and a half up Refugio Road, which leads to President Reagan's mountaintop ranch, they parked, took the shotguns from the backseat, and put them in the trunk. After Rickey set his alarm clock for noon, they slumped into their seats and dozed off.

Passing traffic awoke them before the clock rang. Instead of parking in the gravel lay-by again, they drove another third of a mile past Corral Beach. There the shoulder of the freeway is wide enough for a car to park on. They pulled into a spot marked by a cluster of eucalyptus trees.

Brian's reasoning for not parking in the lay-by was simple: Phillip might recognize the Ford when he arrived at the beach. After all, he had bought it for Stephanie. "If he saw the car, he would be wondering, 'Well, why is Stephanie here?' "

After returning to the beach along the bike path, Brian and Rickey saw no sign of the Bogdanoffs. No brown pickup or lady in a green sun visor. Yet more time to kill. This time

they made even less of an effort to be inconspicuous. They
explored in the opposite direction from their first visit—toward
Santa Barbara. On their way back, about a quarter of a mile
from Corral Beach, they passed through a bottleneck between
a ledge of rock and the cliff face. Perched on the ledge were
two fishermen, Donald Tamayo and Nathan McNutt, who had
come to the beach with their friend, Mark Salas.

Rickey climbed onto the rock. "How's the fishing going?"
Tamayo looked up from watching his line.

"Okay, but we only just got started."

Rickey bent over the bucket beside Tamayo. At the bottom,
a couple of fish squirmed. Rickey laughed. "Hey, Spiderman, Spiderman," he addressed the fish. He looked over at
Brian, who was still on the sand, but his friend just glowered
at him.

"Come on, let's go," Brian said angrily.

The fishermen found the encounter disconcerting. "I thought
something was up . . . They looked out of place to me," McNutt
said later. Mark Salas, who was fishing off rocks just north of his
friends, got the same impression. As Brian and Rickey passed
him, he said, "they just were staring at me really hard . . . It really bugged me." He reeled up his line and rejoined his friends.

Back at Corral Beach, still no sign of Phillip and Diana.
Brian and Rickey scrambled up to the bike path and followed
it toward Refugio. From the path, they took one of the narrow
trails that skirts the edge of the bluffs at the north end of the
beach. A few yards down the trail, they stopped. They had a
clear view of the gravel parking area. Victor Brecht, who was
fishing from the bluff with his friend Robert Rutherford, had
a clear view of them.

"They just stood there," he said later. "I thought they were
trying to get a peek at some nudes . . . They didn't look like
they belonged on the beach that day. They looked like they'd
never seen the ocean before."

Rutherford had gone down to the beach to check on how
another friend's fishing was going. When he got back on the
bluff, he came up behind Brian and Rickey and startled them.
"You seen them two queers looking at us?" Rutherford asked
Brecht when he rejoined him.

The next thing Brecht remembered was hearing the sound of
a vehicle honking. He turned around and saw a brown pickup

pulling off the freeway. Brian and Rickey saw the same thing.
Rickey tapped Brian on the shoulder. "Is that the truck?"

Brian, who was squatting on his haunches, stood up. "I
think so."

A stout, bearded man got out of the passenger side of the
truck. He was wearing shorts and an orange tank top. From
the driver's side emerged a plump, red-faced woman with a
permed hairstyle. She was wearing a white, speckled blouse,
green shorts—and a green sun visor.

According to Diana, they had gotten up at about six forty-five
that morning, although it had to be earlier for Phillip to have
gone before Brian and Rickey arrived at the trailer park. Phillip
didn't bother with breakfast. He showered quickly, put on his
usual casual work attire—tank top, jeans, and boots—and left.
Diana went back to bed.

At the office, Lisa Alviso noticed only one thing unusual,
that Phillip came in about seven. When she asked him why he
was there so early, he said that he was taking the afternoon off
to go to the beach.

Phillip did not go into the field. It was a morning of paperwork and phone calls. At eight-thirty he called his stepdaughter
Cindy to make final arrangements for the planned reunion.
She explained to him that she needed to talk to her church
elders about what form the reunion should take, that he should
probably meet with each of the children individually rather
than all together. The latter might be construed as socializing.
She'd call him Friday morning to let him know for sure.

Around ten, Phillip went downstairs to the office of his
supervisor, Mel Brown, to ask for the afternoon off. As Phillip
had plenty of comp time owed to him, Brown had no problem
agreeing to it. Then his buzzer rang. It was Alviso to say that
she had a call for Phillip. Brown let her page it through to the
office and handed the phone over. He tried not to listen but
guessed the caller was Diana. The only thing he remembered
Phillip saying was, "I think they'll be calling you into work
tomorrow."

Diana told police later that Phillip arrived home about
eleven-fifty, just as she sat down for lunch. She said he
walked in with a can of beer in his hand. She had spent the
morning cleaning the trailer, only venturing outside to sweep

the front step. She made two calls—the one to Phillip and the other to her mother.

While Diana finished her lunch, Phillip got the ice chest ready, packing three cans of Coors beer and Diana's squeeze bottle of whiskey. He changed into shorts. They stuffed two men's bathing suits and a large peach-colored blanket into a pink-striped beach bag. Diana drove them in the pickup, along Calle Real, underneath the freeway, and then back on their tracks to Corral Beach. When they pulled into the parking area, it was about twelve-forty-five.

By that time, it was the sort of day Phillip lived for. The temperature was around the day's high of eighty-three degrees. A feisty breeze whipped up the waves and ruffled the brush-covered tops of the cliffs. The tide had yet to come in far enough to impede access to the coves.

As the Bogdanoffs made their way to the beach, Brian said Diana made definite eye contact with him and Rickey. "It was like [when] you've seen someone or heard something about someone and you finally see that person and you can recognize them from the things you've heard." As she and Phillip rounded the point to the south, she kept looking back. Brian and Rickey waited between five and eight minutes before they came off the bluff and followed the Bogdanoffs around the point.

Diana and Phillip got their favorite cove, the protected spot where they had sunbathed naked, and made love and Polaroid photographs. They stretched out their blanket between a small hump of rock and the foot of the bluffs. They bounded into the water, Phillip naked, Diana still in her bikini bottoms. Brian and Rickey just looked at them in the water and kept on walking down the beach.

Brian could not recall how far they walked, but they do not appear to have made it back to where McNutt and his friends were fishing. They climbed onto some rocks and smoked a joint. "I think we were trying to break the monotony of the situation and we were trying to tell each other jokes to keep our mind off the stuff . . . I was scared, and I think Rick was scared, too."

When they turned back, "we saw this dude there having a little picnic by himself. We thought he was a fag . . . He was just sitting there by himself, pulled up on the blanket reading this book."

The "dude" was Steve Lindgren, a visitor to Corral Beach for thirteen years and the passerby whom Phillip had approached and invited to form part of a sexual triangle. He usually favored the same cove as the Bogdanoffs for nude sunbathing. But this time they had just beaten him to it, so he took the larger cove to the south.

Lindgren was aware of Brian and Rickey. "As I lay there eating my lunch, I noticed these individuals were staring at me. I felt uncomfortable . . . They appeared to be up to something."

Around the point, Diana and Phillip were out of the water. They dried themselves, and Phillip, still naked, lay down on the beach blanket. Diana took off her bikini bottom, put on the sun visor, and joined him.

After about five minutes of staring at Lindgren, Brian and Rickey proceeded north around the point to the next cove. According to Brian, Diana lifted up her visor and watched them go past. They sat down on the rocks at the cove's northern end, only thirty feet from the beach blanket. They had an unobstructed view of this naked, middle-aged couple they had never seen before.

Brian had already taken off his T-shirt. Now, because his feet were wet, he removed his socks. They waited there for a seeming eternity, long enough for Rickey to start worrying again. "Look, Brian, we don't really have to do this, man."

"I made a promise."

"Man, I'm not going to do this. If you're that serious about the girl, here, you do it."

According to Brian, Rickey handed him the .22, and he covered it with his T-shirt. Then Rickey suggested to him just how he should do it.

The true horror of what followed isn't expressed by even the most graphic of the coroner's photographs. But Brian Stafford's description is enough—more than enough.

"Rick walks up to him and then he says, 'Got any cigarettes?' And Diana, she just, she knew what was happening, because she was laying there right beside, and when Rick walked up to her, it wasn't like she was trying to cover herself up, [like] a normal woman would when she's in the nude."

Diana makes no attempt to leave the cove. Phillip sits up on the blanket. It is doubtful that he has time to say anything or make out what is confronting him because . . . "It happened. Pow . . .

"Then when it happened, it wasn't like she screamed or nothing. She just had this look on her face, like, you finally got what you deserved all this time. And when it first happened, it was like, I can't believe it."

Phillip's hands go to his face. Blood streams out through his fingers. "I'm looking at him and I see the blood coming out from underneath his hand. And I look at Diane. And the dude is screaming, 'Oh my God.' "

Brian "could picture this man just laying here in pain, and I felt sorry for him . . . It was bad. I felt sorry for him." He has to put him out of his misery. "I couldn't cope with that man just like that."

Brian puts the gun to Phillip's temple, looks up into the air, and squeezes the trigger again. This bullet tears through Phillip's brain, carving a path of destruction.

Rickey and Brian run off toward Lindgren's cove. Diana never screams. "Being perfectly honest, she stood there. The whole time, she watched. She didn't say a word, she just stood there . . . nude . . . She didn't grab her towel until we were fuckin' around the other cove."

This account of what happened on September 21, distilled mostly from Brian's interview with police and court testimony, raises several puzzling questions:

- If Brian had been told the day before how and when to get to the beach—and Stephanie had even pointed it out to him—why did he need to touch base with Diana?
- Why did he and Rickey bother to stake out the trailer park and the Caltrans office earlier that morning?
- Why did the two of them make no effort to conceal themselves at the beach?

Such questions are not a matter of detail. They go to the question at the heart of this case: Was the murder of Phillip

Bogdanoff "just" a desperate, haphazard, even unplanned act, or was it the expression of a very cold, very deliberate, very nonchalant evil?

Perhaps the best place to look for an answer is in what happened after the murder—the immediate aftermath and during the police investigation. The actions of Diana, Stephanie, and the Bakersfield family during this period betray their nonchalance, their sense of invulnerability, the warped nature of their relationships, even more than what they did before the crime.

PART THREE

A Consummate Actor?

None of the other beach-goers witnessed what had happened in the cove. Steve Lindgren saw Brian and Rickey sitting on the rocks near the Bogdanoffs, but at the time of the shooting, he was several hundred feet away, around the point, talking to Nathan McNutt and the other fishermen. McNutt said he heard what sounded like a gunshot, although it could have been a wave crashing against a rock.

Lindgren did witness the escape. As he walked back to his cove, Brian and Rickey ran past his towel and climbed a trail some fifty feet up the slippery face of the shale cliff. "It looked to me like Rodgers was really freaked out," he told me. "He was way out in front. He looked so panic-stricken, you wouldn't believe it. He was around that corner long before Stafford."

Rickey had no trouble scaling the cliff, but Brian "went about halfway up and started sliding backwards . . . He was really huffing and puffing. His eyes were wide open and . . . it looked like he was hyperventilating."

Lindgren also spotted Diana heading in the opposite direction. "She was running like a wounded animal. It wasn't even a run, it was like running in place." She appeared to be struggling to put on her top. Sensing something was very wrong, Lindgren took off after her.

In the next cove, Phillip lay rigid on the blanket. Walking toward him, Lindgren asked, "Sir, are you okay? Is everything okay?" He soon realized Phillip wasn't okay. It wasn't difficult—a puddle of blood from his head had formed on the sand.

When Lindgren got to Corral Beach, Diana was sitting on her knees on the sand. Another beach-goer had already come to her aid. He and Lindgren asked her several times what had happened. "She looked very upset . . . She wasn't answering," Lindgren recalled. "She was just crying and then she'd stop and look into the sand for a while. Then she'd cry some more . . . She just mumbled a couple of things, something about a black guy and a white guy. We said, 'Which one did it?' She just kind of sat there looking at the sand."

However brief and incoherent, this was Diana's first account of what happened in the cove. Some two hours later, she gave a somewhat different account in an interview with a detective—one that would lay the groundwork for the belief of investigators that she was a consummate actor, not a grieving widow.

By the time Detective Tom Nelson interviewed Diana, the beach was the scene of feverish, chaotic activity. As police, coroner's officials, paramedics, forensics experts, witnesses, curious bystanders, and the media buzz around like flies, the immediate investigation of any murder tends toward confusion. But Corral Beach on September 21 was a study in extreme chaos.

Partly to blame were the murder's peculiar circumstances and the natural hazards of the area. They included the beach's remote location, the high cliffs that hampered radio communication, and the incoming tide threatening to disturb the evidence. Then there was mechanical failure—the van carrying police forensics experts broke down en route to the beach. A railroad worker, a park ranger, a sheriff's deputy, and a detective took turns standing sentry over the body before the coroner was able to remove it.

The first distress call went out from the maintenance crew working at railroad marker 349 on the Southern Pacific tracks above Corral Beach. The workers had seen Diana and Lindgren come running onto the beach. When he found out what had happened, Sal Robles, a welder, radioed a maintenance vehicle farther up the track and told him to call the railroad office in Oxnard, fifty-five miles south. Raul Saldivar, a foreman, waded through the surf to Phillip's body. He covered it with a towel and stood sentry.

From the railroad dispatcher in Oxnard, calls started bouncing around like pinballs. The first officials at the scene were park rangers Mike Lunsford and Linda Rath, who were at the

Refugio State Beach entrance kiosk when they got the news. Lunsford was not given the name of the beach, but he knew the location of railroad marker 349, so had no trouble finding the maintenance workers. They told him they had glimpsed two men running down the bike path toward El Capitan who might be the suspects. Lunsford drove off in search of them while Rath went down to the beach to secure the murder scene.

Three fireman-paramedics arrived a few minutes after Rath got to Phillip. The tide was already so far in, the surf splashing up against the bluffs, that the paramedics stopped to take their shoes and socks off to wade through to the cove. They applied CPR to Phillip, but their efforts were useless. Rath, meanwhile, went back to Corral Beach and got a detailed description of the suspects from Lindgren. He told her about his encounter with a white man and a black man. It was this description that was soon being broadcast over the radios of detectives speeding to the scene.

In a small detective bureau like that of the Santa Barbara County sheriff, all available investigators, not just the five assigned to major crimes, respond to the scene of a homicide. Nelson was working on the fraud detail at the Goleta headquarters when he heard the bulletin. Sergeant Bill Baker, head of major crimes, drove up from headquarters with his most experienced investigator, Fred Ray.

In downtown Santa Barbara, Ray's usual partner, Russ Birchim, had just completed an interview of a crime victim. His car radio's main frequency was jammed with traffic, so he had to call up the dispatcher on a secondary frequency to find out what was going on. The dispatcher gave him directions to the beach.

Birchim found chaos at Corral Beach when he arrived there around 2:30 P.M. "I'll never forget the sight," he recalled. "The helicopter [carrying SWAT team members] was kicking up a dust storm. People were running everywhere."

He drew the unenviable assignment of standing guard over Phillip's body until the crime scene experts arrived. The paramedics had left a towel covering the body from face to ankles. But Phillip's arms stuck out from under the towel, and one of his hands was raised about six inches off the ground, with the thumb pointing upward. Alone with the corpse in the blazing sun, Birchim smoked a chain of cigarettes. His anxiety grew as the tide edged closer to the body—to within six or seven feet at one time. "I was just concerned it was going to come up there and erase any and all evidence," he said.

Another worry was the helicopter, now hovering dangerously close to the crime scene. Cut off by the high bluffs, Birchim was out of radio contact. He tried several times to wade into the ocean to get a message to the pilot to stay away. But each time he failed to get through.

The criminalistics detectives, their van problems finally solved, arrived at 3:34. They took several pictures of the body, including close-ups of Phillip's head. They picked up two men's bathing suits and the cooler containing three unopened cans of beer and a squeeze bottle of a liquid that smelled like bourbon. But they had only been foraging about fifteen minutes when the helicopter, borrowed by the sheriff's office from an oil exploration firm, came in too close. Much of the evidence, including clothing and towels, was blown back against the cliff.

The most important items, however, were left undisturbed. Stuck in the blood five inches from Phillip's head was one .22-caliber shell casing; another was about three and a half feet away on the sand.

At about the same time, Sergeant Baker asked Tom Nelson to take an initial statement from the victim's wife.

Diana had sat on Corral Beach for at least an hour after the shooting. Footage shot by local TV station KEYT showed a fireman-paramedic and a beach-goer kneeling beside her. Looking dazed but not tearful, she mumbled and shook her head or rocked back and forth on her haunches.

Mark Bray, a lifeguard based at El Capitan, overheard some of Diana's mumblings. He heard her tell the paramedic to call someone. "We have that information. You already gave it to me," the paramedic said.

"No, you have to do it right away. He might have something to do with this," Diana insisted.

When Nelson interviewed her, Diana was sitting in the front passenger seat of a fire truck parked on the bike path. A fire department chaplain sat beside her, trying to comfort her. Nelson gingerly leaned through the open door and began to question her.

The interview was spread over a period of about an hour. Nelson had to break off a few times so Diana could collect herself. There was, of course, no suggestion at this time that Diana was a suspect. But Nelson knew that two suspects had been identified—a black man and a white man. The SWAT team members had been combing the cliffs in search of them. The El Capitan State Beach campground had been emptied in case they were in that area.

Diana told Nelson that she and Phillip were just dozing off when a white male approached them. "He said, 'Do you have any marijuana?' Phillip replied: 'What?'" The man asked again, and Phillip said, "No." Feeling conspicuous in the nude, Diana turned to her right to cover herself with a towel. At that moment, the man pulled a gun from his pants pocket and shot Phillip twice. He fled toward Santa Barbara while she ran off in the opposite direction.

Nelson pressed Diana about whether she had seen a black man at the scene. "The only person I saw was the white man who did the shooting," she said. "It was only a white man that was there."

According to Nelson, she described the suspect as a "White male about thirty years old, with his weight appropriate to his height of six feet, and shoulder-length brown hair."

Toward the end of the interview, Nelson asked Diana if she knew of anybody who might have it in for Phillip. She mentioned two possibilities. There was "Sharon," a Caltrans employee who had filed sexual harassment complaints against coworkers. Diana said Phillip was afraid even to be left alone in the office with her. One time he told his boss that he didn't want to attend a meeting with Sharon because he was afraid she was going to come in and blow everybody's head off.

The other possible enemy was "Frank," a water truck driver whom she alleged had lost a four-hundred-thousand-dollar contract with Caltrans because he sexually harassed her. Diana suggested Frank might have wanted to retaliate by killing Phillip.

Nelson included all this information in his initial report. He left out one detail, however—that he had seen no sign of Diana crying while he talked to her.

Breaking the News

After completing her interview with Nelson, Diana was allowed to leave the beach and, escorted by the chaplain, to return to the trailer.

The news had spread fast in the campground. Local radio was broadcasting the story, and some residents, including Al Clarke, had police scanners. At 5:00 P.M. local TV kicked in with footage of paramedics carrying the body through knee-high surf and of an interview with a railroad worker. Police were looking for two suspects, the reports said, in what appeared to be a random shooting.

Campers, most of whom hardly knew the reclusive Bogdanoffs of space E-16, milled around the trailer. The next-door neighbor, Rogena Nutt, made it inside and tried to comfort Diana. "She was crying and she was upset," Nutt recalled.

But Diana was alert enough to arrange for Nutt to take care of a combination-lock briefcase she and Phillip kept in the trailer. "There are going to be a lot of kids around," she told her neighbor. "This has personal items in it, and I don't want anybody to get into it. Can you keep it for a day or so?" Nutt took the briefcase.

With the chaplain's help, Diana also started making phone calls. One went to her cousin's wife Burdeen McCowan in Goleta, another to her sister Kathy in the San Diego area. Most important, she had to speak to her daughter Stephanie and get her to come up from Bakersfield.

Things were similarly chaotic at the Eye Street apartment. Brian and Rickey had returned around five o'clock after an eventful journey from Santa Barbara.

Once they scaled the treacherous cliff at the beach, they ran down the bike path, across the railroad tracks, and onto the freeway shoulder where the Ford was parked under the eucalyptus trees. According to Brian, he still had the gun in his hand. Rickey peeled it from him and threw it in the trunk. He took the wheel and opened the passenger door for Brian. "I curled up in the fetal position," Brian said later. All he could think about was going home and getting a hug from Stephanie. As they drove toward Santa Barbara, they passed police cruisers heading in the opposite direction to the crime scene.

Although they intended to take the same route back to Bakersfield, they strayed off course, ending up in the Los Angeles suburbs. By the time they reached the Grapevine, they were running low on gas and were out of money. They stopped so Brian could call home and get somebody to bring them some money. The phone rang and rang, but nobody picked up.

They only made it to the apartment by coasting much of the way in neutral. When they finally got there, Calvin, barely awake, was on the sofa with Jodie. He had just had a dream in which something bad happened to Brian. Stephanie, sleeping off her crank run, was still in bed.

Almost as soon as he walked through the door, Brian announced the news. He was triumphant, as if he had just pulled off the ultimate drug deal. He had nothing to hide. These were his friends, his family, his audience.

"We did it, we did it, man!" he exclaimed.

"What did you do?" It was Jodie.

"We killed him! We killed Phillip, we killed Stephanie's stepdad."

Jodie could see they were hyper, so hyper it was as if they were amping badly on crank. They had grabbed some cigarettes and were smoking breathlessly. But she apparently still wasn't convinced. "Shut up! You're lying. You didn't just go kill someone."

"Yes, I did. Look at the blood on my shoes!" He pointed to the tip of one of his black and white L.A. Gears. There was a dry red spot.

"That could be catsup."

"No, we killed Phillip. We really did."

As further proof, Rickey displayed the handle of his .22-caliber pistol. It was speckled with red spots, too.

Brian had been behaving as if he expected a round of applause, but Calvin hauled him into a corner of the room and started yelling at him. "You stupid motherfucker! I told you, don't do it. I told you, if she wanted him dead, give her the gun. Now you go and do it your own damn self!

"You're gonna get fucked out of this. You're gonna be used. You ain't gonna get nothing."

Brian wrested himself away from Calvin and went into the bedroom. Stephanie was just waking up, crawling over the foot of the bed. He got his hug and then repeated his story to her. He also showed her the blood on his shoe.

Bleary-eyed and pulling on some clothes, Stephanie staggered into the living room. Rickey, now sitting on the couch, greeted her with an apology. "I'm sorry I saw your mom naked on the beach," he muttered. "I tried not to look. She has nice tits. Next time you see her, tell her I'm sorry."

Stephanie was stunned, silent. After all the talking, all the phone calls, it had actually happened. "I just went into a state of like, 'Oh my God, I can't believe it,' " she said later.

Outside in the hot summer afternoon, normal things were going on, cars grinding by on Chester, people living their usual lives. There in the small cottage, these friends had created a fantasy world. But now a dreadful reality was poking through a crack in the wall of illusion.

Brian's concern was the phone. Why had nobody answered when he called from the Grapevine? Calvin explained that he had turned the ringer off because he couldn't sleep with all the customers calling. Brian switched it back on.

A few minutes later, at 5:28, the phone rang. It was the chaplain in Santa Barbara for Stephanie. He told her that Phillip had been killed, and her mother wanted her to come to Santa Barbara right away.

"Put my mom on the phone," Stephanie demanded.

"Your mom's really upset now."

Stephanie was adamant. "I want to talk to my mom, and I want to talk to her now!"

Diana got on the line and confirmed what the chaplain had said. "I need you to come down here."

"Okay, I'll be down."

Stephanie sat down on the sofa with Jodie. The dreadful reality was sinking in. Perhaps most dreadful of all, she realized she had to see Grandpa before she left.

"Will you come with me to see my grandpa?" she asked Jodie. "I'm real worried about him. I don't want him to get the news by himself."

I asked Stephanie why, if she loved Nick so much, she didn't consider his feelings when she was thinking about helping to kill his son. Without any hesitation, she replied: "I never thought about what it would be like for him. I was thinking about what it would be like for my mom. Stupid, but true."

But the prospect of seeing Nick that evening overwhelmed Stephanie. What could she say to him?

The stooped old man with the sad, watery eyes and deep, resonant voice had always been there for her. His wife had died in her arms. Wasn't he family, too? The only one in her family who treated her as family? Others talked about family, but they had got her in all this trouble. Her mother said they would be family again if Phillip was dead, but now everything had gotten so screwed up.

Jodie agreed to go with Stephanie to her grandfather's. The journey from her apartment normally takes five minutes, but Stephanie was so dazed, she drove in circles. Twice she missed the turn off South H Street.

"I can't believe this has really happened. I can't believe Brian killed Phillip," she murmured.

"Why? You're the one that wanted it done," Jodie said.

"Now I have to tell Grandpa. What am I supposed to do? What am I supposed to say?"

"I don't know what to tell you, Stephanie. If I were you, I'd get to the first church I could and pray to God He forgives me for what I did."

When they finally arrived outside the clapboard house, Stephanie said, "I cannot tell him this. I cannot tell this man that his son is dead. I cannot tell him, especially when I know who really killed him."

They entered the house through the side door. Nick, who hadn't heard anything yet, welcomed her as always and offered her some food. Stephanie was almost mute. "She looked like somebody had just stole her puppy or something," Jodie recalled.

Noticing her strange mood, Nick asked, "Stephanie, what's wrong?"

"Oh nothing, Grandpa, nothing."

"No, Stephanie, there's something wrong," he insisted. "Tell me, tell me what's wrong."

"Nothing, Grandpa. There's nothing wrong."

After a few minutes, Stephanie got up, saying she had to see the neighbors, Tony and Irene Reyes, who rented the house next door to Phillip. The couple recalled her coming over around 6:00 P.M. and telling them what had happened. They lent her about fifty dollars for her trip to Santa Barbara to see her mother. Stephanie showed no obvious signs of distress, they said. In fact, so casual was her demeanor, they thought she was kidding.

Stephanie left without breaking the news to her grandfather. She drove home with Jodie, stopping along the way to buy an eighth of an ounce of weed with some of the Reyeses' money. Nick was so concerned that, at 6:05, he called the trailer in Santa Barbara.

Back at the apartment, Brian had showered and changed, removing any gunpowder residue, and Rickey had cleaned the gun. Calvin was no longer mad at Brian, but he seemed edgy. When Stephanie said she wanted Jodie to go with her to Santa Barbara, Calvin vetoed that. "Uh-uh, I'm not going for that," he said. "I want to go home."

While the girls were away, Calvin had found out more about what happened at the beach, and the more he found out, the more concerned he became for himself and Jodie. Rickey talked about how impressed he was with the impact of the fatal bullet. "I didn't know if you shot somebody in the head, it would do that to his head," he said.

"What did Stephanie's mom do?" Calvin asked.

"She just stood there," Brian said.

"Did she holler or anything?"

"Yeah, she hollered, but not very loud. She waited so we could get far enough away."

Calvin said later that he was wondering, "This motherfucker can kill somebody he don't know, what's stopping him from killing us to keep everybody from talking?" He didn't feel like hanging around the apartment much longer.

Stephanie packed her bag and snorted a line of crank. She and Brian spoke further about what he had done to her stepfather. Finally she dropped Calvin and Jodie off at his sister's house, and the Ford she never liked was heading for Santa Barbara for the second time that day.

She didn't have to go all the way to El Capitan, just to the outskirts of Goleta. During their phone call, her mother had told her she would be spending the night at Burdeen McCowan's home and gave her directions.

Burdeen had taken Diana to her home in the early evening. She described Diana as behaving as if she were on "mental overload." But she was "functioning, she wasn't hysterical." She didn't really discuss the murder except to say the gunman was white and that she was upset that police had already disclosed Phillip's name.

She was also embarrassed about a particular detail. "Burdeen, I have to tell you something," she said. "We were sunbathing in the nude."

"That doesn't bother me," Burdeen replied. "That's your business."

"I just didn't want everyone to know that, everyone in the family to know that."

Burdeen recalled Stephanie arriving around 11:00 P.M. Meeting her mother in the hallway, they embraced. After they all sat down in the living room, Burdeen started, as she put it, "ranting on" about the murder. What she ranted, however, was only common sense.

"This person that did the shooting doesn't know that you can't identify him," she said to Diana. "Anyone that would come up and shoot somebody and leave a witness had to have been a dopehead or really ignorant."

To her surprise, Stephanie interjected: "Come on, not necessarily. I wouldn't say that."

When they were ready to turn in, Stephanie and Diana were given a guest bedroom. They got into bed together. It was just the two of them again, just like it was way back in Colfax, just like it was before Phillip came along and separated them. But as Stephanie recalled it, the reunion was more tense than cozy.

Stephanie wanted to know what happened on the beach, but her mother didn't want to talk about it. "Brian already told me. I want to hear it from *you*," she persisted.

Diana relented and gave her a host of details. They saw Brian and Rickey from the water, and Phillip asked something about the "nigger" on the beach; she had told him to hurry up and go to sleep so she could fall asleep to his snoring; it was Brian who came up and asked for something; after he was shot the first time, Phillip looked at her like, "Oh my God, I can't believe this just happened."

At the apartment, Brian had told Stephanie that her mother had agreed to leave the cove and "act like she was going to the bathroom" when it was time for the shooting. But Diana denied that. She did say, however, that "she gave them time to get away."

They discussed the future. Diana said she was going to keep the house in Visalia, and she wanted Stephanie to move in with her. But her daughter wasn't too keen on the idea. Stephanie preferred Bakersfield to Visalia; that's where most of her friends were. She didn't want to be uprooted all over again.

Well after midnight, they fell asleep. It was the end of a long day, the end of what was supposed to be the nightmare of Phillip. It was the beginning of something far worse.

Taking Care of Business

The morning of Friday, September 22, the Bogdanoff murder led the front page of the *Santa Barbara News-Press*—under the headline "Authorities Seek Two Suspects in Slaying at Beach"—and was being carried by wire services to newspapers around the country.

One of only ten homicides in Santa Barbara County the entire year, it apparently defied logic. "It seems to be totally senseless," the *News-Press* quoted a sheriff's spokeswoman as saying. "Most [killings] are, but this one more so." Around town, it was hard to believe such an act could have been committed in such an idyllic place. Somehow the virus of Los Angeles–style random violence had crept up the coast and destroyed the immunity of Santa Barbara.

"This incident tells me that you're not safe in these coves anymore," a Corral Beach fisherman said.

The *News-Press* reported that the Bogdanoffs were approached by the two suspects, and the shooter asked for some marijuana. When they said they had none, "the man was shot twice in the head." The shooter was described as a white male, about six feet tall, who was accompanied by a black male of similar height.

The newspaper published two large photos from the crime scene on the front page. One showed Phillip's body being removed from the beach. The other featured a woman sitting on the sand, her head bowed over her knees. A bystander crouches beside her, his hand on her shoulder, while a sheriff's deputy looks on. The caption went: "The victim's wife, Diana Bogdanoff, is comforted after the shooting."

That morning Diana was up early as usual, plunging into life after Phillip. The most pressing matter was financial.

Burdeen McCowan had asked Diana the evening before about how she planned to deal with all the expenses of Phillip's death. Diana said they had some money in a checking account and a little in a savings account. "Oh, and there's a check. Phillip had a check in the trailer. Almost twelve thousand dollars."

It was the check Phillip had received in May from the tenant paying off the IOU on his Shingle Springs lot.

"Why was he keeping it?" Burdeen said.

"I don't really know why. He kept talking about investing it, maybe buying some property at Big Bear. He just hadn't gotten around to doing anything with it."

Diana added that she was worried about leaving the check overnight in the trailer.

"What can you do with it?" Burdeen continued. "I really think you should talk to an attorney and see what you can do with that check."

"The only one I know is Judge Pattillo. He's a judge. He's the one that married us."

Diana felt it was too late to call him, but Burdeen said, "I think this is important enough that you should talk to him tonight."

The judge was leaving town the next day, but he had no trouble thinking of a referral for Diana—his son, James Pattillo, Jr., who happened to specialize in probate cases.

At around 9:00 A.M. on September 22, Diana returned to the trailer to fetch the check and then set off for her bank. She was with Burdeen, and Kathy Markwell and her husband, Stan, who had driven up from San Diego.

The younger Pattillo, a gangling, mustached man who writes detective novels in his spare time, was waiting for the others at the First Interstate bank in Goleta when they arrived at around 10:00 A.M. He noticed that Diana's eyes were red, her face puffy, as if she had been crying.

Diana asked him what she should do with the twelve-thousand-dollar check, a cashier's check made out to Phillip. Pattillo advised her that, as Phillip's spouse, she could endorse and deposit it herself. The lawyer did not notice that Diana deposited the check in her personal checking account.

At First Interstate, Diana also entered a safe-deposit box which she and Phillip had started renting in February. With

Pattillo observing, she removed documents including escrow papers, deeds, IOUs, and a copy of Nick Bogdanoff's will. There was no will by Phillip.

From the bank, Diana returned to the trailer with the Markwells so she could pack some things to take with her to Bakersfield, where the funeral would be held. Some strange things also happened at the trailer, after two of the last people to see Phillip alive stopped by to visit.

Mel Brown had learned of the murder the previous day and was as shocked as everyone else who worked with Phillip. Although he had never been that close to him, it was hard to believe that the gruff guy in the orange tank top wouldn't be around anymore, that he had been killed so randomly.

Diana called Brown at the office around 8:00 A.M. He remembered that she cried on the phone and said something like "He did it for me." He presumed she meant he took the afternoon off for her. She suggested he come to the trailer about 1:00 P.M. to handle some business matters.

Brown took Lisa Alviso with him so she could drive Phillip's state-issued car back to Caltrans. They sat around the trailer talking for a while, Diana tearfully going over her story of the murder. Stan Markwell was outside with Al Clarke, listening to the police scanner in Al's pickup. Suddenly Stan burst in. There was something on the scanner about two suspects being cornered nearby, he announced.

"They've come back to get me," moaned Diana, looking very surprised.

"Why don't you pack your things so we can get out of here?" her sister Kathy suggested.

But the panic ebbed quickly. "Don't worry about it," Diana said. "Just sit back and relax."

Another odd thing involved Phillip's El Camino. The previous Saturday, he and Diana had taken the car to the home of a Kasler carpenter, Kevin Arrowood, who had agreed to sell it for him. Arrowood lived off the busy Highway 33 that connects U.S. 101 in Ventura to Ojai, a popular tourist destination. For a commission, he let friends use the front of his property as a showcase for items they had for sale. Phillip wanted about thirty-six hundred dollars for the El Camino; Arrowood figured he could get at least three thousand.

There hadn't been any takers during the past week, so, on Arrowood's behalf, Brown asked Diana what she wanted done with the vehicle. "Don't have him sell it," she replied. "I'll take care of it when I get back on Tuesday."

The most important thing she had to take care of in that period of time was the funeral. There again, her behavior was bizarre.

Certainly the funeral was more of an ordeal than most widows have to bear. The body was released by the coroner's office the day after the murder and taken to a mortuary in Bakersfield. In accordance with Russian Molokan custom, it lay in an open casket for public viewing from Friday evening until the interment on Sunday afternoon.

At the mortuary, three rows of seats were arranged on each side of the coffin. The Molokan mourners—women in off-white dresses and lace head coverings, men in tunics and loose white pants belted by a sash—sang and chanted in Russian.

For most of the wake, Diana sat in the front row of mourners, just inches from the casket, with Nick Bogdanoff at her side. She wore a Russian scarf knotted around her head and an off-white suit. She accepted the hugs and condolences of family members, dabbed her eyes with a tissue, put her hand on Phillip's, and said a prayer. She seemed every bit the grieving widow, struggling to bear up under the strain.

"She went right through the whole thing like she should have, A to Z," recalled Tommy Byford, Phillip's friend.

Phillip's first wife and children weren't sure what to make of her. Admittedly they were all a little peeved to start off with because of the way they heard about the murder. Diana had supposedly asked Phillip's brother on Thursday evening to tell them. Instead they didn't find out until the next day, and then only through a family friend whose daughter had seen a TV news report.

Nicki managed to get hold of Diana at the trailer on Friday afternoon and asked her what happened. She was very curt, prefacing her account by saying: "I'm going to tell you once, and that's it. You tell the rest of the family."

Still, they all picked up on similar things at the funeral. Maybe Diana was sedated, but she was too composed, especially when you considered that, only two days before, the man in the casket was killed in front of her. "I never saw tears come out of her eyes," Cindy Cook said. "She would have a tissue and cover her face . . . She was more concerned about my grandfather than anything."

Diana also made little comments that disturbed them. As she hugged Kay, Diana whispered in her ear, "Jehovah is my strength." To Christy she said, "Don't worry, Jehovah will bless you, He will get you through this." That was how a Witness would talk, referring to God as Jehovah. What was Diana doing? She wasn't a Witness and never had been.

When Cindy leaned over the casket to touch her father's head, Diana grabbed her hand. "Don't touch him," she warned. "If you touch him, his head will split apart and pus will come out. The skin is so tight, it could burst."

Another mourner, Tommy Byford, felt troubled by Diana's behavior. She had said some strange things when she called to notify him of Phillip's death. She described how happy she and Phillip were, how they had just bought her daughter a car and fixed her up with an apartment. She went into graphic detail about the murder, telling him "how they put the gun on his temple and blew his brains out." The police, she said, thought it was possibly gang-related.

Then she told Byford that she thought of him at the time of the shooting, that "I could have been of some help if I'd been there." That really made him wonder. He hadn't seen her or Phillip since they moved to Visalia two years before. Why think of him?

On the Saturday evening, taking a break outside the mortuary, he had another odd conversation with Diana. "If they find the person who did it, will you call me collect please?" he asked. "Immediately. You will be able to just walk in and identify him, won't you?"

"Well, Tommy, I was putting a towel around me and I could recognize the back of his head. I could tell you what kind of gun he had and all of that."

The more he thought about it, the more it puzzled him. If these people walked up to them on the beach and spoke to Phillip, how come she couldn't identify anyone?

There was something else. Byford, who was in the trailer business himself, asked Diana if she would like him to pick up her trailer in Santa Barbara. She said

that wasn't necessary, but she would like him to stay
in touch and come up to Visalia and see her sometime.

The inferences of Kay Bogdanoff, the children, and Byford
were perhaps oversubtle, those of people who were over-
wrought at the time. What nobody at the funeral could over-
look was the behavior of the widow's daughter.

Stephanie had returned to Bakersfield on Friday. Diana
wasn't around to see her off or give her some money to
tide her over for a while. Burdeen ended up lending her
one hundred dollars. She had bridled when Diana asked her
to go to the funeral, but her mother insisted because "it would
look better."

Her mood worsened on Saturday when her apartment was
robbed while she was out with Brian and Amy Baca, her
friend from Visalia, who had agreed to accompany her to the
funeral. "Every piece of that house was upside down," Baca
recalled. The main item missing was her stereo—the rumor
in the complex was that the burglar was looking for dope and
stole the stereo as a smoke screen. After sitting around in the
debris for a while with Brian and Amy, Stephanie got up,
screamed, "You can both go to hell!" and marched into the
bedroom, slamming the door behind her.

When she got to the mortuary on Sunday morning, Stephanie
acted as if she were about to be pushed out of an airplane at
fifteen thousand feet without a parachute. "I was tripping,"
she recalled. "I didn't want to walk down the aisle and
see him."

Elaine Kosareff, the wife of Phillip's cousin, took her arm.
"Come on, you've got to go down there," she urged. "You
need to be brave."

"I can't look at him."

"Come on, go sit by your mother. I'll take you."

When she saw the embalmed corpse, "It was like 'uuugh.' I
couldn't handle it." Her mother put her arm around Stephanie
and sat her down in the front row of mourners. She was now so
hysterical, Nick had to intervene. "You've got to calm down,"
he whispered.

"Stephanie totally unraveled," Kay Bogdanoff recalled. "She
couldn't look at Phillip. She came in more torn up than her

mother." Kay reckoned Stephanie only stayed an hour. She had gone by the time the body was taken away for burial.

Phillip Bogdanoff was buried beside his mother in a cemetery just outside Shafter, a few miles up the road from the farm where he grew up in Rosedale. The two graves are in a corner of the cemetery reserved for Russian families. They both carry the same inscription in Cyrillic Russian script. Roughly translated, it means:

> *Here rests the body*
> *Peace to the ashes*
> *Until the appeal*
> *of the archangelic trumpet*

Smelling a Rat

After the burial, Diana invited Phillip's daughters to stop in Visalia on their way back to northern California. It was the first time they had been to the house on Tulare Avenue. Now their father wasn't even there. They chatted uncomfortably with Diana. At one point, Nicki casually mentioned that Santa Barbara detectives had spoken to her.

Diana appeared startled. "Oh really? What did they ask? What did they want to know?"

"Just about the case," Nicki replied.

"Well, what did you tell them?"

"Just what I knew about, what I knew about my dad."

Diana didn't take it further with Nicki. But the next day—Monday, September 25—at about 11:00 A.M., she called Detective Russ Birchim in Santa Barbara. She wanted to know how the investigation was going.

Since the frenetic activities at the crime scene, it really hadn't gone very far, and Birchim was beginning to wonder when the first break would come. Things were looking as frustrating as they had on the beach, when he had kept vigil over the body, cut off from radio communication.

A lot was riding on the case for Birchim—it was the biggest homicide the forty-year-old investigator had ever handled. A native of Lone Pine, near Death Valley, he joined the sheriff's department in 1976 after working for a private store security firm and made detective in six years.

The work was often routine in a community where violent crime is relatively rare. But that suited Birchim fine. No one could mistake him for an abrasive big-city cop. He is much closer to Sheriff Harry Truman of "Twin Peaks" than Dirty

Harry. Soft-spoken and tanned, he fits the laid-back, semirural ambience of Santa Barbara. He and his wife—his childhood sweetheart from Lone Pine—built a house in a secluded canyon, where they live with their three children and a menagerie that has included goats and pigs. About the only dents in the image are the cigarette habit and the gray hair, which lends him a passing resemblance to the actor Steve Martin.

When the big cases came along, he often took a backseat to his more experienced colleague, Fred Wayne Ray, a twenty-year veteran of the department. Birchim didn't mind that. Besides identical mustaches, they have a lot in common. Ray is also from rural California, from Fresno, in the heart of the San Joaquin Valley, and has a folksy, easygoing manner. They share the cop's sense of humor—the mixture of merciless teasing, gruesome anecdotes, and scatological commentary that provides the outlet for the tension of their work. Call Birchim just about any time and he's fending off an attack of rubber-band missiles from his partner.

Working together, they had a knack for making unconventional methods work and being in the right place at the right time. On a robbery case, instead of conducting a standard covert surveillance of a grocery store, they parked right outside it. "If the robbers drove by and saw us, they'd think, 'Those guys aren't on a stakeout,' " Ray explained. They arrested the suspects after one of them came up to the car and poked his head through the window.

On a murder case, they were looking for a suspect who had killed his victim at a home where he rented a room. As they were interviewing the suspect's landlady, he called to ask her husband to sign a forged document showing he had not stolen the victim's car. He would stop by shortly. Birchim and Ray were waiting for him when he did. "Every time we went looking for someone, we caught him," Ray said.

At the time of the Bogdanoff murder, Ray was heavily involved with another homicide case. So their supervisor, Bill Baker, made Birchim the lead investigator, with Ray available as backup when needed. Four days into the investigation, Birchim was feeling the pressure.

Virtually all the resources of the Santa Barbara sheriff's major crimes and forensics units had been put at his disposal. There had been dozens of leads from the public and supposed sightings of the suspects; dozens of reports had been filed and hours of overtime logged. Birchim himself had hardly got any sleep. Using Lindgren and the fishermen, detectives had made composite drawings of the suspects. That of the black suspect was almost a work of art, so complex was the rendering of the hairstyle, with its flat top, V-shaped lines, and tuft at the nape.

One possible clue had been overlooked initially. Herman Devine, one of the fisherman-witnesses, had left the beach before the shooting. But he called the police when he heard the news later on Thursday and told them about the white guy urinating against the wall and ditching his soda cup on the bike path. It wasn't until two days later, however, that Ray called back and took Devine to the beach to find the cup. It was still on the bike path, but there was little hope of lifting usable fingerprints off it.

Detectives had identified Diana's possible suspects as Sharon Borege and Frank Dominguez, but not bothered to interview either of them. In the case of Dominguez, they had received an anonymous tip that the water truck driver might be involved. A Santa Barbara policeman familiar with the alleged sexual harassment of Diana sent a memo to the sheriff's office, noting that "Dominguez has a questionable past and may have had a contract on Bogdanoff." But Birchim thought the whole thing was "kind of flaky . . . It really didn't take priority."

The autopsy revealed plenty about the nature of the shooting. Pathologist Dr. Robert Failing found the two slugs in Phillip's head. He established that one entered below the right eye, passed through the cheekbone, and lodged in the soft palate of the mouth. It had been fired from at least two to three feet away. If promptly treated, it would not have been fatal. The second bullet entered the left temple above and in front of the ear, plowed through the brain, and concluded its journey in the right lobe. The condition of the skin around the entrance wound indicated the gun was touching it when the shot was fired. Death would have been almost instantaneous. But the slugs were so badly damaged, it would be impossible to identify them exactly. They were small-caliber but so lightweight that they virtually exploded on impact. They now looked like lead mushrooms.

Usually, in a murder investigation, the first few days are crucial. But here, despite all the hard work, nothing substantial had surfaced. Things were getting gloomy around the airy, high-tech headquarters of the Santa Barbara sheriff's office opposite the county jail.

Publicly the story was still that it was a random shooting. On September 23 the *Los Angeles Times* weighed in with a story similar to that in the *News-Press* the previous day. Under the headline "Murder of Beach-Goer Shocks Santa Barbara," it stressed the nude beach angle and characterized the killing as "an apparent random act of violence in an unlikely place."

The sheriff's spokeswoman was again quoted, this time saying: "There were no sexual overtones. Nothing more to it. Just a random, violent act . . . We don't expect this kind of thing to happen around here. It woke up a sleepy county."

Birchim was now starting to think about talking to the widow. She had only been interviewed by Tom Nelson, and then only right after the homicide. He and Ray had some vague suspicions about her story, a gut instinct that everything was not as it seemed. "It didn't sit with us that the guy hadn't killed her," Birchim recalled. "Fred kept saying, 'I smell a rat.'"

"The guys were not dressed to be at the beach," Ray explained. "They didn't sound like local people. Why were they waiting around? Why then did they go up and shoot a guy for no reason?"

The detectives had also spotted the inconsistency of Lindgren and the fishermen seeing a white guy and a black guy at the beach, and Diana maintaining that a white guy alone approached her husband and shot him. "Just a little flag was waving in the air," Ray said.

On the morning of September 25, contacting Diana Bogdanoff was on Birchim's list of things to do. She saved him the trouble by calling him.

"I was just calling to see how the investigation is going," Birchim recalled Diana as saying.

"We're stymied," he replied bluntly. "We have no idea who did this."

Then he had an idea. "You know, we haven't spoken before. Could you run through for me what happened?"

She basically repeated what she had told Nelson. She wouldn't recognize the suspect if she saw him again, she said. She went on again about Dominguez, alleging it was common knowledge on the work site that he dealt drugs. If the murder was not "just a bizarre thing," she said, it had to have been at Dominguez's bidding.

There was one discrepancy in her account. She said the suspect drew the gun from his jacket pocket—in the interview with Nelson, it came from the pants pocket.

Birchim said he would like to talk to her in person as soon as possible. When would she be returning to Santa Barbara from Visalia? Then the conversation got heated.

She was afraid to come back, she said. What if the murderers were looking for her? She didn't even feel safe in Visalia. Several reporters had found her there. If they could find her there, anyone could. Birchim tried to reassure her. After all, if the suspects had wanted to kill her, they had ample time at the beach. "You don't have anything to fear from these people."

Diana flew off the handle and started yelling at him. "You don't understand! I've worked in hospitals. I've seen people die. When that man saw what he had done, he got scared. That's why he ran and didn't kill me, too."

There was no reassuring her. She kept saying, "You don't understand!" Birchim said it might be possible to interview her in Visalia instead. He'd have to get permission from his supervisor and call her back. Diana wanted an immediate decision, so he put her on hold and spoke to Sergeant Baker. It was agreed that he and Ray would drive up later that day and see her the next morning.

Birchim was really puzzled. "Her reaction about coming to Santa Barbara didn't make sense," he recalled. What was the widow's problem? An anonymous tip they received just before leaving for Visalia was the first real clue.

At 3:15 P.M. an unidentified female code-named "Joe" called Bakersfield police's WE-TIP hot line with information about the Bogdanoff case. Joe said "the wife had the husband murdered. Big inheritance for her." A friend had told her seven or eight months ago about being asked by the wife to kill her husband for ten thousand dollars. The murder was supposed to happen on the beach. Joe didn't come forward at the time because "this friend is a known liar." But after reading about the murder, she felt she had to.

Bakersfield police passed the information on to the Santa Barbara detectives at four o'clock. Now they had something to work on. During the long drive to Visalia, Birchim and Ray talked about little else. It was certainly going to make their interview with Diana more interesting. "It gave us a little more positive frame of mind," Ray said later with diplomatic understatement. A larger flag was waving.

The detectives met her at 1620 Tulare Avenue at 11:00 A.M. on Tuesday, September 26. She showed them through the dining room and into the kitchen. They were impressed with how immaculate everything was. "You could eat off the kitchen floor, it was so clean," Birchim recalled. They noticed an expensive dining room set and a glass-fronted china cabinet. Inside the cabinet was an antique Russian samovar.

They sat down at the kitchen table. It was oppressively hot indoors. Diana had the air-conditioning off. She was planning to spend that night in Bakersfield and then leave for Washington state the next day, she explained. "I don't want to turn everything on and then have to remember to turn everything off."

They interviewed her on tape for three and a half hours, covering almost every aspect of the case. Although Diana was generally cooperative and made no glaringly obvious mistake that incriminated her, the interview was what Ray would later call a "turning point."

She talked freely about the marriage. "Phillip did have a drinking problem" and a temper—"That is the Russian thing, very volatile." He "was the one that had to have total control of everything. He like had to tell you what to do all the time." It was very demanding, but she complemented him. "I'm very calm. I was the opposite in so many ways—that's what made us a good team. I was patient enough to listen to what he was saying even though he was yelling."

He did get physical with her, but not very often. The problem was "very temporary." She recalled three incidents, including one in Visalia in 1987 when he gave her a concussion, and another in Santa Barbara when he gave her a black eye. She didn't report anything at the campground because "if anybody in the park knew, we would have been kicked out of the park."

"Would you classify your marriage as a good marriage?" Ray asked.

There was no hesitation. "Absolutely . . . Phillip would do anything for me."

"How about you doing things for him?"

"Vice versa, vice versa."

She added: "It takes three years, I think, for a person really to know the ins and outs of the other person. And it was like everything was coming together for us."

She poignantly recalled Phillip's battle with cancer. "He fought for his life so hard. That's why it's so devastating to see something like that [the murder] happen to a survivor, you know, just terrible."

For most of the interview, the detectives probed her account of the murder. She deviated little from her prior statements but supplied a wealth of detail.

When they arrived at the beach, she said, she saw two fishermen on the bluff, presumably Brecht and Rutherford. There were two other people in the distance, "but I didn't pay any attention." While she and Phillip were swimming, they saw a white guy and a black guy walking along the sand. Her impression was that the two guys were just tourists. They were "clean-cut, didn't seem a threat, in other words, and Phillip was very perceptive . . . He didn't get upset, he wasn't worried . . . There was no feeling of fear."

After they got out of the water and lay down on the sand, the last thing she said to him was, "You better hurry up and start snoring, because you know I can't sleep till I hear you snoring." The next thing she knew was the voice asking, "Hey, man, do you have any marijuana?" She stuck to her story that the gunman was white and she did not get a good look at him. "I just saw his hand. That's how I knew for sure it was a white person."

Ray tried to trip her up. He asked if the gunman was the same white guy she had seen walking along the beach with the black guy when she and Phillip were in the water. "I'm not sure . . . I don't know if it's a blank in my mind or if I just didn't notice, didn't pay any attention to him."

"You know what his name is?" Ray wondered casually.

"What whose name is?"

Ray covered himself. "The guy, I'm sorry, the guy that was on the [railroad] tracks that came back to help you."

There was only the odd inconsistency. For example, while listing Phillip's vehicles, Diana mentioned the El Camino. They had taken it to a Kasler carpenter called "Keith" to be sold. After the murder, he "called me and wanted to know, what do you want me to do with it? I said, 'Sell it.'"

She also inadvertently filled a key gap in the murder chronology. She knew at 3:30 P.M. on September 20 that she would not be working for Lash the next day. But how did she know when she called Stephanie two hours later that Phillip might also be free on September 21? If she called Stephanie before he got home from work, how had she managed to clear things with him?

Diana told the detectives that while she worked for Lash, she would park her truck at the union office, because there was no space available at the jobsite. Phillip, who drove to work in his state car, would relay her the few blocks to the jobsite in the morning and then take her back to the union lot at the end of the day. After work on September 20, she said, "He came and picked me up at this corner where I was flagging and drove me back to the union office, and I picked up my car."

That drive would have given her time to discuss plans for the next day, suggest that Phillip take some time off. He may not have needed much persuading. As Diana told the detectives, they were overdue for a trip to the beach—"we hadn't been to the beach since Labor Day." And Phillip was such a beach bum. " . . . He's always acting like a little kid when he's going to get to go to the beach. I mean, it's his favorite thing. He loved to go to that beach."

But none of this registered with the detectives—that was the first they had heard of the El Camino. Throughout the case, the possible significance of Diana's parking arrangements would be overlooked. As a result, no jury was ever told how Diana may have contacted Phillip on September 20 before she called her daughter.

What stunned Birchim and Ray during the interview was not *what* Diana said, but *how* she said it. "It was more the atmosphere and a feeling," Birchim recalled.

Sometimes she appeared cheerful, almost perky, rattling along in her chirpy, lilting voice as if marveling about the weather. There were jokes—about a Tulare County town called Goshen ("My sisters married brothers from that great city"), about her friend Judy Chojnacki marrying "a real Polack," about Phillip taking ice home from work rather than paying $1.50 a bag for it at the campground.

Most remarkable was her description of Phillip's death spasms. The language alone conveys the demeanor:

When Phillip was shot the first time, he put his hand up to his face, she said. It was, "like, oh my God, I've been shot."

Next, "the guy just stuck the gun over to his head and just blew him away. I was screaming . . . I just couldn't believe my eyes. And it was total shock. All of a sudden, I look at Phillip and his whole side of his head's just going [she made a *whut* sound] right into the sand. You know, it was gushing everything, and I was totally freaked out . . . I was looking at Phillip and I could see his body just start going through these tightening-up things, you know, convulsion-type things."

She was "totally freaked," but she threw some clothes on before running off for help. "I can't run down the beach nude," she explained.

She felt so helpless, she went on. "My thing in life has always been to help people, you know . . . dialysis people that are dying, you know. I couldn't do anything.

"I knew he had to be gone, you know, when that all just came right out of his head."

In two other areas, Diana was conspicuously vague. One was her own daughter. She gave her name, but when Ray asked for her phone number, she paused for several seconds before saying it was "323-1301, I think. I don't even remember. Too many numbers in my head." Stephanie had just moved, so she didn't have an address for her.

She was the same way when any financial question was raised. "Did he leave you any insurance or anything like that?" Ray asked.

"I don't know," she snapped.

"Can you get—"

"I don't know."

A few questions later: "Do you know if he had any life insurance at all?"

"I don't know. I just don't know."

At one point in their discussion of financial matters, she said, "Maybe I should have my attorney present. Maybe I shouldn't even be speaking."

But Diana was very definite about one thing. "I'm not ever gonna let this house go," she said. "One way or the other, I *will* maintain this house . . . The payment was five hundred a month, and I can make five hundred a month some way.

"This house means a lot to me," she told them.

Relating the story of how she and Phillip obtained the house, she said the owner "sold it to *me* [italics added]" for seventy thousand dollars. "Well, you know what it's worth now, it's double that," she added. "Unreal."

Unreal, indeed—the house would be appraised at only eighty thousand dollars a year later.

Toward the end of the interview, Ray gave her his view of the case. "We don't have any evidence," he said. The various descriptions of the suspects didn't match. "Everything's all mixed up."

"You're kidding," Diana said.

Ray continued: "I want you to know that . . . there's not much we're going to be able to do. It looks like it was maybe a couple of bums walking down the tracks or something."

"I don't believe they were bums . . . I do believe they were like from somewhere else."

"Yeah?"

"I don't believe they were from Santa Barbara. I mean, it could have been, but I just don't think—"

"Why do you say that?" Birchim interjected.

"I just kind of get that feeling. I don't know. I deal with people every day."

In his report on the interview, Birchim wrote: "It should be noted . . . that during the entire interview, Diana did not show any remorse, nor did she shed any tears and never expressed any fear of someone being after her."

The detective noticed something else at the house that day that he did not include in the report. It didn't show up on the tape either. When he adjourned to the rest room, he looked down into the trash basket. There was a Polaroid photo of Phillip, torn into four pieces.

Dear Daughter

Diana had a lot more to worry about during the interview than the detectives' questions. As she was speaking to them, her daughter appeared headed for a nervous breakdown.

Since the funeral, Stephanie had remained on the verge of hysteria. "I couldn't handle it," she said. She used crank to escape, but "I wasn't escaping . . . I wasn't going anywhere. It was all staying there right in my mind. I wanted to forget it like it never happened, but I couldn't."

Brian's attitude also didn't help. "The first day [after the murder], he was real quiet. After that it was just like nothing ever happened and it was normal. He expected things to be normal . . . I was crying a lot. He was back to business."

Apart from crank, the only thing Stephanie was ingesting was soda. In the absence of any food, she was suffering severe stomach cramps. While her mother was talking to the detectives, the pain was becoming intolerable. In fact, she called and interrupted her mother's interview three times to find out when Diana was coming to see her.

During the first call, Diana was reassuring. "I'm still here at the house because the detectives are here with me . . . As soon as they're finished, then I'll be able to take off. Probably in another half an hour." About half an hour later, Stephanie called again. Diana told her to go to Nick's house, where Dorothy Bogdanoff, his other daughter-in-law, was visiting.

"She's having a physical problem," Diana explained to the detectives. "She said she's got a real bad pain somewhere. She said she needs to go to the doctor. I wonder what that's all about . . . She is totally stressed out."

Just before the end of the interview, Dorothy called to say Stephanie hadn't shown up. "If necessary, you just take her to the emergency at the hospital," Diana told her. "She had major stomach problems a couple of years ago, but I don't see how . . . It might have flared up again." No sooner did she hang up than Stephanie called again. Diana was starting to sound impatient with her daughter. Dorothy was going to pick her up, she said.

"She's gonna go to the emergency," Diana said when she got off the phone. "She has terrible pains in her stomach."

In fact, Stephanie had just told her to forget about Dorothy: Brian was taking her to the hospital. She wanted her mother to meet them there.

Birchim and Ray finally left just before 2:30 P.M. Diana set off minutes later for Bakersfield. But she was apparently so flustered by the interview and Stephanie's condition that she soon ran a STOP sign and hit another vehicle. With the delay, it took her twice as long as usual to make it to Bakersfield.

When Diana eventually showed up at the emergency room of Kern Medical Center, Stephanie and Brian were sitting in the waiting area. As if the encounter on the beach weren't sufficient, Stephanie introduced her to Brian.

After Stephanie was called into the treatment room, Diana was left alone with the young man who had freed her from her husband. She didn't exude gratitude. According to Brian, "She was trying to tell me I should leave for a while and stay away from Stephanie. And I kept telling her, 'You don't understand. We're intact.' "

Diana tried another tack. Stephanie had a sexually transmitted disease when she was younger, she told Brian. But he "just shook it off. It wasn't like it was nothing to me. It was something that had passed. I didn't really have too many words for Diane."

Apparently she also tried reassuring Brian. She told him about the descriptions she had given the police. "I think it was either a white guy or two white guys," Brian said later. "I don't think she told them a black guy was there." She also said "when she came back from Washington, she was gonna fucking get Stephanie an apartment. If Stephanie and I wanted to be together, we could stay there with no problems. She'd help us out and she was gonna give me the El Camino and all this. It seemed like, you know, the perfect picture, like nothing had ever happened."

Tired of waiting with Brian, Diana then marched into the treatment room. Stephanie had yet to be diagnosed or given a prescription. But Diana said the hospital was a dump and the staff didn't know what they were doing. It was time to leave. Stephanie, who had been feeling better since eating a bag of chips, agreed.

They all drove back to Eye Street. Stephanie had with her something Diana had given her at the hospital. A week late, it was an eighteenth birthday card. The printed inscription read:

> Dear Daughter,
> I'm proud of the way you've grown up.
> I admit I still worry at times
> because the world has changed a lot
> since you were born.
> Many of the choices you've had to make
> have been more difficult
> than those I faced when I was your age.
> I haven't always agreed
> with your decisions,
> but I hope you know
> that I respect your courage
> and independence in making them.
> You're doing all you can
> to be the person
> you want to be,
> and I admire that . . .
> And remember—
> no matter what life brings,
> you will always be my daughter,
> and I will always love you.

That evening, Diana took them out for a meal. Stephanie and Brian went in the Ford, Diana following in her truck. He and Stephanie "were having a blast," Brian said, kidding around and smoking joints. The fun ended when they sat down at the restaurant, a Chinese place near the McLeods' house.

Diana got things off on the wrong foot. "Stephanie, are you going to say grace? You always used to do that so good."

"No, Mom, I'm not going to do that."

Both Stephanie and Brian were quiet. Diana chatted about incidents from Stephanie's childhood, which made Brian feel left out. "It was like, 'Remember how we used to do this and how we used to do that?' " he said later. " 'We're going to do this all again.' It was like she was trying to alleviate [sic] me out of the picture.

"That was wrong, because she had ran out on the girl once," Brian testified. " . . . I was possessive over Stephanie, and her mom was intruding on that."

Stephanie just felt out of it. She was thinking about Brandon, about how they used to come to the same restaurant all the time for fried rice. At one point she did confront her mother about something—the El Camino.

"Are you going to give him the El Camino?" she said. "You promised him the El Camino."

"No, we're going to sell the El Camino."

"But you promised."

"Well, yeah. But what would it look like if I gave him the car and Phillip was just killed? We'll sell the car and either give him the money or get him a new car." She was hoping to get four thousand dollars for the El Camino.

It was all very uncomfortable, Stephanie said. "It was like a dream dinner." She corrected herself. "A nightmare, not a dream. I didn't know what to say. There wasn't anything you *can* say after something like this." If this was a taste of family life after Phillip, it was as bad as the food they were eating.

At least they didn't have to put Diana up at the apartment that night, her last before leaving for Washington. Instead, she stayed with Nick Bogdanoff, the man she called "Pop," the man who had just lost his son.

The next day—Wednesday, September 27—Diana had another confrontation with Stephanie and Brian before she caught her plane from Los Angeles. She went over to the apartment to ask Stephanie to come with her to Washington. "We got into a big argument about that," Brian recalled.

According to Brian, Diana used "all kind of things" to lure Stephanie away from him. "She was like, 'If she stays here, they're going to arrest both you guys. They're going to come questioning you guys. If Stephanie's with me, they can't find you.' " But it was no use. "Stephanie kept telling her no, because she wanted to be with me . . . and she told her mom, 'You ran out on me once. I just met this person and I love this person, and he's been here for me all this time.' And her mom couldn't comprehend that."

Stephanie's recollection was quite different. She said she was ready to go with her mother, but it was Brian who insisted otherwise. "He was saying that I was going to run off and that he was going to take the fall for everything, and my mom was saying, 'No, she's got to go with me,' and so he's saying, 'No, you've got to stay here,' and they were fighting over me, and I just didn't know what to do."

She told me that fear was the main reason she opted to stay with Brian. "I didn't know he was capable of something like that [the murder]." What if he thought she might be ready to turn him in?

According to Stephanie, the whole point of her mother's mission to Bakersfield was to "get me to go with her to Washington . . . When she couldn't do that, it was time to go." Diana left a parting gift. She gave Stephanie one hundred dollars so she could buy herself some new shoes as a birthday present. Then she looked at Brian's shoes—the same L.A. Gears he had worn at the beach. She asked to see the soles. Oily black tar still clung to them. "You better get rid of them," she said, offering him one hundred dollars to replace them.

"You can't buy me with money," Brian blustered. But he took the hundred dollars. Later he bought new shoes and threw the L.A. Gears away.

Her mission unaccomplished, Diana drove to Los Angeles to catch her flight to Washington, where she would spend the next ten days with her daughter Christine. Stephanie's decision not to go with her would turn out to be crucial. Together they might have been able to exert some control over events. But apart, they were like two ships heading for the same reef.

Hide-and-Seek

The anonymous tip, the off-key demeanor during the interview—Diana was now at the center of the detectives' case, a position she would occupy until its conclusion.

The question they were now asking each other was: Who in the world would do this for her? After all, the suspects from the beach had been identified as a young black male and a young white. How in the world would she connect with that age group and with black people?

Birchim and Ray were now so suspicious that, after the interview, they followed Diana as she made her way to Bakersfield. But they lost her on a rural road through cotton fields some time before she had her accident. They then returned to Visalia, where they noted down pay phone numbers near Diana's house. If she had solicited someone to kill Phillip, they reasoned, maybe she didn't use her home phone. They also researched the deed on the Visalia house and interviewed Judy Chojnacki. Diana's closest friend was nervous and noncommittal.

On the morning of September 27, they arrived in Bakersfield. They researched Phillip's property records, interviewed Tommy Byford, even cruised down Nick Bogdanoff's block, taking down license plate numbers. Stephanie Allen was not on their list of people to contact. They didn't even know how old she was or that she had a boyfriend.

But by the time they returned to their motel in the late afternoon, the WE-TIP informant had come through again. At 3:15 P.M. "Joe" called Santa Barbara and spoke to Gregg Weitzman, another major crimes detective. She added detail to her story of an unidentified male friend being solicited to kill Phillip—that Diana told the friend she would be with her husband on the beach so he could recognize them; that she had requested Phillip be shot in the head.

Most important, Joe brought Stephanie into the murder mix for the first time. She said her friend was an old boyfriend of Stephanie's. In fact, he and Stephanie had gone to Santa Barbara six or seven months ago at the time he was solicited by Diana. Weitzman asked if Stephanie had any black friends. Joe said she did not know any names, but "Stephanie had a lot of black friends."

Joe's latest revelation was relayed to Birchim and Ray at their motel in Bakersfield. Ray dialed the number for Stephanie that her mother had given them. A well-spoken male answered the phone. He said his name was Brian and he was minding the apartment while Stephanie was at the store. Ray left a message for her to call him at his motel when she got back. Around 7:00 P.M., he and Birchim hadn't heard anything, so they decided to go looking for her. They didn't have her address, but Nick Bogdanoff gave them a rough idea where the apartment was. They also had a description and the license plate number of her car. "We have this luck," Ray recalled. "We just drove over there."

As they cruised in the murky twilight up North Eye Street, they spotted a skinny girl standing on the sidewalk. She had angular features, studs curving around one ear, and shoulder-length, permed brown hair. She flagged them down.

"Who are you?" they asked.

"I'm Stephanie Allen."

She was expecting them. She had just called their motel, but when there was no reply, she figured they were coming to see her in person. She showed them inside her apartment. There was no sign of Brian. She apologized for the mess, but she had just been robbed. She had a large fan going and incense burning in the living room—anything to hide the marijuana smell, the detectives guessed—and she was baking a cake for a friend's birthday.

During her interview, Stephanie lied more convincingly than her mother. "She never stalled once," Ray said. "She never showed the kind of reaction I would look for. She really fooled us. Her mother was too cold."

She lied from the outset. She identified Jodie Davis and Diane Muilkey as friends of hers. "How about boyfriends?"

Ray asked. "Looks like you're going steady . . . You're wearing a ring on your neck."

"Kind of," she replied.

"Okay. What's his name?"

"Brian Duileky . . . D-U-I-L-E-K-Y."

"And how long have you been dating Mr. Duileky?"

"I don't know if I'm still dating him, to tell you the truth, because I haven't talked to him. But it's been about three weeks probably . . ."

"You must be. He answered the phone."

" . . . No, that wasn't him . . . That was a different person in here."

Armed with the WE-TIP information, Ray soon cut to the chase. "We're starting to pick up some rumors that are a little more than rumors . . . that your mother hired some people to have Phil killed."

Stephanie sounded aghast. "Say what?"

"You heard me." Then Ray took a real flier. The rumor, he told her, was also "that you knew about it."

"That *I* knew about it?"

"Uh-huh."

"No. I don't know who you heard that from, but that's a wrong answer. That's a very wrong answer. My mother wouldn't do something like that, and I sure wouldn't be involved in it."

For the next hour, the detectives tried every trick in their book to pry Stephanie open. There was the avuncular tone—"You seem like a real nice girl, you've got a lot going for you, and you don't want to get jammed up behind something that's not your fault"; there was the menacing—"We've got to resolve Phil getting his head shot in, and that's not right . . . I'm having a very difficult time with it, thinking about that man sitting there and someone just blowing him away like that. And, Stephanie, how can you live with it either?"

Birchim and Ray devoted most of their efforts to easing a wedge between Stephanie and her mother. "We've worked cases like this before where blood relationships get involved for stupid reasons and . . . it makes it tough, very, very hard and difficult to deal with," Ray said.

"If your mother did do it, it's *her* problem, it's *her* situation," said Birchim. "If she drug [sic] you in somehow, if

you tried to help her because you felt sorry for her or wanted
her out of a jam, still she's an adult and knew what she was
doing, and there's no reason for you to spend the rest of your
life regretting it."

Stephanie was resolute. "I don't know anything about it . . .
I don't know who did it . . . I stay out of trouble, and besides
that, I wouldn't be a part of something like that."

They asked if she had any black friends. She identified
Brandon, Calvin, three girlfriends, and twin brothers who had
a painting business. But since she and Brandon broke up,
"I don't talk to as many black people as I used to." How
about black acquaintances who might run around with a skinny, long-haired white guy? "Not in Bakersfield," she replied.
"Black guys, they stick to their people."

"Well, they must not; they run around with you, and you're
white," Ray pointed out.

"Well, I'm different . . . I'm not a prejudiced person." You
certainly wouldn't see a long-haired white guy around black
people in Bakersfield, she said.

"That tells me it's kind of a drug culture . . . If you have the
drug culture, there's that lack of boundaries. You know, they
kind of intermix sometimes."

" . . . There's nobody [black] that I know that would run
around with someone with long hair," she insisted.

But on a couple of occasions, Stephanie wavered in her reso-
luteness, giving equivocal answers. For example, Ray asked,
"Has your mother ever asked you, jokingly or inquiring, 'Do
you know anyone that can do this?' "

She replied: "Not that I can remember. But if she did, I
wouldn't take it seriously and, you know, put it in my mind
and remember it. That's not something I would expect to come
out of my mother's mouth."

"But she did say it, didn't she?"

"No, she didn't . . . She could have, okay, but I didn't, I
cannot remember her saying anything to that nature."

Later Birchim asked: "Would it surprise you that your mom
might have done [this], knowing that Phil was brutal with her
at times?"

"Two years ago, when me and my mom were really close
and I knew everything my mom did . . . it wouldn't have been
possible. But I don't know what she's been through since I

haven't been with her. I'm not going to say it's not possible, but I'm saying that from my point of view."

A glimmer of light shone for the detectives—enough for them to suggest Stephanie take a lie detector test the next day. "The issue would be whether you know anything about the murder of Phillip Bogdanoff or not," Ray told her.

"If my mother's ever mentioned anything to me about killing Phillip Bogdanoff or having somebody do it?"

"Yeah."

"That is fine," she said quietly. "You can do that."

The detectives left the apartment just before 9:00 P.M. As they did after the interview with her mother, they decided to conduct an impromptu surveillance. It became an almost farcical game of hide-and-seek.

Birchim and Ray drove around the block and parked on H Street, parallel to Eye. They positioned themselves a few feet apart behind the wooden fence that separates the apartment complex from the rear parking lot of a realty management firm on H Street. Stephanie was pacing around her backyard. Then she looked over the fence and spotted Birchim cowering like a cornered fox. "His gray hair looks like a neon sign at night," Ray joked later.

Birchim retreated through the parking lot and walked south toward Brundage Lane. He turned around. Stephanie was following him. He darted down an alley. She was still after him, the hunted suddenly the hunter.

Meanwhile, Ray returned to H Street and waited by the car for his partner. As he was standing there, he scanned the license plates of passing traffic. He recognized one as Stephanie's. The car, a Ford Fairmont, was moving slowly and being driven by a black guy. The driver "was looking real intently or real hard at me," Ray recalled. He ran to his car and started up, expecting a pursuit. But the driver just pulled over to the curb. They met on the sidewalk.

The driver identified himself as Brian Bishop. He admitted he was driving Stephanie's car and that she had made him leave the apartment before she was interviewed. She had paged him after the detectives left. He chatted amiably with Ray, saying he had served in the military and wanted to be a child psychologist. When Ray told him he was conducting a murder investigation and showed him the composite of the black suspect, the driver was very cooperative. "It looks like a guy called Shalamar Fields," he said.

"He was just as cool as she [Stephanie] was," Ray said, recalling the sidewalk interview.

While Ray was questioning Brian, Birchim rejoined his partner after his tour of Bakersfield's alleyways. He still hadn't managed to elude his pursuer. She was standing at the intersection of Brundage and H, watching. Then she walked up to them, looking somewhat peeved. "What's going on?"

"We'll see you tomorrow," the detectives said.

So Stephanie did have black friends, after all, including one who drove her car around. That wasn't enough for the detectives to make her or this Brian Bishop suspects. But there must be a connection with the murder somewhere in this racial "intermix" in Bakersfield.

On their way back to the motel, Ray chanted: "Fee, fi, fo, fum, I can smell blood on this one."

The detectives' euphoria faded quickly the next day—Thursday, September 28. Stephanie wouldn't take the polygraph examination.

Lie detector tests are not admissible as evidence in U.S. courts. But police commonly use them in investigations—sometimes the mere threat of one will induce a suspect to confess. In Stephanie's case, it seemed that Birchim and Ray might have no other way of finding out whether she was being truthful or not.

They arrived at the Eye Street apartment around 11:30 A.M. Stephanie said she had to speak to her mother in Washington before she took the test. After talking to Diana briefly, she handed the phone to Birchim.

If Diana was alarmed about her daughter implicating her through a polygraph, she didn't show it. She was concerned about Stephanie's health, her "nervous condition." Birchim assured her that, if the girl showed any signs of distress, they would stop the test and get her medical attention. Not once did Diana ask why her daughter was being tested.

They drove Stephanie to the Bakersfield Police Department, part of the government complex in the center of town. They had arranged for a state Department of Justice examiner to conduct the polygraph in an interview room. For a few minutes Birchim and Ray left Stephanie alone in the assistant police chief's office while they spoke to the examiner. When Birchim returned to the office, he found Stephanie on the phone talking to her mother.

After she hung up, he asked what she had been discussing with Diana. "I just called her because I'm afraid I might go to jail."

"What do you mean?"

"Well, I'm afraid that if I fail the test, I'll be arrested."

"Do you think you'll fail the polygraph?"

"No."

"Then you have nothing to worry about. Besides, we couldn't arrest you because of how you did on a polygraph."

Stephanie didn't last long with the examiner. He was asking her questions she didn't want to answer, probing into her personal life. After about ten minutes, she stood up. "You know what? Forget it. I don't want to take this."

Her change of mind was hardly surprising. She told me that during the conversation with Diana in the assistant chief's office, her mother said, "You don't have to take that polygraph. Just go home or something."

The polygraph option precluded, the detectives decided to try something less formal. Maybe they could get further by establishing a rapport with Stephanie and Brian, showing them they were human beings, not just cops. They said they would treat her to lunch. She insisted on bringing Brian along. So they picked him up on a street corner near the Village Lane apartments—he had been there to see Rosalyn and Kerisha Bookout. As they ate at a barbecue restaurant, there was no more probing about the case. "We just laughed and told jokes," Ray recalled. "It was casual lunch conversation. We were teasing him about his beeper."

When Brian went to the rest room, they asked Stephanie, "Is he a drug dealer?"

"Of course he is," she replied.

At 2:00 P.M. they interviewed Stephanie briefly, asking her if she knew of anyone with the hairstyle of the black suspect in the composite. "I know a guy named Shalamar that wears his hair like that," she volunteered. She added that Shalamar had met her parents when they lived on Planz Road and that she had also seen him recently with a white male biker called James. She and Brian took the detectives to Village Lane, where they said Shalamar lived. But they couldn't quite remember which apartment it was.

That afternoon Brian also volunteered his real name. He explained he had given them an alias because there was a warrant out for his arrest in Bakersfield. He had violated probation in the burglary case again, this time by failing to show up for a drug test. His probation officer had issued the warrant on September 20, the day before the murder.

The detectives seemed to have been parried effectively. After five days on the road, they returned to Santa Barbara late on Friday, September 29, without gleaning more from Stephanie and Brian. But if the young couple had any feeling of security, it was built on sand. The threat was not from without, from these middle-aged cops from a different world 150 miles away on the coast. It was from within their own world, from within the cocoon of their "loyal" family.

"Nobody Made Him God"

Stephanie actually suspected something was up during her interview with the detectives on the Wednesday evening. They had dropped all these clues in her lap. "We've been getting phone calls from people . . . Our guys are flooded with them in Santa Barbara," Ray told her.

" . . . We're not saying that your mother did it," Birchim said. "People that are calling us are saying that . . ."

"People from Bakersfield?" Stephanie asked.

"This was in the Bakersfield and Visalia papers."

The detectives were bluffing, of course—the only "people" to whom they were referring was "Joe." But Stephanie didn't know that, and by the end of the interview, she was ready to do her own investigative work.

"Could she [Diana] have gotten any of your friends jammed up into this thing?" Ray asked.

"No, but if she did, I'm going to find out."

"What are you going to do?"

"Well, I'm going to ask . . . the people that know her. There's not many of my friends she even knows . . ."

Birchim tried to put out the fire. "Do me a favor. We can't tell you not to . . . but if you stumble across the guy that did this, you're probably gonna be next if you start asking questions. The guy that did this is a cold-blooded killer. Didn't bother him at all to pump two bullets, execute Phillip . . . Be careful, that's all I'm saying to you. If I were you . . . I'd let us handle it."

But after the detectives returned to their motel, she and Brian immediately set off to confront their likely suspects, the "people" who might be making those calls to the police.

*   *   *

It is not clear how many members of the Eye Street "family"
knew about the murder and who had committed it before
anyone was arrested. Stephanie insisted that knowledge was
limited to the five of them at the apartment on September 20
and 21—herself, Brian, Rickey, Calvin, and Jodie.

Some of those familiar with Brian say it would have been
impossible for him not to tell anyone else, particularly the
Bohlingers and Steve Emmons. "They [Gator and Steve] knew
everything Brian was going to do, and he knew everything
they were going to do," Rosalyn Bookout said. "They were
too close not to know."

"Gator and Mike might have known it was going to happen,"
James Oliver said. " . . . They definitely knew what he [Brian]
did before he was arrested."

Rickey said later that he told Mike Bohlinger about the mur-
der shortly after it happened. Court testimony would implicate
Gator in the disposal of the murder weapon. He allegedly
helped Brian and Rickey saw it up at his parents' house.
The pieces were then tossed into a remote canyon outside
Bakersfield.

A lot of this is speculative. What is certain is that Stephanie
and Brian didn't focus on the Bohlingers or Emmons as possible snitches. Rickey also seems to have been ruled out. He
had continued to "shadow" Brian after the murder. While
Stephanie was being interviewed on September 27, Brian was
with Rickey at his mother's beauty parlor.

If anyone was talking, it had to be Calvin and his girlfriend,
Jodie. After all, it was Calvin who had told Brian he would get
"fucked out of this"; it was Calvin neither of them particularly
liked. Maybe if he had talked, he had even gotten Jodie to go
along with him.

"Me and Brian both did [suspect them]," Stephanie told
me. "We wanted to scare them, find out if they were the
ones."

Calvin had gone to the police by then—but the police had not
gone to him.

He had asked his mother what to do as soon as Stephanie
brought him and Jodie home from Eye Street after the murder.
He "came in and looked at me real funny," his mother, Ollie

Williams, recalled. She asked him, "Calvin, what's wrong with you? I know something's wrong."

"Mama, I want to tell you something," he said, and proceeded to describe the murder and the abortive shotgun trip. "Brian blew that man's brains out," he told her. "When he came home, he had blood all over his shoes."

When she advised him to call the police, he said, "Mama, I'm scared."

"You got to go. Sooner or later, they're going to find out you knowed about it. Your conscience will whip you."

"Mama, I don't know what to do."

All he did at first was try to keep himself and Jodie away from the Eye Street residents. "Stephanie was calling me on the phone and wanting me to come over to her house because she wanted to talk to me, because I was her best friend," Jodie recalled. But "Calvin didn't want me around her, did not want me around Brian . . . because they just killed somebody, and we knew about it, and he was afraid that they were going to kill him or me."

Calvin paced around the backyard of his sister's house, weighing his options. Even at night he couldn't get any peace. He had nightmares about Brian coming after Jodie and his family. Others were about what happened to his father. "I remembered the pain, how he was hollering, how he was crying," he said. "For me, that man [Phillip] didn't holler or cry. But it felt the same way."

If his mother was arguing in favor of him going to the police, his sister and Jodie were against it.

On Sunday, September 24, Calvin made up his mind. Without telling Jodie, he contacted Bakersfield police and arranged to meet them at Bakersfield High School. But the police never showed. Frustrated, he then placed an emergency call to his younger brother. Myers Monigan, also known as "Herk," was in the county jail at the time for violating his probation on a car theft conviction. Herk told him not to do anything until he got out.

Calvin, therefore, hadn't implicated anybody when Stephanie and Brian pulled up outside his sister's home around 9:00 P.M. on September 27. But he had every reason to be anxious.

Jodie answered the door. "I want to talk to you," Stephanie said.

"About what?"

Calvin, who had been getting ready to go to bed, came into the hallway and looked on curiously.

"Come on, let's all go for a ride."

Jodie and her boyfriend approached Stephanie's Ford as if it were their hearse. She insisted on going back into the house to fetch her purse and put some shoes on. "Take me to the store. I need to get a pack of cigarettes," Jodie said when they got in the car. Stephanie was driving, but she didn't seem to be headed anywhere. She turned the radio down and told them about the encounter she had just had with Santa Barbara detectives. Somebody was talking to the police, she said.

"Man, we didn't say anything," Jodie insisted. "We haven't told anybody."

This wasn't like the last time the four of them went for a drive, when they had their "shotgun trip" to Santa Barbara to kill Phillip. Then they were all friends; there was an implicit trust between them. But a lot had changed in only two weeks. There had been a murder in the "family," and now Jodie and Calvin didn't feel trust, but fear.

Jodie was particularly scared because she was sitting next to the door in Stephanie's car that wouldn't open. She even wondered if they might drive them up Round Mountain Road and dump their bodies in one of the canyons.

"You guys really ought to leave town," she suggested. "You guys need to do something or you'll get caught."

"No, they're stupid. They don't know what they're doing," Stephanie assured her.

"Oh, you think you're smarter than a police officer? They're trained for stuff like this."

Stephanie brought up the alibi. "I gave them your mom's number, so they should be calling your mom."

"Why did you do that?"

"Because they needed to know who my friends were and an alibi and all this other stuff. Just tell them that you spent the night with me and that you guys were asleep in the living room, and we stayed up and watched a movie. Just tell them nobody ever left."

Stephanie and Brian brought their friends home that night safe and sound, but scared. They were so scared, Jodie recalled, that "Calvin was like wanting to call the police right then."

Coincidentally, Herk was released that evening from jail. Over the next few days, he questioned Calvin about his knowledge of the murder. "He was saying, 'Don't be lying to me. Tell me if you were with them,' " Calvin recalled. When Herk was convinced his brother hadn't done anything he could be arrested for, he advised him to go ahead and call the police again.

A week after the drive with Stephanie and Brian, Calvin made that call.

Early on Wednesday, October 4, Detectives Birchim and Ray were in Visalia, still struggling to break the case open. It was approaching two weeks since the crime—the freezing point, many detectives say, for a murder investigation.

They had made some further headway with their informant "Joe." On September 29 she had given Birchim the key to unlocking the identity of the friend allegedly solicited by Diana. The friend has a lengthy arrest record and went with Stephanie to the hospital when she took a drug overdose, she said. Birchim and Ray then spoke to Nick Bogdanoff, who gave them the name Tim Gray and said he used to live across the street from him.

It seemed like a breakthrough. They rushed back to Santa Barbara with a mug shot of Tim obtained from Bakersfield police. On September 30 they paraded it in a photo lineup to two of the fisherman-witnesses. But neither recognized Tim as the white guy from the beach.

He was now eliminated as a suspect. As a witness to a prior conspiracy, there were problems with Tim Gray, too. In San Luis Obispo County, the detectives found his grandmother and uncle, who told them they had heard a similar story to "Joe's," either from Tim himself or other members of the family. But it didn't sound as if Tim would make the most credible of witnesses. "Joe" told them he "was known to be a drug abuser, and many of his ramblings were found to be untrue," and Nick Bogdanoff said he "had a reputation for using dope and breaking the law."

On October 4 they still hadn't found Tim, and they knew that, even if they did, a defense lawyer might have a field day with him. In Visalia that day they were groping for leads, trying vainly to contact Stephanie's friend Amy Baca. Then, at 9:45 A.M., they got a message from Sergeant Baker to contact the Kern County sheriff's office. A detective there told them he had received a call from a Lewis Calvin Monigan in Bakersfield relating to the Bogdanoff murder. Monigan had only said, "I didn't do the murder, but I know who did." He had left a phone number. They called immediately. Monigan said he would wait for them at his sister's house.

They arrived about 11:40 A.M. A slim, rangy black guy in stone-washed jeans and high-top sneakers was sitting in a chair on the front lawn, munching crackers out of a box. The detectives had been expecting nothing more than a casual conversation. But the first thing he said to them was: "I didn't do it. Brian did it."

"Wait a second. Let's go in the house and get all this on tape."

For an hour, as small children ran around the house, as the phone rang almost continuously, Calvin related the key events of the past three weeks or so. He implicated Diana, Stephanie, and Brian in the murder, while putting most of the blame on the two females. "It's really not Brian's fault," he said. "Stephanie and her mother put Brian up to it."

Sometimes he was frustratingly vague. For example, Ray asked him, "Did Brian tell you if he was going to get any money for it?"

"Whatever half is, whatever that man [Phillip] had, Brian is getting half," he replied. "They got to split it between really three ways . . ."

There were some strange discrepancies. He said Brian told him he shot Phillip three times, including once in the chest. He thought Brian's nickname was "Batman."

Unaccustomed to Calvin's peculiar drawl and street slang, the detectives had trouble even understanding him. "Every white guy was 'dude,'" Birchim recalled. Calvin identified Rickey only as "some white dude."

After finishing with Calvin, the detectives turned to his girlfriend, who had been playing a Nintendo game in the next room. Calvin had only informed Jodie half an hour before they arrived that he had called the detectives. He told her he would do all the talking, that he would keep her out of it. "You're a fool," she said, embarking on a lecture in common sense. "Do you think these people are going to believe you? You've been in prison. You think you can tell your story and Jodie Davis doesn't exist? You have left me no choice."

As a witness, Jodie was "a breath of fresh air," Birchim said later. She went into far more detail than Calvin, even telling them about cow shooting. She identified the "white dude" as Rick, although she could not recall his last name. Where Calvin had difficulty sustaining an answer for more than a few sentences, she rattled on ad infinitum, almost without prompting. "Do you realize that she's been talking for an hour and we haven't even had to ask her anything?" Ray said to Birchim at the end of the interview.

Calvin and Jodie gave the detectives a bonus. After the interview, they took them to the Royal Palms apartment complex, where the "white dude" and Calvin had both once lived. The manager identified him as Rickey Rodgers.

Then they went on an expedition up Round Mountain Road to search for spent shell casings from the cow-shooting trip that might match those recovered from the murder scene. In the remote canyon where Rickey shot his .22, Jodie pointed out the butt of a cigarette she had smoked. The detectives couldn't find any casings, however.

Kern County officers would later track some down with a metal detector. Tests showed that the casings were not fired from the same gun as those found on the beach. Rickey had taken another .22 to Santa Barbara.

Calvin Monigan's decision to come forward on October 4 was undoubtedly the pivotal event in the investigation of the murder of Phillip Bogdanoff. Without him, the police may never have penetrated the Eye Street cocoon.

Calvin didn't quite see it that way at the time. He felt no great sense of relief. He was, in fact, even more worried that Brian would come after him. "If he think that I was telling you all right now, he'd probably kill me," he said to the detectives.

By the end of the interview, he was really fretting. "Suppose this fool get whacked out and starts getting paranoid . . . See, Brian, he got friends. That's what I'm worried about. He got friends."

The detectives weren't very reassuring. "You do whatever you have to do to protect yourself," Birchim suggested.

But amid all his fear, Calvin seems to have realized that he had not only done the expedient thing, but also maybe even the right one. There was the glimmer of a moral rationale—something that would really justify betraying his friends, that he could hold on to in the difficult days ahead when he would wear the "snitch" label like a tattoo and wonder whether his cooperation had been worthwhile.

"He [Brian] killed him and he didn't even know that man," Calvin told the detectives. " . . . I could understand if the man had did something to Brian . . . You know, he my friend. Then again, he's not my friend, because I don't know no friends that goes around killing people . . . I wouldn't have said nothing if he would have gave me some kind of reason why he did it. I can't understand it."

In one of my interviews with Calvin, he was more lucid: "I guess I decided to myself nobody made him God . . . There's a limit to everything."

The Army Moves In

The detectives wasted little time acting on the disclosures of Calvin and his girlfriend. They called for reinforcements. On Thursday, October 5, a small army from Santa Barbara assembled in Bakersfield. It included five members of the major crimes unit. Birchim and Ray had been joined by Baker, Weitzman, and Detective Ed Skehan. Assistant District Attorney Pat McKinley, the third-ranking prosecutor in Santa Barbara County, was there, too.

At around 3:20 P.M., McKinley, Birchim, and Ray called Municipal Court Judge Frank Ochoa in Santa Barbara to obtain search warrants for the Eye Street apartment and 1620 Tulare Avenue, and arrest, or Ramey, warrants for Diana Bogdanoff, Stephanie Allen, Brian Stafford, and Rickey Rodgers.

"Detective Birchim, on those Ramey warrants . . . do they all charge a violation of [California] Penal Code, Section 187, murder?" McKinley asked.

"Yes."

"We believe at this point that Brian Stafford and Rickey Rodgers were involved in the actual killing in Santa Barbara," Birchim told the judge.

"And that Stephanie and Diana Bogdanoff are implicated in the murder as either principals or aiders and abettors," McKinley added.

In a tape-recorded affidavit, they summarized for the judge the evidence for the warrants. They referred mostly to the statements of Calvin, Jodie, and "Joe." After an hour and a half, Ochoa issued the warrants.

The next day, the army launched its attack. They were fortunate to be dealing with at least three suspects who apparently had no idea what was coming.

*   *   *

It had been more than a week since Stephanie and Brian had
seen or heard from the Santa Barbara detectives. Their lives
seemed to have settled down again.

They were convinced after the September 27 drive that it
was Calvin and Jodie who had been talking to the police. "I
knew it was them when we got home [that night]," Stephanie
said. "I just felt it." Brian noticed how reluctant Calvin was
about going on their little drive. "It gave me a funny feeling
right off the bat," he said. "[He was] looking for a million
things to do, and he had never done that before."

Despite these feelings, they had not even threatened their
friends since then. Stephanie told me that Brian discussed
taking Calvin out, but "I think it was just an idea that came
and went."

The couple took some precautions. According to Jodie, they
wouldn't talk on their phone, because they thought it was
bugged. "They didn't want to talk about Diane, they didn't
want to talk about Rickey, they didn't want to talk about
drugs, they didn't want to talk about anything on their phone
anymore."

But Brian, for one, felt secure in Bakersfield, as if it were
an impregnable fortress, as if nothing could touch him there.
"I was in my home," he explained. "Bakersfield is my home.
I know that town. That town is like an energy for me."

If either of them thought of escape, it was Stephanie, who
had never had a hometown. But she seems to have been more
anxious about escaping from Brian than the police.

Brandon McLeod and his mother recalled Stephanie coming
over several times just before her arrest. They did not know
about the murder but could tell something was wrong with
her. "She started coming around a lot more," Brandon said.
"She had this look in her eyes, man, like it wasn't right. I kept
asking her, 'What's your problem?' She was like, 'Nothing,
nothing, it's bad, but I can't tell you.' "

One time they were talking in his bedroom, and she kept
looking nervously out the window. "What are you looking
for?" Brandon asked.

"Brian. He's out there somewhere. He left the house walking
with his guns. If he catches me over here, he said he'd kill both
of us."

Another time, Brandon said, she came around and showed him five hundred dollars in cash. That was up-front money, she said, to leave town with her, "as in leave for good." He would get another thousand dollars later. She would pay for everything. "I had the five hundred dollars in my hand," Brandon said. "I took a long think. Nah. I took a twenty and stuck it in my pocket." He didn't want "nobody looking for me nowhere."

Other clues as to Stephanie's state of mind were provided by Jodie. On October 3 they finally spent some time together away from Calvin. They drove around all day, running errands and shopping. According to Jodie's account of their conversations that day, Stephanie was more concerned about her conscience and Brian than the police investigation. At one point Jodie told her friend that the police hadn't called her yet.

"Oh, I don't think they're going to do anything about it anyway," Stephanie predicted. "I don't think they found anything out."

Jodie recalled how afraid she was the other night when they went on that drive. "You scared me. You know, it was like you guys were accusing us of it. The reason me and Calvin don't hang around you anymore is because of what happened. It's hard to trust somebody or be around somebody that just could cold-bloodedly kill somebody like that."

"Brian scares me, too," Stephanie replied.

"What do you mean, he scares you, too?"

"I never thought Brian would really do it himself. I thought he might have somebody else do it."

Stephanie went on to say she just wished it had never happened like it did. Jodie was blunt with her. "You're going to have to live with that the rest of your life. Because you cold-bloodedly planned, plotted, and killed somebody."

"I know. My conscience is really bothering me."

On Friday, October 6, Stephanie was still with Brian and getting ready for the next step in their life together. They had been up all night, snorting crank and packing up her apartment. Her deadline for eviction was coming up in two days. They were planning to go apartment-hunting that day and find something before the deadline.

"I wasn't concerned about getting caught until the day I got arrested," Stephanie said later.

*   *   *

Since flying into Washington on September 28, Diana had been staying at Christine Allen's home, a frame bungalow in a rural area outside Tacoma. She hadn't seen Christine, who had just turned twenty-two, since her daughter's affair with Al Clarke ended the previous Christmas. She had hardly seen her grandson since he was born in December 1987.

According to Christine, her mother was still genuinely grieving and in shock over Phillip's death. She recalled Diana crying while they watched the video footage of Phillip at Thanksgiving the previous year. She said Diana also had nightmares and even broke out in a rash.

Stacy Stewart, Gary Wymore's daughter, got a different impression when she ran into Christine and Diana at a shopping mall in Puyallup one afternoon. She hadn't seen either of them in years. "Mom's just visiting from California," Christine explained. "Her husband just got murdered. She was right there when it happened."

"I've just been walking around the mall all day shopping, going in circles," Diana chimed in. "That's why I look the way I do."

According to Stacy, Diana "looked great, she looked really good. She showed no sign of mourning . . . She showed nothing, no sign of emotion. She just had this look, kind of a smirk look."

Diana also kept busy going through her address book, taking a pilgrimage through her past, as if a networking ghost had returned to haunt Pierce County. Often using Christine as her go-between, she tried to contact her two ex-husbands. Steve Allen, who had remarried and built a successful career at Boeing, got a message from Christine, saying Diana wanted him to call her. "By that point, I wanted nothing to do with her," he told me. It wasn't that he suspected her of anything. He was still seething over how she had treated their kids, particularly Bryon, when they all lived in Colfax.

Gary Wymore told me that when he and Diana were going through their last breakup, they visited a bar in the Seattle-Tacoma area. When Gary returned from the rest room, Diana was talking to the bartender. He overheard her say to him: "I'll be back. I have future plans. I'll be back."

Some four years later, Diana was back and trying to contact

him. She left a message for him to call. But life had moved on for him, too—he was now living with his girlfriend in Puyallup—and he wasn't interested in being part of Diana's nostalgia trip.

Another name in the address book was Debra Brown, her onetime babysitter. Brown, who, as a teenager, lived for a few months with the Allen family in Washington, said Diana was at times cruel and hurtful toward her. Once she lied to their pastor, saying Brown was having sex with a boy. The youth pastor even implored her to leave the family. "He kept calling and saying, 'Debbie, I want you to get out of there; there's things going on, and you need to get out of there.' "

Now, over ten years later, Diana wanted to see her. She was asked by Christine on Diana's behalf half a dozen times. She ignored the requests. "I knew nothing about what happened. I just felt really funny about it," Brown said.

Diana was more positively received by one old acquaintance, Dick Corey. One evening she had dinner with him at a restaurant. On October 2 Diana called again and asked him to take her on some errands. They went to a post office and a bank, where Diana wired $345 to Stephanie to pay off her daughter's overdue traffic tickets. Then they had lunch.

Of course, amid all this activity, she couldn't completely forget about the investigation of the tragedy on the beach. She had that difficult interview with the detectives to think about, the attempt to put Stephanie through a polygraph. At 1:30 on September 29—while Stephanie and Brian were having lunch with the detectives—Diana called the sheriff's office in Santa Barbara and served up a new red herring.

She suggested they contact a foreman from the Caltrans assignment in Springville, where she and Phillip had worked in late 1987. She said he was a drug dealer, and supplied the phone number of his supervisor. "She had no particular reason to suspect [the foreman] of any involvement in the [murder], but was responding to questions by investigators regarding drug activity," the police report noted.

Even more bizarre was a favor she asked of Bryon Allen while she was in Washington. She wanted her son, now nineteen, to cut his shoulder-length brown hair and shave off his beard. He looked "exactly like" the white suspect whom the police were looking for, she explained.

There is no evidence, however, to suggest that Diana feared imminent arrest. On October 6 her main concern appears to have been a splitting migraine headache.

Russ Birchim began the attack that day by calling Diana at 9:35 A.M. In a friendly tone, he asked how she was doing. "I feel terrible. I've never had headaches like this before," she told him, sounding very subdued.

He just wanted to know what her plans were. She was flying back at noon the next day, arriving in Los Angeles at 3:10 P.M. on Continental Airlines. Then Birchim tried a bluff, something that might just rile her up, make her do something stupid.

Stephanie had told them she hadn't been to Santa Barbara in the weeks before the murder, he said. But rangers at El Capitan State Park note down the license plate numbers of overnight campers, and Stephanie's had shown up in a check of early to mid-September.

In fact, rangers had done nothing of the sort, and the license plate had never been recorded. But Diana fell for it. After a long pause, she said: "She came to work with me . . . She stayed at the [trailer] park."

"No, this is across the highway at the state park, and it was just one evening, one date."

Diana sounded rattled. "Oh well, she probably went over there."

"She went over there to crash for one night?"

"I don't remember . . . I can't place that at the moment . . . I'll have to get back to you on that."

"Did she bring anybody with her when she made the trip to work in September?"

First Diana said Stephanie came by herself, then that "she had a girlfriend, um, living with her."

"Did she ever bring her boyfriend with her?"

"I don't know. Not into the park . . . If she did, she didn't let us know she did . . . You know how kids are."

Diana had a new theory about the murder. "I think they thought we were somebody else."

" . . . You think they were sent there to get somebody and they got the wrong person?"

"I really do."

There were a few more questions. Asked about Brian, Diana described him as "really a nice guy . . . He comes from a nice family. Really nice family." When Birchim mentioned that Stephanie was getting evicted, Diana put him straight. "No, it's not really evicted, but she didn't like living there . . . I'm signed onto the apartment with her and Brian."

They hung up after some final platitudes. "Have a nice flight," Birchim said.

"I'm glad you called, and you know, keep in touch."

"Okay. I will, I promised you I would. Try to get some rest."

"Oh God, it's these headaches . . . Must be the change of weather up here . . ."

"Yeah, it's very possible. Be nice to get home."

The bluff seemed to have stuck. Now the army turned to its most accessible targets—the youthful tenants of 107 North Eye Street, Unit B.

At 10:45 A.M. Brian and Stephanie got a strange phone call from Jodie. Brian answered the phone, and she asked to speak to Stephanie. "Do you want to go to a pay phone and call me back?" Jodie said to her girlfriend.

"Why? What's the matter?"

" 'Cause, um, I just woke up, and Peaches [Calvin's niece] told me that those detectives were over here . . . and they said that they're gonna come back . . . They told Peaches something about being in Santa Barbara in September."

"You guys?"

"Us. All four of us."

"But that didn't happen, so what are you tripping on? Don't trip."

"Stephanie, just go to a pay phone and call me back. They're gonna come back, Stephanie."

Stephanie was getting angry. "So what?"

"So what do you want me to tell them?"

"Tell them exactly what you know, Jodie—nothing. That's all you have to tell them. They're only trying to find out what they can. They're gonna say anything and everything they can say to find out. Don't you know that?"

"So?"

Now she was indignant. "So when they say, were you guys

in Santa Barbara, you tell them, fucking no . . . They're just detectives."

Jodie said Calvin wanted to talk to Brian. But Stephanie wanted to know if he had said anything to the police.

"He asked me, was we up there?" Calvin said. "I said no, but—"

"That's all that matters." In a "you better not" tone, she added, "Just don't forget that, okay?"

Stephanie put Brian on the phone, and Calvin told him the police knew the four of them were in Santa Barbara. "I'm gonna tell them we went up there for the beach or something like that . . ."

Brian had another idea: "If they ask, we just went up there like, we were just visiting, we were up there with some friends, fuck that. 'Cause Patrick [Brown] and them took a road trip with us, and I can fucking convince Patrick . . ."

Calvin wanted to know what happened to the "dude that went up there with you and did this shit."

"He's gone."

"Where?"

"Way out."

Calvin just sighed.

"Look, check this out. Why don't you come by here?" Brian suggested. " . . . Let's make it at exactly eleven-thirty."

"Okay, but they coming back to talk to me."

"Well, fucking after you get through talking to them, come by here. Or you can come by here before you get a chance to talk to them. Okay?"

Calvin sighed again. "Brian?"

"What?"

"I think you fucked up, man; you shouldn't have did that."

"Dude, dude, Calvin, Calvin, come by here and talk to me. Okay?"

Another sigh. "They asked me some questions about what's-his-name [Rickey]. I don't know what to tell them about that fool. Well, should I tell them that I don't know him?"

"Calvin, Calvin, Calvin, Calvin, come by here and talk to me. Okay? Trust me, Okay?" There was a long silence. "Hello?"

A final sigh. "Okay."

They hung up. Calvin and Jodie turned to the guests in their living room, the guests who had orchestrated and taped the entire conversation—Russ Birchim and Fred Ray.

The army headed for Stephanie's apartment. There had been some debate among its troops over tactics. Knowing Brian's passion for sawed-off shotguns, Bill Baker favored using a SWAT team to make the arrests. Birchim and Ray argued for using a feather, not a hammer. Why not make the most of the rapport they had established with Stephanie and Brian during their previous visit to Bakersfield? Why not just stop by as if for a friendly visit, tell them they were only wanted for questioning? As far as the suspects were concerned, they were still dumb cops. "They didn't even know we were on to them," Ray said later. If things got heavy, then they could arrest them on the spot. They got the go-ahead.

Birchim and Ray arrived at the bungalow around noon. As they walked up the cement path, Ray put his arm on his partner's shoulder. "It's okay, I'll protect you," he said, only half joking. From a bank parking lot across the street, the other detectives and McKinley watched intently.

Stephanie asked them to wait outside a few minutes. She had to finish a phone conversation, one with Jodie in which her friend was apparently making a last-ditch effort to save her. "She told me to hurry up and come over and bring her some cigarettes," Stephanie recalled. "I said I would leave them in the mailbox outside the door, because I was getting ready to go with the detectives."

She and Brian also needed to stall awhile so they could tidy up the apartment—Brian had just concluded a crank sale, and an eight ball was spread out on a mirror.

For three minutes or so, the detectives waited nervously on the threshold behind a screen door. When Stephanie let them in, they found Brian in only his pants. "What do you want? I'm in a hurry," he said.

"We'd just like to ask you a few more questions, clear a few things up. We can do it at the sheriff's office. It's only going to take half an hour."

"Can't we do this later?"

"No, we need to do it before we leave town."

Brian had more excuses. "I got so many things to do, I got job interviews. I haven't even taken a shower."

"Come on, it won't take that long. We'll have you back in half an hour."

Stephanie did her hair and grabbed a Dr. Pepper. Brian took cigarettes. They were still technically free, not under arrest. After Birchim and Ray drove them off, the other detectives moved in to search the apartment.

The detectives put Stephanie and Brian in separate interview rooms at the Oildale headquarters of the Kern County sheriff. At 12:30 P.M. they began interviewing the teenage girl. Ray, the more experienced interrogator, did most of the questioning while Birchim took notes. They also had a tape recorder going. The tables had been turned since the September 27 interview. Now Ray had the advantage of knowing the answers to his own questions in advance.

Ray advised her of her rights as a suspect. He then posed the same puzzle to her that Birchim had tried out on her mother. How did she explain rangers finding her license plate at the state park in September? She couldn't understand it, she always stayed across the street with her parents when she was in Santa Barbara. "I've never stayed there [at the park]," she insisted.

"Now, we talked to your mother this morning, and she said that you were there one time with one of your girlfriends and stayed over at the state park," Ray said.

"That's Christine [Ferman]."

"But Christine was already gone by then . . . up north."

"But I didn't come up and stay with anybody in September besides them [her parents]."

" . . . You're saying you weren't there at all? In September?"

"I was there to work for that time, but I stayed with my mother . . . I didn't stay over at the state beach."

"Why would they have your license number?"

"That's what I'd like to know."

Stephanie then denied Brian had been out of town since they had been together. She didn't know who Rickey was— "There's people that come over that I don't know that Brian knows. Now, that could be who that is." Had she come to Santa Barbara with Tim Gray as his grandmother had told them? "Tim Gray is like insane," she said indignantly. "He's always on drugs . . . He told a lot of people a lot of things that never were true. So this question is totally off the wall and not true. Next question."

By the end of the interview, she was testy, especially when they asked about her new shoes—so new, they still carried the manufacturer's tag. "A new pair of shoes for my birthday and you need to know when I got them, where I got them, and how much they cost, too? Doesn't make sense. This is ridiculous." Her last comment was: "Come on, you guys. I need to find me an apartment. I should have been out looking already."

They concluded the interview after half an hour and told her to stick around while they talked to Brian. As they left, she tried to dash into his interview room to see him. All she managed to say to him before they pulled her out was, "They know we went to Santa Barbara."

They began talking to Brian at 1:10 P.M., and the same trick question soon paid dividends. Yes, he had stayed at the state park in September with Jodie, Calvin, and Stephanie. He described how they drove to Santa Barbara in Stephanie's car. But they only went there because "Stephanie wanted something to do."

It was the first of a series of lies as obvious as Stephanie's. He and Rickey had gone out the night before the murder, but only to see Steve Emmons and his wife; he then went to bed, and Rickey drove to Tehachapi, about forty miles east of Bakersfield in the mountains; he spent the morning of September 21 looking for his mother; his mother had paid for his new shoes.

Ray finally confronted him. Deliberately he asked: "Isn't it true that when you and Stephanie and Jodie and Calvin went over to the state park that night, that you guys took shotguns with you to kill Phillip Bogdanoff?"

"No, not even close."

"You took shotguns, though, didn't you?"

"No, Calvin took his little toy, but—"

"You had a toy, didn't you?"

"No, I can't carry one," he said, referring to the terms of his probation in the burglary case.

"Okay. He took two toys."

"No, he only took one. That was his twenty-gauge."

" . . . And what were you guys going to do with the twenty-gauge?"

"Nothing. That's protection."

Even more deliberately, Ray then asked: "Brian, isn't it true that you went on Thursday morning on the twenty-first and shot Phillip Bogdanoff?"

"Not even close. It's against everything I was brought up to believe."

The detectives had more than enough evidence for a prosecution of both Stephanie and Brian. But they wanted to keep talking to Brian. He had been calm and self-possessed until Ray accused him of the murder. Now they had him on the run. He was bathed in sweat, as if he had just popped out of the shower. This was probably their one chance at getting him to confess. Maybe he could even help them achieve what is usually the toughest objective in the investigation of a murder conspiracy—building a case against the mastermind.

Confessions

The murder warrant gave the investigators a basis for arresting Diana, but not for a successful prosecution.

In the warrant, she was an aider and abettor, like her daughter. Under California law, there is no distinction between those who actually commit a crime and those who aid and abet it. They are all "principals," subject to the same charges and penalties. In practice, however, it is nearly always harder to convict the aider than the executioner. Where forensic or eyewitness evidence can often link the executioner directly to the crime, evidence against the aider is usually circumstantial.

Before October 6, the only evidence Santa Barbara detectives had on Diana was vague and circumstantial. They couldn't go to a jury solely with testimony about her demeanor in the September 26 interview. Calvin and Jodie could testify about what their friends said or did. But anything they testified to concerning Diana's involvement would be worthless without corroboration. It was hearsay—Brian and Stephanie telling them what Diana had supposedly told them. The warrant affidavit said that "Diana Bogdanoff had told Stephanie and Brian Stafford that if they killed Phillip Bogdanoff, she would give them half of any estate she inherited"—but it was quoting Calvin.

If Brian or Stephanie broke down and implicated Diana, then the detectives might have a workable package.

In his most avuncular tone, Fred Ray launched a full-frontal assault on Brian to induce him to confess, the main thrust of which was that Brian was almost a victim himself, a victim of a setup by Diana and Stephanie.

251

"You know you're being suckered into this thing," Ray told him. " . . . [Do] you think Stephanie's gonna take care of you or . . . let you fry for what they orchestrated, what they did? And you are gonna be the patsy behind the whole thing? . . . They have had you do this foolish thing, and now they're gonna leave this poor black kid in Santa Barbara in jail and they're gonna be off spending the money and laughing at you . . . These people got you by the balls right now, and they're gonna let you fall."

When that didn't work, Ray suggested Diana was also going to desert her daughter. Groping for some black argot, he said, "She's laughing at you. She be up there in Washington right now going 'Ha ha ha' . . . You guys are fools to believe that woman is coming back . . . You think she's gonna come back to this, this godforsaken town of Bakersfield?"

"No, because she ran out on Stephanie before," Brian interrupted.

"That's right . . . She gonna be going, pssh, gone . . . Nothing is gonna keep her here, including Stephanie, and you're gonna be the one sittin' in jail."

Brian fended off the barrage. Almost as an afterthought, they placed him under arrest. "Warrant. Murder."

"Can I kiss Stephanie?" was his immediate reaction. He was sweating so profusely, he had to ask for a paper towel.

Ray kept going at him, laying bare the strategy. "You don't have to implicate Stephanie," he assured Brian. "All we want to do is know about Mother, and how Mom orchestrated this thing . . . I'm not even gonna ask you about Stephanie, because I know where your heart is. I'll ask you about Mom, what Mom's part, Diana's part, was in this whole thing."

Birchim joined the chorus. "What we're trying to do is get you to say you did it and save, help save yourself and get her. We know she's the one who orchestrated it."

"Can we stop this [the tape recorder] for a minute?" Brian said.

The detectives didn't like having the recorder in the room in the first place—the device can often be a psychological barrier for a suspect under interrogation. The interview rooms they were using were hooked up to an external recorder, but the system was malfunctioning. They shut the tape off for the next twenty-three minutes.

According to Birchim and Ray, they continued to apply pressure to Brian, telling him that Diana had conceived the murder and used him and Stephanie to commit it. They promised no leniency and made no threats.

"They were trying to convince me to go ahead and tell my side of things, because regardless, I was going to jail," Brian recalled. "So why not get a chance to tell my side?"

At 2:25 P.M., when they turned the tape recorder back on, Brian was ready to talk. His first words on the restarted tape were: "As I was saying prior to this, Stephanie's mom had just kept calling constantly, every day, twice a day, asking Stephanie had she heard any news." It came out piecemeal—the El Camino payoff, the call to Diana from the Thrifty gas station, the description of the murder itself, the hospital encounter with Diana. Sometimes Brian threw in homemade analysis—Stephanie was "some little girl inside trying to find her mom." He delved into irony—Diana had said if Phillip was killed, "everything would be good for everyone . . . There was no everyone."

It was the first time Russ Birchim had heard a murder confession, and he was so enthralled, he forgot to keep taking notes. "It was probably every detective's dream," he recalled.

Brian equivocated in only one area—who actually shot Phillip, him or Rickey. Initially Brian seemed to be hinting at Rickey. "I don't want him to think I'm selling out on him because he did it, because he's a friend of mine and he wouldn't want to see me get in any trouble," he said.

"Who shot him, you or Rick?" Ray asked.

"Can we leave that invalid?"

"No, because you got to think of yourself."

" . . . If it wasn't for him being a friend—"

"I know, but if you pulled the trigger, I can understand you being reluctant about saying anything, okay? But if he pulled the trigger, come on, you got to think of yourself, you can't be thinking of him right now . . . I want to know who Diana's gonna lay it off on, which one of you guys pulled the trigger."

"Nine times out of ten it'll be put off on me."

"I know . . . I want to know who pulled the trigger."

"Being honest, God as my witness . . ." He paused. "Stupidity pulled the trigger."

Then Ray asked, "You?" and Brian nodded. "Okay. That's the information that we had, that you pulled the trigger."

At about three o'clock, the interview concluded and the detectives went back to Stephanie. Ray readvised her of her rights, but she was now in no mood to be questioned further without a lawyer present. "I mean, I'm sitting here for hours, answering a bunch of questions about something I have nothing to do with . . . I guess I should get a lawyer to defend myself."

She was evidently not expecting Ray's blunt response. "Okay, we will stop the questioning right now, and you're under arrest for murder."

"I'm what?"

"And Brian's under arrest for murder, too."

"Now, wait a minute. I don't understand that."

Stephanie started crying and fumbling with her purse. Without any further explanation, the detectives handcuffed her and shut off the tape. Birchim then told her they had promised Brian that he could see her. Did she want to see him? She said yes, but could she see him alone? Birchim escorted her into the room where they had left Brian.

The detectives said that putting Stephanie and Brian alone in the room together wasn't a cunning ploy. They were just doing them a favor. As far as they were concerned, the questioning was over. They had cracked the case. Baker and McKinley had arrived at the sheriff's office, and the four of them were jubilant, exchanging high fives as if they had just won the World Series. A Kern County deputy was on his way to transport Stephanie and Brian to the jail in downtown Bakersfield, where they would be booked and fingerprinted.

But after the couple had spent about five minutes alone, a deputy notified Birchim and Ray that they were asking for them. "I want to talk to you now," Stephanie said as they entered the interview room.

"But you already waived your rights."

"I want to talk to you now," she repeated.

Stephanie told me that she felt compelled to follow Brian's lead and confess. The detectives had "scared the shit out of me. You try being arrested for murder . . . You cannot imagine what it feels like to be arrested for murder . . . I'd never been to jail. I thought they were going to kill me in jail." On top of that, while she was alone with Brian in the interview room, he kept telling her that she, too, had to come clean.

Ray made it clear that they were primarily interested in what she knew about her mother's role in the murder. "The important thing is . . . that we establish the pressure that you were under as a little, young lady and the influence that your mother has had on you . . . I'm not trying to pit you against your mother . . . But your mother's not here right now . . . She's not facing the music on this. She's letting you and Brian face the music on this."

For the next hour, Stephanie really didn't say very much. She covered the Tim Gray solicitation, the shotgun trip, and the events surrounding the murder. She made numerous references to the pressure her mother exerted on her, back to when she lived with Nick Bogdanoff. But her answers were generally brief, hardly surprising since she was crying almost the entire time.

Sometimes what she didn't know was more revealing than what she did. Did she know, Ray asked, that over a year ago, Diana and Phillip "weren't legally married. She could have just walked out of the relationship. Did you know that they didn't get married until . . . December of eighty-eight?"

"No, I didn't know."

"So after the phone calls started to you, she got married to him. Do you see a pattern?"

"Yes."

When asked, "What did she [Diana] tell you you would get from it?" Stephanie broke down. "Her happiness," she sniffed. "It's so hard."

Much of the "confession" was dominated by Brian, soothing and cajoling his girlfriend. Maybe he was just acting the gallant lover. But a lot of it sounded like someone who was already refining his defense.

"What was my reason for doing it?" he butted in at one point. "That I told you?"

Initially Stephanie rebuffed him. "Don't say that."

"But it's true."

"Don't say that."

In a whisper he continued: "What did I say? Come on, don't quit on me now . . . This is all-important. In the long run. Okay? Come on, be strong. What did I tell you when you asked me that?"

Finally she said: "You said you'd do it 'cause you loved me and that was hurting me, what was going on . . . ."

Things got particularly torrid when the detectives took a break and left the couple alone again—with the tape still running. Brian tried to soothe her in what sounded like his best child psychologist manner. "You don't even know," she protested.

"Yes, I do, Stephanie."

"Brian, that's my fucking mom," she wailed.

"It's just me and you," he went on, "just like it's always been since we've been together. No one's ever really been that close." There was a lot more in that vein. "The only thing that's important to me right now is you. And I hope you can believe that. Remember I said I'd give my life for you?"

He gave her his summation of the case. "I think we were both getting used like two chess pieces in this. You because you wanted your mom, and me because I was tired of seeing you get hurt." As Ray returned to the room, he added: "All you wanted is for your mom to be happy. Well, maybe she's happy."

All Stephanie said that was audible during the monologue was, "Oh God, Brian," "I'm gonna get sick," and "I swear to God, I can't handle this."

Stephanie made her most important contribution to the case after she finished her confession: She agreed to McKinley's suggestion that she call her mother.

Diana had actually called the Eye Street apartment at around 3:23 P.M.—almost exactly the same time that Stephanie was making up her mind to confess. Ed Skehan, who was still searching the house, answered the phone. Diana asked to speak to Stephanie.

"She's not here," Skehan said. "She's gone to the store."

"Who are you?"

"Oh, just a friend of the residents."

"Have her call me right away, as soon as she gets in."

The detectives weren't sure that Diana was still going to catch the flight to Los Angeles the next day. Stephanie had told them during her confession that she was supposed to pick her mother up at the airport, but "she won't show up if she doesn't talk to me." Maybe Stephanie could also get her mother to incriminate herself. At 5:23 P.M. she dialed her sister Christine's number in Washington, and the detectives started taping.

Christine answered and passed the phone to her mother. Diana hadn't changed her plans. She told Stephanie that she didn't want her to arrive too early in Los Angeles. "I don't want you driving around L.A., okay?" Also, "there's probably still detectives following you everywhere anyway."

Then she mentioned the strange question Birchim had asked her that morning. "I don't know if he was just trying to get me to say that you did it . . . but he said sometime in September that . . . because of the license plate, they knew your car was in the state beach park . . . When was it when you were on the state beach side?"

"I don't know," Stephanie replied.

"Well, think about it. I need to know 'cause they're gonna ask me again."

"I went up there with Calvin and Jodie and Brian, and we stayed across the street in the car."

"Overnight?"

"Yeah . . . Remember, I called you and told you that we were there to do it. They were supposed to do it when he came out." A pause and a sigh. "Oh, man."

" . . . Well, I just told them I didn't know anything about it, but you know kids, run here and run there. So they're gonna ask, and you're gonna have to say, 'Yes, we came, we spent the night there.' "

"I will, but I'll tell them you didn't know about it."

" . . . I would not say that Brian was with you. Okay?"

"All right."

"Totally omit, omit that."

"Okay."

"If they say, 'Why were you there?' what are you going to say?"

"I don't know." Stephanie paused. "I'll say, 'I came up there to kill my stepdad.' "

Diana reacted as if she were trying to douse an inferno. "Hey, cool it!"

"Why?"

"Cool it, Steph! I don't want to hear about that."

"If that's what makes you happy."

Stephanie had a message for her from Brian. He wanted to know about the El Camino. "I'll know about it Tuesday when I get in town. I have to go to Santa Barbara on Tuesday."

"What will you know about it?"

"Anything about it—if it's sold, or if it's not sold, or if I'm going to take it back to Visalia and try to sell it or what."

"I thought you told Brian he could have it."

"I did. Everything's cool."

Stephanie was now vehement. "He took care of your problem, and you said you would give him a damn car!"

"I'm going to! Everything is cool. You just can't do things overnight like that. You gotta be very careful. You know that."

Then, as if speaking to a three-year-old, Diana told Stephanie, "Your brother's here. You want to talk to him?"

"Not right now. I gotta go."

Bryon Allen took the phone. Stephanie was so abrupt with him, he could sense something was wrong. She was in a hurry, she had people outside waiting for her, she explained. "Well, they're going to have to wait. I don't talk to you that often," he said.

"That's because you never call me."

"Well, I'm sorry if I don't have your number."

Diana got back on the phone. She said she could get Tommy Byford to pick her up at the airport if it was too much for Stephanie. "No, I'll be there," her daughter said.

At the end of the conversation, Stephanie had a surprise for her mom. "Brian's coming with me." Silence from Diana. "Okay?"

"Okay."

"Excuse me! That didn't sound very promising."

"I said, okay."

After the phone call, it was time to transport Brian and Stephanie to the Bakersfield jail for processing. Brian asked for one more look at his girlfriend.

Stephanie really didn't look like much. The weeks of drug abuse and inadequate rest had overwhelmed her once wholesome, youthful features. Her hair was unkempt, her face was haggard, and her eyes were bleary. She had lost so much weight—down from her normal 135 pounds to below 110—that she appeared almost anorexic.

But Brian wasn't interested in the overall picture. "Can I just have one last look at your tits?" he asked. Stephanie dutifully raised her top.

As the deputy drove them to Bakersfield, Stephanie cursed her mother: "Goddamn my mom! That bitch! It should be her ass that's in this car."

They spent their first night in custody at the Kern County jail. The next day—Saturday, October 7—they went on a road trip to the Santa Barbara County jail, handcuffed in the back of Gregg Weitzman's car.

Ducks in a Row

By any standards, the detectives' attack had been remarkably successful. They had arrested two suspects without any hassles, obtained two confessions, and tricked another suspect into incriminating herself.

The search of the Eye Street apartment had also turned up a hoard of evidence. Skehan and Weitzman found the sawed-off shotguns, crank supplies, newspaper clippings of the murder, even the *Leonard, Part 6* videotape. They also had a list of Brian's and Stephanie's associates who called the apartment during the search. Gator Bohlinger had actually walked in on them. They drew their guns on him, and Skehan searched him. He found a small quantity of whitish powder in Gator's fanny-pack, but decided not to arrest him.

None of that would be worth much, however, if Diana eluded the detectives.

Pat McKinley said later that he wished they had played a few more games with Diana before arresting her, strung her along to lure her into more incriminating statements. They could, for example, have put a wire on Stephanie and had her meet Diana at the airport. But back in Santa Barbara, political pressure was mounting to tie the case up—Undersheriff Jim Vizzolini was in the middle of a close election for the vacant sheriff's position. "Solving the case would be a good thing for Vizzolini," McKinley said. "It was, 'Let's go, let's make everything public.'"

To add to the urgency, news of the arrests of Stephanie and Brian had been leaked to local radio in Santa Barbara on Friday, and the *News-Press* ran a front-page story the next morning. The sheriff's office in Santa Barbara was trying desperately to keep the identity of the other suspects secret.

"At this time, Diana Bogdanoff is not a suspect?" a reporter asked Vizzolini at a news conference late Friday afternoon.

"I didn't say that," he replied. "I just said we can't release" the identities of the two suspects still at large. "She may be involved in the case, but at this point we have not made any contact with her."

Against this background, Birchim and Ray drove from Bakersfield to Los Angeles International Airport on October 7, hoping nobody else had contacted Diana either. Maybe Washington was far enough away for her to remain not so blissfully ignorant. They arrived in plenty of time at the gate for Continental flight 60 from Seattle-Tacoma. They had worked out a scenario in advance for their target, one they hoped would "really shock her."

They paced nervously around the gate waiting area, Birchim chain-smoking. The plane was right on time. The passengers began filing out—and there was Diana. Quickly they approached her. Looking startled, she asked, "Where's Stephanie?"

"She's got car problems. She couldn't make it," Birchim replied.

"What kind of problems?"

"We've impounded her car."

"Why?"

They told her that both Stephanie and Brian had been arrested for murder. "We have a warrant for your arrest, too." Then they handcuffed her. As they led her away, Diana said: "I had nothing to do with the planning of the killing of my husband. You guys better make sure you have all your ducks in a row."

After allowing Diana to collect her baggage, they searched her at the airport police station. Among the items they found were Stephanie's eviction notice, the business card of Kevin Arrowood (the Kasler carpenter), and thirty-two hundred dollars in cash.

Then they took her into an interview room. At 3:45 P.M. they advised her of her rights, and she agreed to talk to them. It soon became clear, however, that this suspect wasn't going to confess to anything. The interview was a complete about-face from the cordial chat in her kitchen just ten days before. The detectives fired verbal bullets, and she scrambled for cover.

Diana soon got in a terrible muddle after Ray asked about the call she received on the morning of the murder from a pay phone at the Thrifty station on Milpas Street. Phillip had called from there, she said, to say that he still wanted to go to the beach. But how did she know he called her from a pay phone and not his office?

" 'Cause he said something about he was getting gas, and that meant that he must have been at a pay phone."

Okay, Ray said, Phillip was driving his state car that day, wasn't he? When he bought gas for the car, he paid with a credit card, didn't he? "So the credit card [bill] would show which station he purchased gas at."

"That's true." But then Diana added: "That doesn't mean he got gas that day."

" . . . You said he did, though."

"He said he was at the station, he didn't say he was buying gas, that I remember. He just said—"

"But you said he was buying gas."

"I guess I assumed he was buying gas."

"Brian didn't call you, did he?"

"No."

"From that station?"

"Absolutely not."

The onslaught was relentless. They confronted her about Tim Gray telling his relatives that she had solicited him. "Tim is mentally insane. He is insane for Stephanie," she replied.

"How convenient for you," Birchim said.

" . . . You look at him, and then you put yourself in my position . . . If you were gonna hire somebody, would you hire that guy to do something?"

Another key question was, why did she say the white guy shot Phillip? She had a new answer—she had her sun visor on when Phillip was shot. Ray batted that one back. The gunman was still white, wasn't he? "Why is it that Brian tells us last night that he's the one that killed Phillip and not the white guy, he's the one that shot the gun?"

They hurled Stephanie's confession at her. "You tormented Stephanie to the point in her life where . . . the only relief she could get from her loving mother was to have your husband murdered," Ray said.

"That's not true," she replied vehemently.

"Stephanie said every time that you called her for a year, you said, 'When are you going to kill Phillip?' "

"That's not true."

She was going to let her own daughter take the fall, wasn't she? "You're gonna fry your daughter, huh?" Birchim said.

His partner stepped in with, "You're gonna let your daughter cook over this whole thing because you could care less . . . about anything but yourself."

Nothing broke Diana down. At the end of the interview, she told the detectives she was prepared to go before a judge and jury. "I don't believe she [Stephanie] had anything to do with it, and I know as a fact that I didn't have anything to do with it."

She went on, almost screaming at them: "None of this is easy. Laying there, seeing somebody murder your husband, is not easy . . . Especially when I am the kind of a person that saves people's lives. I don't kill people, for crying out loud."

"Well, you're killing your daughter," Birchim said. "You don't seem to care about that. She seems like a real nice gal, but her life's over. You're gonna have to live with that."

Finally they asked about the El Camino. "Did you offer to give Brian the car?"

"No."

They shut off the tape. "Diana, that one's going to hang you," Ray said.

At about 4:30 P.M. the detectives began driving Diana the one hundred miles up the coast to Santa Barbara. Ray told me that he felt frustrated after the interview. "I felt I should have been more patient. She was thinking on her feet. I thought she coped pretty well with it." But before the end of her first full day in custody, Diana would make a critical mistake—one directly connected to the questions she parried at the airport.

In the Santa Barbara County jail, a modern cinder-block facility overlooking U.S. 101, Diana was reunited with her daughter, who had arrived from Bakersfield a few hours earlier. They were close again, separated by a few feet. But the closeness was only physical. As for communicating, they could have been light-years apart.

Both were housed in single cells in the isolation tank of the women's unit. The unit consists of parallel rows of cells. The single cells—most of them seven feet by twelve—barely have room for a toilet, bunk bed, metal table, and stool. Diana got FI-14 in the "S" row, giving her a view of frosted windows from her cell. Stephanie was behind her in FI-7 of the "R" row. They were divided by the aisle of "R" row and a thick brick wall.

Communication between adjacent isolation cells is quite straightforward. The cells are sealed only by bars running from ceiling to floor. Inmates can communicate through the bars and extend their arms to pass items. But contacting an inmate in a separate row of cells requires more ingenuity. Inmates exercise only with members of the same row. They are fed in their cells, not the dining hall used by the general population. They can yell at each other through the walls, but that attracts the attention of guards and isn't exactly confidential.

Of course, seasoned tenants of the jail have found ways to close the communication gap. They use a trusty—an inmate who helps clean and maintain the facility—as a go-between. A sympathetic guard might even forward a message. But inmates unfamiliar with jailhouse ways, especially those in high-profile cases, take a major risk if they trust anything to anyone.

Diana Bogdanoff took that risk. On Sunday, October 8, she tried to pass a note through her neighbor to Stephanie. The note never got to her daughter.

That first exposure to jail—the clanging doors, officious guards, leering inmates—must have filled Diana with panic and apprehension. The detectives' questions must have been swirling in her brain. The temptation to communicate with Stephanie, just the other side of the back wall of her cell, must have been overpowering. Since it was a weekend, she had yet to be assigned an attorney to relieve her anxiety or advise her as to how to behave in jail. She hadn't even been formally charged.

When she first arrived, Diana was not in a talkative mood. When her neighbor in FI-15, Chrisia Curry, asked her what her name was, she replied: "I don't have a name."

The next day, Diana was more friendly with Chrisia. She could hardly have chosen a more unlikely friend.

Chrisia, then thirty-two, was a black woman of prodigious girth and gab. Five foot eight, she weighed in the region of three hundred pounds, her ample frame making an isolation cell a tight fit. Her coiffure was topped with orange streaks. She had been employed as a housekeeper by ailing old women, but got into trouble because of her habit of forging checks in their names. In 1985 she had forged a check from a Santa Barbara woman. Four years later, she had just begun a six-month sentence for violating her probation in that case.

Before she knew who her neighbor was, Chrisia had read about the murder on Corral Beach. On October 8 she found out Diana's identity when another inmate on the row called her name. She started talking to her notorious neighbor. To pass the dreary hours, the two wrote each other some notes. As she did for everybody on her row, Chrisia made Diana a bracelet out of pieces of string.

Diana appreciated the gift. "Could you make Snuffy one?" she asked.

"Who's Snuffy?"

"Stephanie. My daughter. She's in the next section."

Chrisia agreed to make Stephanie one, but then Diana asked: "How I am going to get it to her?"

"Sometimes you can get an officer to take things over there. Even though they're not supposed to pass things from section to section, sometimes they will."

"Do you think you could get a note to her?"

"Sure. I can do that."

While Diana wrote, Chrisia created another bracelet. When they were done, Diana handed Chrisia two notes through the cells' bars. On one she had drawn a teddy bear and written only, "I love you, Mom." The other note covered both sides of a sheet of yellow paper. Diana told Chrisia she could read it.

"Is that all right?" she asked when Chrisia was finished.

"Yeah," Chrisia said.

Chrisia then wrapped the note and the teddy bear missive in the bracelet for Stephanie and put the little package in her Bible. "After Diana let me read it, I figured it might have something to do with the case," she said later. That was putting it mildly.

The note, written in pencil in a small, printed hand, went as follows:

Do not try to send me a note. Tim told me he would do it for 2,000.00. I did not ask him too [sic]. I told him no! He was crazy about you & [you] did not like him. He is nuts remember? I never asked him anything, he was always following you—I know he told everyone I asked him to do that but I didn't! And I know you didn't either. You were always trying to hide from him. Pop was afraid of him. What I told Brian was that I would not let you have the car but if he wanted it he could steal it in 3 weeks if it wasn't sold by then. I would get him some keys because I was so mad at Phil for getting you a car you didn't like, and because he yelled and said all those mean things to you. He said he could sell it in LA for 6,000.00 enough to get a car & a new apartment. But that is not what he told you I said or anyone else I guess. He called me on Thursday morning said he was in Santa Barbara and wanted to see the car. I told him it was in Ohi [sic] and gave him some directions. I thought he was checking it out to steal, but he wasn't, he wanted to know if I was working, I wasn't, he followed Phil I guess or took a chance and went to the beach hoping to catch us there, he did! I said that the white man did it because when I saw his black hand I realized he could be a friend of yours, and got scared for you. Now I have to tell them it was him because when I got to your house I saw his shoes & put some money on the table for groceries & he took it and bought new shoes. He saw me looking at them and new [sic] he was in trouble. But he new [sic] he had told everyone that I hired him, so he thought he was safe. I did not tell on him because I had never seen his face. But now I have to. Stick with me I was scared for you. Put in toilet.

Chrisia Curry's motives for handing over the note are uncertain. She testified that she cooperated with law enforcement for unselfish reasons—"because an innocent person was dead." She insisted she was not hoping for favorable treatment of her case in return for her information.

That may sound disingenuous coming from a veteran offender like Chrisia. At the time she received the note from Diana, she had recently been disciplined for "getting into it" with a guard and was still awaiting a release date. So there was ample incentive for her to make the most of being lodged next to Diana Bogdanoff.

Whatever the incentive, on Tuesday, October 10, Chrisia removed the note from her Bible and gave it to a guard. Later that day, she was interviewed by Detective Skehan and agreed to make a note of anything else Diana said to her about the case.

By then, Diana had retained Santa Barbara attorney Steve Balash to represent her, and he had counseled her not to discuss the case with anyone. Over the ensuing days, Diana couldn't resist making comments when items about the murder were aired on the local TV news. She said that maybe Brian killed Phillip to save Stephanie; she complained about the mug shots of herself and Stephanie being aired, and not that of Brian; she didn't believe Brian was her daughter's boyfriend; she admitted Phillip had slapped her around a couple of times, but it wasn't that bad.

Chrisia dutifully noted these things down and handed what she could to guards. But nothing would come back to haunt Diana as much as her note to Stephanie. Here she was, addressing the key questions raised by Russ Birchim and Fred Ray in the airport interview. Did you offer Tim Gray money to kill Phillip? Did you offer Brian the El Camino? Did Brian call you the morning of the murder? Why did you say the white guy shot Phillip?

It read like an obvious and transparent attempt by Diana to coordinate stories with Stephanie. Trying to manipulate her daughter one more time had given the investigators the nearest thing in the case to a smoking gun.

At the end of the week, the "white dude" joined the other defendants at the Santa Barbara County jail after a dramatic nighttime arrest. Like Diana, he spent his last days of freedom with his family, what he called his second family.

Rickey Rodgers fled Bakersfield shortly after Brian and Stephanie were arrested. He said his friend Richard Gee told him about the arrests and advised him to go "somewhere where nobody knows you." The next morning, Gee suggested he go to Gee's parents, George and Estalita Diggs. On October 9 he arrived at their residence in Roseville, just northeast of Sacramento.

They were glad to have Rickey. "George and I have been kind of like a mom and dad to Rickey, and he is like a son to us," Estalita said later. " . . . We just became a family-type thing." They had gotten to know Rickey when they lived in Bakersfield, but had not seen much of him since they left the city around 1988. At the time, they had outstanding warrants for their arrest in Kern County. George was wanted for possession of methamphetamine, and he and his wife had also skipped town on bad check charges.

The Diggses said Rickey told them when he arrived that he needed to get away from Bakersfield because of some family trouble. The next day they became curious after Rickey's mother left a phone message, saying an all-points bulletin had been issued for his car. Rickey assured them he wasn't in any real trouble.

According to the Diggses, it wasn't until Thursday, October 12, that they found out about the murder. The conduit was Rickey's natural father, who had leapt into action after a visit from Russ Birchim and Fred Ray.

The Santa Barbara detectives had been searching intensively for Rickey since they arrested Diana. They first contacted his mother, who denied any knowledge of his whereabouts. They were not convinced. They conducted a stakeout of her beauty parlor, knowing it sometimes doubled as Rickey's crash pad, but he never showed.

On October 9 they met Rickey's father in Tehachapi at the mobile home where he lived with his wife, Barbara. Donald Rodgers told them he did not know where his son was, but if he saw him, he would turn him in. After the detectives left, he called Rickey's mother. "I'm scared to death," he quoted her as saying. "We got to get him an attorney and help him out." She said that Rickey was at the Diggses'.

Rodgers called his son in Roseville and told him that neither he nor his ex-wife would turn him in. On October 10 he wrote a note to Rickey in which he advised: "Remember not if but when the law cach [sic] up with you, throw your hands as high in the air as you can." He did not advise Rickey to surrender, but pointed out that "as time goes by the thing get [sic] worse." He mailed the note to Rickey, along with a wanted flier he had obtained from his daughter Cheryl Dotson. She was Rickey's half sister, the one who worked for the Kern County sheriff.

On October 12 Rickey showed the flier to the Diggses. It said he was wanted for murder in Santa Barbara. He told them he wasn't involved, that he was in Bakersfield at the time of the shooting. He asked George, who worked at an electrical company, to forge several weeks worth of time cards for him as a phony alibi. George only filled in the dates on the cards, not Rickey's name. Estalita said later that Rickey agreed to turn himself in to Roseville police the next morning. He was saved the trouble.

Rickey had finally been traced that day after Fred Ray spoke to Cheryl Dotson in Bakersfield. She had just become the beneficiary of a strange transaction in which Rickey granted her title to some land in Tehachapi, the land their father lived on in the mobile home. The deed was signed early on October 12 at a notary's office.

The timing alone is strange. Rickey could not have signed the deed, because he was in Roseville at the time. According to the notary, the "Rickey" in her office had no ID, but Barbara Rodgers vouched for him.

Like her relatives, Dotson told Ray she didn't know where Rickey was. The breakthrough came when he asked her for the names of anybody Rickey might be close to. She mentioned a couple called the Diggses. Something clicked for Ray—the Bohlingers had said that he had a "second family." Maybe that's who the Diggses were.

After finding their address through court records, Ray asked Roseville police to check it out. The officers spotted Rickey's car in the complex parking lot.

Birchim and Ray sped over three hundred miles up the San Joaquin Valley to Roseville. At around 10:00 P.M. on October 12, they arrived at the Diggses' complex, joining a SWAT team of local police officers. They weren't taking any chances this time. In addition to a sawed-off shotgun, Rickey was believed to be armed with an Uzi assault rifle.

As the SWAT team took their positions, George Diggs and his wife left the complex and were taken into custody. The couple's young son was still at home with Rickey, so police got Estalita to call the boy and tell him to go to a neighbor's.

Rickey followed the boy onto the walkway outside the apartment. He surrendered immediately, his hands high in the air. He was staring down the scope of a laser rifle. Its beam ended in a red dot over his heart.

Rickey wouldn't speak to the police. The laser rifle "was all he could babble about," Birchim recalled.

On October 24, 1989, the four defendants were arraigned in Santa Barbara County Municipal Court. A crush of spectators, relatives, and media packed the courtroom. Diana was composed, at least compared with her first court appearance on October 11. Then, on her way to the courtroom from holding cells across the street, she collapsed in full view of TV cameras and two of Phillip's daughters.

The district attorney had thrown the book at all four of them. They were charged with first-degree (premeditated) murder and special allegations that the murder was committed for financial gain and while lying in wait for the victim. If convicted of the "specials," they would face either the death penalty or life in prison without parole. Stephanie, who was only three days over eighteen at the time of the crime, was in the same boat. Brian was also charged with conspiracy to commit murder for his role in the shotgun trip.

It was hard for some to fathom such a bizarre plot. Nick Bogdanoff told a reporter: "Phil loved Diana, and Diana loved Phil. I can't believe it. I can't think of any reason for it. Diana almost worshiped Phil. She always told me how much she loved him." He said he was fond of Stephanie. "If you see her, tell her I miss her," he asked.

The defendants all pleaded not guilty to the charges. It would take a year and nine months, some seven hundred thousand dollars in taxpayers' money—and the painstaking work of an unusual prosecutor—to bring them to justice.

PART FOUR

Murder and Mirth

Patrick J. McKinley's office is decorated with legal diplomas, family snapshots, a framed newspaper front page, pictures of his hometown Pittsburgh Pirates, even some baseball cards. Two items are more distinctive—a hangman's noose attached to an antique Pittsburgh streetcar meter, and a sign of the word "Psycho" in purple neon.

The meter once counted incoming and outgoing passengers. Now McKinley uses it to tally the annual total of prison time to which defendants in his cases have been sentenced. Pull the noose and a new number slots into the meter.

The "Psycho" sign hails from an incident during his early days as a Santa Barbara deputy district attorney. One day sheriff's deputies at the county jail, tipped off about a possible escape plot, secretly taped a conversation an inmate was having with a former inmate out on bail who was visiting him. They began discussing their prosecutors, and it turned out they had both been assigned to McKinley.

"What's he like?" one asked.

"He's a fucking psycho," the other replied. "All he cares about is putting people in prison."

"Psycho" stuck. McKinley even started driving around with 5150 DDA on a vanity license plate—the number referred to a California law concerning mentally disturbed people who are a danger to themselves or others; the letters were his job acronym. In those days, the "Psycho" epithet seemed more than apt.

After getting his law degree in 1968, McKinley, fired up with the idealism of the age, intended to become a defense lawyer. His plans changed when he went looking for a job in, of all places, Bakersfield. Unable to find the public defender's office, he asked a janitor for directions. He still couldn't find the office. More directions, another futile search. Finally the janitor suggested he see the district attorney. He couldn't miss that office; it was right upstairs. The DA offered him a job, and McKinley, then a virtual pauper, accepted.

In 1970 he moved to Santa Barbara, where he acquired a reputation for almost fanatical prosecutorial zeal, every case a crusade and every defendant a "sleazebag." Sometimes defense witnesses felt the sting of his sarcasm. He even had one arrested for perjury when the witness left the stand. He frequently clashed with judges trying to keep him under control.

At the 1982 trial of Robert La Cava, accused of killing his live-in girlfriend, McKinley was on a roll. Frustrated by the memory lapses of a witness, he put a gruesome autopsy photograph of the victim in front of her and asked if that refreshed her recollection. For good measure, he accused the defense lawyer, Steve Balash, of "shyster tactics."

"McKinley in those days was just vicious," Balash told me. "For a long time he was known as a dirty fighter kind of attorney." One attorney claimed he suffered so much verbal abuse from McKinley at a court hearing that he was brought "near to the point where I was prepared to engage fisticuffs with [him] in the courtroom."

Some defense lawyers also felt that McKinley was too close to the police—a cop's prosecutor. It was standard procedure for police to clear arrest warrants with a DA before presenting them to a judge. But McKinley was wont to accompany police when they served warrants, even on small drug cases. He also socialized with them outside work.

He was perhaps most notorious for his handling of the case of Barry McNamara, accused in 1985 of killing four members of his family in the worst mass slaying in Santa Barbara history. First McKinley tried to have the defense attorney removed from the case, alleging the lawyer's incompetence was jeopardizing the defendant's right to a fair trial. Then he was reprimanded for composing a ballad about the crime based on the 1917 song "MacNamara's Band." It went: "My name is McNamara, I'm the killer of the clan; I killed my parents, sis, and niece, just before I ran." A very unamused judge called it a "sick" joke.

McKinley, forty-nine, now has the stooped posture, wire-rimmed glasses, and receding hairline of an aging academic. A veteran of over three hundred jury trials, he has won enough of them (about 80 percent) to boast a solid track record. The eccentricity is still there, along with the "Psycho" sign. He hands out an official bio which states that he lives with—in this order—"his dog, Tascha, and his wife, Esther."

But some of his critics say that McKinley has mellowed in recent years, the vitriol has diluted. "Right now he's a very professional prosecutor," said Balash. "I have a lot of respect for McKinley now."

Deputy Public Defender Michael McMahon says the prosecutor has a very distinctive, disarmingly confident courtroom style. "It's not surprising in a very important case for him to accept the first twelve jurors who are randomly selected. The theater that goes to the jury is: 'We have a very strong case' . . . It's also possible for him to get through an entire trial without objecting to anything, once again reflecting his self-confident style . . . He's very unusual."

The Bogdanoff case would be a stern test of his mellowness and his self-confidence.

When McKinley heard about the murder on the beach, he didn't think much of it. "I just thought it was a psycho," he recalled. It wasn't until the detectives called him on October 4 and asked for help with their warrants that he knew there was more to it. Although he had curtailed his habit of riding along on arrests, he decided this case was big enough to justify going to Bakersfield himself.

It was certainly the most complex he had handled since McNamara. Instead of four victims and one defendant, he had one victim and four defendants, three of whom were from out of town. The Bogdanoff case also involved informants, reams of telephone records, and obscure financial data. Then there was the headache of intense publicity. The tabloid TV show "A Current Affair" had got in on the act with a segment called "Murder on a Nude Beach."

In the weeks after the arrests, McKinley played his cards very close to his chest. He publicly said little more than "No comment" about the case. He even joined the defense in getting a court order to allow the voluminous search warrants, normally public record, to remain sealed. "There are major portions of this that if [made] public, would try the case in the newspaper," he said at the time.

In the new year, McKinley finally aired out the basis of his case, and the public found out just how unusual it was. The occasion was a preliminary hearing that began on January 8, 1990. Such hearings in California are a bridge between a felony criminal defendant being charged and being brought to trial. To cross that bridge, the prosecution has simply to show a crime was committed and that there is a strong suspicion the defendant committed it. The prosecution presents its case in public before a municipal court judge, and its witnesses can be cross-examined by the defense.

Usually "prelims" are brief and routine, a bout of sparring before the big fight. Rarely is an entire case dismissed by the judge, although sometimes individual charges are reduced or eliminated before going to the superior court level for trial.

There wasn't much that was routine, however, about the preliminary hearing in *The People of the State of California v. Diana Bogdanoff et al.,* held before Santa Barbara Municipal Court Judge Arnold Gowans. It was "better than daytime television," one spectator said.

The four defendants seemed to have little more in common than the handcuffs they all wore to court. Seated at the defense table with their lawyers were the prim, portly mother with the double chin; her pale, fidgety daughter, who looked like a dissipated cheerleader; and the stocky black guy with the Fu Manchu nails. In the jury box with his lawyer was the long-haired, skinny white guy.

The setting was more appropriate for a PTA meeting than a capital murder case—the courtroom was a converted modular classroom in the parking lot of the municipal courthouse. It was so small that McKinley and Birchim sat in the jury box. Relatives of the defendants and the victim, plus media and curious spectators, filled four rows of gallery seats.

What really set the hearing apart was McKinley's cast of witnesses. They blurted out one surprise after another, prompting either peals of laughter or stunned disbelief among the audience. "I've never seen a case in which there were so many surprises," one lawyer said.

Top billing went to the five young Bakersfield witnesses, now collectively known as the "Bakersfield Bunch." All of them testified only because McKinley had given them immunity from prosecution for any crimes they might describe on the stand; all of them seemed to have come from a different world. Their life-style "can only be described as pointless," the *News-Press* reported.

Calvin Monigan and Jodie Davis were a conspicuous presence. The couple, then living together in east Bakersfield, drove into the courthouse parking lot in his new red Mustang convertible. Calvin, clad in blue turtleneck sweater and gold chains, was somewhat baffling on the stand, although it was hard to tell what was responsible: his drawl or his vagueness. A frequent response was, "I can't say yes, can't say no."

His diminutive girlfriend was more precise and lucid, but greeted many questions with a roll of her eyes, as if her interrogators were morons. What was the purpose of cow shooting, she was asked? "There was no purpose whatsoever," she replied, the eyes rolling.

She dropped startling nuggets of information as if they were confetti. Where had the Mustang come from? She had just turned eighteen, she explained, and had received a thirty-six-thousand-dollar damages settlement held in trust since her father's death. So she had spent a large chunk of that on buying the car for Calvin. The settlement was now down to about six thousand dollars. In the same matter-of-fact manner, she revealed that her parents had supplied her and Stephanie with crank.

Taking mindlessness to new levels were two witnesses who showed up at court wearing garish Oakley sunglasses: the Bohlinger brothers. After his gunpoint encounter with Ed Skehan, Gator had not warmed to law enforcement; nor had his older brother Mike. They were extremely reluctant to talk to Birchim and Ray in Bakersfield, and at one point, their father refused to allow them to be interviewed without a lawyer present.

McKinley had given them immunity, too; now he hoped the oath would induce them to testify truthfully. It was soon clear that the oath meant ludicrously little to them.

On key points, both were consistent. For example, they denied knowing anything about any murder until after the arrests. Mike said he heard before the murder that "somebody, no name or nothing, was going to get hurt." But he didn't know "where, who, when, or nothing."

But there were so many contradictions that it was hard to believe anything they said. Mike claimed he didn't know what happened to the murder weapon, even though he had told police he heard it had been destroyed. The brothers admitted that Stephanie, Brian, and Rickey had called them from jail after they were arrested. Gator testified that he never discussed the case with them and they never asked him to lie for them, but Mike conceded that Rickey asked him to say that Rickey didn't go cow shooting.

It was obvious that the brothers were still close to their friends and willing to protect them. Gator frequently flashed his bad-toothed grin at Brian from the witness stand, or tugged his beard in what appeared to be a code gesture. He even minimized Brian's role as a drug dealer. What did Brian sell you? McKinley asked.

A: Some pot.

Q: Anything else?

A: No.

Q: . . . Was he selling crank?

A: Not to me.

Q: To other people?

A: [Gator hesitated] It's possible.

Q: Did you see him sell crank to other people?

A: No.

Q: Why do you think it's possible?

A: Well, if I had it, I would be selling it to people that wanted it to make money.

Gator also said under direct examination that Rickey was not involved in any drug sales. But under cross-examination, he blatantly contradicted himself:

Q: About how many times did you ask Rickey if you could buy a quantity of drugs from him?

A: I couldn't even count. Over nine years, there could have been a few times.

Q: . . . And what is the largest amount of drugs that you bought from Rickey?

A: Maybe a gram.

Q: A gram of what?

A: Crank.

Despite such obvious inconsistencies, Gator appeared enamored of his own cleverness, even accusing McKinley of "not asking the most brilliant of questions."

Inadvertently, the truest insights that the Bohlingers provided were into the emptiness of their values and the aimlessness of their life-style. Mike claimed he stayed awake three weeks on a crank binge. Why did he do that? he was asked. "I wanted to see if I could do it." The only reason he spent so much time at Stephanie's apartment was boredom, he explained—"I didn't have anything to do."

Gator stopped at one point to admire the twenty-gauge sawed-off shotgun that McKinley had asked him to identify. He gazed at it like a child looking at wrapped presents on Christmas Eve. "That one is cool," he said.

"It may be cool, but I am going to move it out of your way," McKinley said hastily.

Gator portrayed violence as an everyday feature of life in Bakersfield, like drug use. "People in Bakersfield talk about tearing people up all the time." It was mostly talk. When it wasn't, "A lot of times once you get there to do it . . . if you hit them in the mouth once or something, they just quit. It's over. It's not really people getting beat up." A lot of guys in Bakersfield carry a gun "because if you don't have it and somebody else does, you are going to tend to do what they want."

But there was something he wanted to explain: "The first day I came here, I was standing up on the [courthouse] stairs and wasn't even in this guy's way and he told me, 'Excuse me,' and I did not know what to say to him, because in Bakersfield, they either tell you to get the hell out of the way or they would move you."

Had Gator learned any other lessons? Apparently not. He had given up crank, he said, but now he was using cocaine. "I just like it better than crank. You can eat on it, where you can't eat on crank. Doesn't make you feel like shit when you're coming down."

How about killing someone? Gator had already said that some people deserved to get beaten up. Are there some people who deserve to die? a defense lawyer asked.

A: Depending on what they do.

Q: Do you feel you are capable of killing somebody if they deserve it?

A: [Gator ruminated] I don't know if I should answer that question or not. I mean, it depends on what they did to me or my family. If they did something bad enough where it was really driving me crazy, I'd probably do it.

The fifth Bakersfield witness put on a virtuoso performance that cast doubt on his sanity. Stephanie and Diana's comments about him to police seemed only too true.

Since his last trip to Santa Barbara, with Stephanie a year before, Tim Gray's life had become even more chaotic. He was arrested four times, apparently attempted suicide twice by stabbing himself in the arms, and spent time in four mental institutions. One arrest, in March 1989, stemmed from an attempt to break into Stephanie's trailer—she was away at the time. He was sentenced to six days in jail in that case. One psychiatrist who examined Tim diagnosed him as schizophrenic, another as a borderline personality. Another thought what he needed was some basic care and attention. "Rather than psychotherapy, he needs some environmental support and manipulation to help him," he recommended.

Unfortunately, Tim did not get much of that. On September 16, staff at a mental hospital in Los Angeles noted that he was talking about "going to Hollywood to be a movie star and make some big money and buy a big house and a car." On September 22—the day after the murder—he was still fearful and delusional. But the next day he was discharged to his sister Tammy, who took him to Visalia.

That was where Russ Birchim and Fred Ray finally located him on October 10. They interviewed him that day at the house of Diane Gray, now estranged from Tim's father. Three months later, to ensure he showed up for the preliminary hearing, they drove three hundred miles and picked him up in a small Valley town near Modesto where he was staying with an aunt. They found him on her porch, hung over and vomiting.

Under his grant of immunity, Tim testified over two days, longer than any other witness. He appeared sober at the time, but his idiosyncrasies still overshadowed his tale of being solicited by Diana and Stephanie to kill Phillip. Profanities flowed in torrents, and the laugh punctuated his testimony so often that one defense lawyer asked if it could be reflected in the court record. One exchange with McKinley was from the Theater of the Absurd. It concerned his alleged meeting with Diana in Stephanie's trailer:

Q: What was the first thing that was said?

A: ... I can't remember the first thing that was said.

Q: What is the first thing you remember being said?

A: I don't remember the first thing that was being said.

Q: What is the first thing that you remember?

A: I can't remember.

Not surprisingly, the defense attorneys used their cross-examination to probe Tim's story and psyche. Some of his answers were odd, to say the least. Here he was being questioned by Steve Balash, Diana's lawyer, about precisely when the trailer meeting took place:

Q: Do you recall what time of year it was, what season it was?

A: Yeah. It was rainy season and the sun was shining.

Q: It was rainy season but the sun was shining?

A: I remember riding my bike in the rain ... and it was pouring down rain, but the sun was shining, and I felt good, you know ...

Q: Do you recall if it had rained the day before?

A: No. I prayed that night or that day, I was praying that it fucking rain. You know, I was praying, "Jesus, hey, we need some rain and make it different."

Religious references dominated his account of his personal
torment. "I had had enough, man," he said, explaining one
apparent suicide attempt. "I was going through too much hell
at the time to stay here in this shitty, fucked-up place." He
recalled praying, "Now, Jesus, I'm tired of this. I just want
to go to Heaven." Was he treated in the mental hospitals for
schizophrenia? "They were treating me so I couldn't pray to
Jesus, man. I couldn't be myself. I had to be all doped up, so
I couldn't be me."

The schizophrenia question loomed when Tim recalled how
he learned to steal a car. He was five or six years old and
watching a TV show about a "repo guy": "It was kind of like
the power of thought. He was like telling me how to steal a
car, but he was telling a totally different thing when the TV
program was going on."

Michael McMahon, representing Stephanie, asked Tim to
elaborate on what he meant by "the power of thought":

A: . . . when I talk out loud, the only people that can hear
me [are] you. When I use my thought, the whole world
hears me.

Q: Can you sometimes hear what other people are thinking?

A: Oh yeah, of course. I hear other people's thoughts a lot
of times.

Q: Can you hear what I'm thinking now?

A: Uh-huh . . . power of Satan. That's what you thought.

Q: When I said power of thought, what I really was thinking
was power of Satan?

A: Well, actually, at first, your mind went blank, and you
weren't thinking shit, and then you thought power of
Satan.

Tim also told McMahon that Jesus spoke through him. "Like
a few minutes ago, me and [another lawyer] were carrying on
a conversation . . . and I think I called him a dirty name. I was
talking, you know, but it was like Jesus said that for me at that
time, but it came out my voice." Some of his answers were
coming from Jesus rather than his own mind, he said.

But at other times, he was sharp and logical, suggesting that the "Crazy Tim" persona was an act, a way of attracting attention. That didn't always help McKinley, however, particularly when Stephanie's guilt was at issue.

In his interview with detectives on October 10, he had never said outright that Stephanie wanted Phillip dead. "It was just she was all uptight," he told them. "You know, because her mom was fucking riding her ass. Telling her, you know, 'Get a boyfriend and have him do it' . . . She was just emotionally all fucked up." At the end of the interview, he lamented: "She's too good to spend her life in the can."

He stuck to that line at the prelim. During the trailer meeting, he was asked, did Stephanie say anything about killing Phillip? "Not too much. I mean, shit, if she did, I can't remember a word of it." On the trip to Santa Barbara, he said, Stephanie did nothing toward killing Phillip.

His loyalty and ardor were undimmed by all Stephanie's rebuffs. He kept glancing at her at the defense table. It didn't seem to matter that she had a boyfriend. In fact, the boyfriend—whom he actually identified as Brandon McLeod—was sitting there with her. When Balash asked him about his feelings for her, he was emphatic:

Q: You loved Stephanie at that time [of the Santa Barbara trip], didn't you?

A: Yeah, I did.

Q: And you still love her, don't you?

A: Yeah. I can honestly say I love her.

There were further revelations from people who had no connection to Bakersfield but had somehow been swept up in the maelstrom of Phillip's murder. Foremost among those was the pencil-tree man.

Al Clarke had originally been interviewed by Ed Skehan on September 25 with his "wife," Sylvia, but gave very little useful information. There was no mention of any affair with Diana or solicitation by her. "I wasn't going to come out and say, 'Well, I am having an affair,' with my wife standing there," he explained later. "That is kind of embarrassing. It is already embarrassing enough."

Then Stephanie landed him in the soup. Late on October

7, she had another interview with Birchim and Ray in the Santa Barbara jail—the detectives had just returned from Los Angeles with her mother. There was something she hadn't told them the day before. "My mom and Al talked about killing Phillip all the time," she said. "Al was, I think, trying to find a way to help my mom." Not only that, she thought they were having an affair.

Stephanie wasn't sure if Al would cooperate with police. "Al is an older, wiser man."

On October 18, Clarke, reinterviewed by Skehan and Weitzman, corroborated Stephanie's story. Two weeks later, he wrote a statement detailing the affair with Diana and her alleged solicitation of him.

Testifying at the prelim, Clarke was so uncomfortable, he seemed ready to flee to the South Pole at a moment's notice. His brow so furrowed, it looked like it had been plowed, he averted his eyes from Diana and jutted his jaw out as if it could somehow deflect incoming questions.

Al's main problem was the mystery of Diana's briefcase. While she was in Washington, Diana had called Al and asked him to pick it up from Rogena Nutt. Al duly stored it away in his tool shed. On October 7 he saw police searching the Bogdanoffs' trailer. The next day, he jammed the briefcase open with a screwdriver and then turned it over to police. It contained such "personal items" as several dildos and numerous Polaroids of Diana and Phillip having sex in their favorite cove.

What defense lawyers wanted to know was, why did Al open it himself? Was he concerned it might contain something to implicate him, something "in there with your name on it that might drag you into this?"

He groped for an answer. "I think I was thinking there might have been something in it . . . hidden weapon or something." He did not mention that it was the same case Diana had shown him once before they made love.

Al survived the witness stand, but his ordeal had only just begun. Soon after he testified, the owner of the trailer park fired him, and his "wife" left him.

After two weeks, the preliminary hearing ended. Whatever the difficulties, McKinley had got his case on the record and his witnesses on the stand—particularly significant in light of his fear that some might not be available for later trials. Judge Gowans ruled that all four defendants be held to answer in superior court, and left the special allegations in place that made them eligible for the death penalty.

The *News-Press* summed up the hearing in a story headlined "Strange Case of Murder and Mirth." The atmosphere was almost festive, it said. Lawyers, spectators, even defendants, were laughing—"possibly all the way to the electric chair." Brian and Stephanie, in particular, seemed oblivious to their predicament, smiling and giggling.

No one knew exactly what was so mirthful. But some guessed the case might be too terrible to take seriously.

"Mommie Dearest"

It was the moment everybody had been waiting for. A week had passed since testimony in Diana Bogdanoff's trial began in the historic Santa Barbara County Superior Court building. The gallery of Judge William Gordon's courtroom had been at least three-quarters full as the first thirty or so witnesses testified. But on the afternoon of Tuesday, September 25, 1990, there wasn't a spare seat for the star witness. An overflow of spectators lined up in the corridor for any seats that might become available.

At 2:00 P.M. a bailiff escorted the girl out of a side door that led to the jury room. She was wearing a purple corduroy skirt and matching vest, and her hair was neatly arranged, bangs cascading over her forehead. She swore the oath, anxiously gripping the hem of her skirt. Then she unsteadily mounted the witness stand and sat down. She gnawed her lower lip and blew out her cheeks, the nervousness intensifying. She cast furtive glances at Diana, apparently composed at the defense table.

Pat McKinley stood up from the prosecution table, chewing gum as usual to lubricate his throat. His arms crossed, he looked down at a list of questions on the table. He had total silence. He asked the girl her name, where she went to school, the names of her brother, sister, and father.

Then: "And is your mom the defendant in this case?"

The answer was a husky, quavering murmur: "Yes." The girl was biting back tears. She looked beseechingly at her lawyer, seated a few feet from her beneath the blackboard.

The prosecutor resumed: "Using September 21, 1989, as a fixed date to work from—that is the day that Phillip was killed over here in Santa Barbara—prior to that date, had your mother ever said anything to you regarding having Phillip killed?"

Again, a murmur. "Yes."

A year after participating in an act supposedly calculated to help Diana, Stephanie Allen was in a position to help convict her mother of murder. She had faced a reality that overwhelmed her solidarity with her mother.

"I thought I was going home," Stephanie told me. "The whole first six months, I thought they were going to let me go. It was just a denial of belief that I could actually be in jail for murder, and actually be convicted and go to prison. I didn't believe that at all."

She added: "I knew I was guilty of what they were saying. But to a certain extent, I thought it was excusable because of the circumstances. I didn't understand that it's not excusable." She was still a long way from "accepting the reality of it. I knew I was guilty, but I didn't know that I couldn't be excused for the reasons I did what I did."

As the hours of monotony in a seven-by-twelve cell dragged by, reality sank in. "The more I got into the jail scene, the more it just started hitting home . . . If I was to really believe it when I got arrested, I would have overloaded."

Reality also meant conceding that a jury might not find her conduct excusable. Her lawyer, Michael McMahon, had been busy preparing a defense for her, sending his investigator as far as Washington in search of evidence. His defense was going to be: Although Stephanie said and did many things that made her look like an aider and abettor, she did not really believe the murder would happen. She did not believe the talk about murder was "anything more than a fantasy game," the public defender said at the prelim.

But there was no guarantee a jury would buy it. "I saw some serious marketing problems at trial selling that view of the facts," McMahon told me. "If she walks like a duck, talks like a duck, the jury will think she is a duck."

If the jury didn't buy it, Stephanie at least would no longer face the gas chamber. In February 1990 McKinley decided not to seek the death penalty against her and Rickey—in their cases, there were too many mitigating factors. But she and Rickey still faced first-degree murder charges and, with the special allegations, could be sentenced to life in prison without parole if convicted.

In that harsh context, a plea bargain, even if it meant implicating her mother, began to look attractive. She talked it over
with a fellow inmate, who helped her understand the legal
issues and encouraged her to take a deal. She also had an
unexpected reunion with her mother in which the subject of
a deal came up.

On June 25, 1990, the wind-whipped Painted Cave fire
swept down from the San Marcos Pass area, cutting a swath
of destruction along the drought-stricken hillsides of Santa
Barbara and threatening the county jail. As a result, all inmates
were evacuated. Diana and Stephanie were still being kept
apart at the jail, but during the evacuation, they spent several
hours together at the women's honor farm.

Stephanie mentioned to her mother that a deal was in the
works, though nothing had been finalized. "Don't take a deal;
everything's going to be okay," Stephanie recalled her saying.
"Just trust me." But what if Stephanie had no choice but to
take a deal? Diana said she wouldn't blame her. "I got a good
lawyer and I'll be all right."

As Diana's trial approached, the key question was, would
McKinley make Stephanie an offer she couldn't refuse?

The direction of his case dictated that he should. Diana was
still the centerpiece, the linchpin who could only be convicted
on circumstantial evidence. Key components of that evidence
were the portions of Stephanie's and Brian's confessions in
which they incriminated Diana. But under California law,
McKinley could not use those statements in a trial of Diana
unless the confessors testified. The prosecutor might convict
Diana of first-degree murder with one of the confessions, but
with neither, he would be on thin ice. Stephanie was the
obvious target for a plea bargain, because Brian was still a
death penalty case.

In April 1990 the presiding judge of the Santa Barbara
Superior Court granted defense motions for each defendant
to be tried separately. The next month, the court granted
Steve Balash's request that Diana go first. "I feel the whole
case revolves around her," Balash explained at the time. The
trial was expected to start around September. Any deal with
Stephanie would have to be made before then.

After talking it over with Russ Birchim and Fred Ray,
McKinley decided to offer Stephanie a plea to second-degree

(unpremeditated) murder. He reckoned she would have to take it. "We thought that if she went to trial, she would get a conviction of first-degree and maybe life without parole," he explained. "She really couldn't afford to roll the dice."

But the prosecutor and Stephanie's lawyer took their time coming to the table. "I think we were both playing hard to get," McMahon said. In an ironic twist, it was Diana's lawyer who finally prompted them to make a deal.

Balash had filed a motion to exclude Stephanie's confession from Diana's trial on the grounds that it had been coerced by the detectives. He had also subpoenaed Stephanie to testify on that issue. But at a pretrial hearing on August 6, McMahon refused to let her take the stand, prompting a lengthy legal argument with Balash.

During a recess, McKinley and McMahon started talking about a deal. Negotiations continued over the lunch break. Stephanie got a second opinion from a colleague of McMahon's in the public defender's office. "He told me I wasn't going to make it [at a trial], and the best thing for me was to take the plea bargain," she said.

That afternoon, sobbing and distraught, Stephanie pleaded no contest to second-degree murder. The charge carried a possible sentence of fifteen years to life or, under very rare circumstances, probation. Stephanie also agreed to "testify truthfully if called by any party to this action." The wording avoided saying she was a prosecution witness, but the *News-Press* hedged nothing the next day with the headline: "Daughter to Testify Against Mother."

The deal assumed additional importance two days later, when McKinley suffered a significant setback to his case.

At the prelim, two of his most effective witnesses were Steve Allen and his sister-in-law Dwylene. The one a licensed minister and the other the wife of an ordained minister, they had impeccable credentials compared with many of the other witnesses. Their story—that Diana had told them she tried to have Steve killed during their marriage—sounded fantastic. But what juror could imagine the straitlaced, wholesome Allens making it up?

On August 8 Judge Gordon, ruling on another motion from Balash, excluded the Allens' testimony from Diana's trial. He accepted Balash's contention that Diana should not have to

defend herself against an alleged crime with which she had
not been charged and that might well prejudice jurors against
her. "I can just see this being called the 'black widow' case,"
Balash told Gordon.

The ruling gutted an entire dimension of McKinley's case,
a dimension suggesting that Diana might just be inherently
evil. And as Balash pointed out at the time, it really put
Stephanie on the spot. "Stephanie is the star witness now,"
he said.

On August 9 a *News-Press* columnist stoked the fires further.
Diana's trial, the columnist somewhat flippantly said, would
be "a replay of *Mommie Dearest,* Santa Barbara–Bakersfield
style."

The overture to Stephanie's appearance was protracted. Jury
selection alone took five weeks. The lawyers and the judge
waded through a pool of over two hundred potential jurors,
far larger than normal since this was a death penalty case.
If Diana was convicted of first-degree murder with special
allegations, the jury would have to come back for a separate
proceeding to decide whether she should be sentenced to death,
or life without parole.

A jury of seven women and five men was finally seated on
the morning of Monday, September 17—almost exactly a year
after the murder.

The atmosphere was solemn and subdued, certainly when
compared with the preliminary hearing. There was no room
for "festiveness" in Department 6 of the Superior Court. With
its high ceiling, oak fixtures, and towering velvet drapes, the
courtroom had the appropriate air of judicial gravity. Peer-
ing over his glasses from behind the bench was crew-cutted,
gruff-voiced Judge Gordon, who looked no more likely to
tolerate nonsense or frivolity in his courtroom than he would
a cabaret act.

McKinley, wearing one of his customary Paisley ties, rose
to make an opening statement. The prosecutor had devised
a simple theory of his case—Diana wanted to leave Phillip
because of his physical abuse but chose to kill rather than
divorce him, because otherwise she would be left destitute.
As he stated in a pretrial brief: "Phil was murdered because
Diana did not believe in divorce."

In his statement, he elaborated on that, fitting Stephanie into the picture: "The murder was committed because Phillip was beating the hell out of Diana periodically, getting drunk, beating her up, but she didn't want to leave him because if she left him, she'd leave with virtually nothing, so she kept calling her daughter, 'Get someone to kill him. Get someone to kill him. Get someone to kill him. If we don't kill him, he's going to kill me, and I'll be left with nothing.'"

McKinley had flirted with the idea of calling Stephanie as his first witness; that way, he would be sure to grab the jury's attention from the beginning. But he decided instead to spend the first week establishing the background of the murder and the conspiracy through such witnesses as Calvin, Jodie, Brandon McLeod, and Al Clarke.

The prosecution had a headache with Calvin: not what he said, but what he was wearing. Gone were the turtleneck and gold chains of the prelim. This time he was clad in jailhouse blues.

Calvin was a convict again, serving a six-year prison sentence for child molestation and arson. He allegedly committed the former crime on New Year's Eve—before the prelim—by having sex with a thirteen-year-old girl at a Bakersfield motel. On January 19 Jodie left town with another man, and three days later, Calvin allegedly burned down the home of a woman whose daughter dated his brother Herk. He claimed the motel girl duped him with a fake ID; evidence linking him to the arson was circumstantial. But he pleaded guilty in return for a lenient sentence.

McKinley wasted little time getting Calvin to describe his crimes and his sentence. But he couldn't stop Balash raising the issue three times during cross-examination.

Calvin also didn't help himself on the stand by suffering some strange memory lapses. Questioned by Balash, he could not remember exactly when Diana called Stephanie to tell her where she and Phillip would be on September 21:

A: I know she called. I know that Stephanie was relaying to Brian where they was going to be. It could have been a day or two [before the murder].

Q: You just don't know. Is that correct?

A: I can't say.

The problem with such vagueness was that Calvin claimed earlier in his testimony that he had a perfect memory.

Still, most of McKinley's early witnesses were unchallenged. The fishermen and Steve Lindgren painted the scene at the beach the day of the murder; Lisa Alviso and Kevin Arrowood testified about the El Camino. A handwriting expert confirmed that the jail note was written by Diana.

A series of officials from state agencies and financial institutions listed Phillip's assets at his death. Excluding his three houses and the Shingle Springs land, he was worth around one hundred thousand dollars. That included his sixty-three thousand dollar retirement fund (of which Diana had a quarter share), the IRA, and over nine thousand dollars in unpaid salary and overtime. In a divorce, Diana "would have lost virtually all of the assets shown by the evidence," McKinley alleged.

By the time Stephanie made her long-awaited appearance, the prosecutor had set the scene.

Stephanie was torn by conflicting emotions when she took the stand. On the one hand, "I didn't want to testify at all. I was scared and I didn't want to do that to my mom. I felt like I was telling a secret I wasn't supposed to tell." But she was also upset and angry with her mother because of things she had recently learned from detectives: "[They] were telling me that my mom was telling them, if I did it, I did it on my own and that I had a nervous problem."

What particularly upset her was the revelation that Diana had asked her brother Bryon to change his appearance because he looked like the white guy on the beach. It seemed that Diana was trying to suck Bryon into the case. "It really pissed me off that she couldn't take responsibility and she wasn't trying to help me," Stephanie told me.

Another consideration was her own fate. She was supposed to have been sentenced before the hearing. But Judge Gordon postponed a decision for at least ninety days so Stephanie could be psychiatrically evaluated. She was still, in theory at least, a candidate for probation, rather than a shoo-in for fifteen years to life. Could her testimony influence Gordon's eventual decision on her punishment?

Stephanie didn't know what to think on the stand. "It was

like, I know she doesn't want me to do this and I don't want to do this, but I'm going to do this anyway; I have no choice . . . That's what I had to remind myself: I'm not doing this because I *want* to, I'm doing this because I *have* to."

She could barely look at her mother in court. Diana had an expression on her face "like she was pleading with me not to do it. Maybe not that extreme, but just maybe 'Watch what you're saying.' "

It took more lip biting and cheek blowing, but Stephanie managed to control her emotions under McKinley's direct examination. Some of her answers came as laboriously as blood from a stone. It seemed she might still be trying to protect her mother wherever possible. Here is a typical exchange with the prosecutor:

Q: What kind of things would she say regarding killing Phillip?

A: I don't understand.

Q: Can you give us an example of some of the things she would say, what her words would be?

A: Just that she wanted somebody to kill him.

Q: What words, what words came out of her mouth? Give us a quote or an approximate quote of the kind of things your mom would tell you regarding killing Phillip.

A: She would ask me if I found anybody who would kill Phillip. She would just say that she wanted somebody to kill him.

Stephanie said Brian spoke to her mother on the phone, but she wasn't sure about what.

Q: Did you . . . talk to your mom on the telephone and/or in person about what she and Brian were talking about?

A: I think, I'm pretty sure that I talked to my mom about it. And she just said that he said he was going to take care of it or something. I can't answer that for sure.

Vaguest of all was her recollection of the phone call with her mother on the afternoon of September 20, 1989. Did she

tell Diana that Brian and Rickey were going to come to Santa
Barbara the next day to kill Phillip? McKinley asked.

A: I think she asked what was going on or if anybody was
coming . . . or if there was any plans yet.

Q: What did you say?

A: I could only imagine what I said. I can't tell you for
sure.

Q: What do you generally recall saying?

A: Um, telling her that Brian and Rickey were leaving that
night . . .

Q: At some point . . . you told your mom that the die had
been cast, so to speak, that Brian and/or Rickey was
coming down there?

A: Right . . . I would imagine.

That call had particular significance because it was the
only one in the twenty-four hours before the murder that the
prosecution had found on a phone bill. Investigators had been
unable to trace the collect call Brian placed to Stephanie from
the Thrifty station the next morning or the subsequent call he
made to Diana. And Stephanie couldn't remember anything
about the call from Brian.

Still, the gist of her testimony was clear—that she was
pressured almost constantly by her mother for about a year
to find someone willing to murder Phillip Bogdanoff. There
was enough emotion to suggest she was telling at least most
of the truth. It burst through when McKinley asked her why
she made the taped phone call to her mother after her arrest.
"When they [the detectives] were questioning me, I was upset
and I was crying, and they were telling me . . . that my mom
used me and that I was going to go to prison for the rest of
my life because of it, and that she was going to go scot-free,
and she used me." Stephanie sobbed, trembling. "That's what
they kept telling me, was that she used me."

After about an hour and a half, McKinley finished his questioning of Stephanie. It was time for the stiffer test of cross-
examination. In a sense, she was now on trial, a tenuous hope
for a hamstrung defense.

The Defense Dilemma

Even at this early point in the trial, it was clear that Steve Balash faced a dilemma, one of the more excruciating of his nineteen years in criminal defense.

Balash is a genial, balding man with a gray beard, twinkling eyes, and a passion for Harley-Davidsons. His legal career was the exact opposite of that of his adversary in Department 6. He had started out as a prosecutor and had briefly worked at the Santa Barbara district attorney's office, where he first met McKinley. But he felt stifled by all the regulations and politics of life as a DA, so in 1971 he quit and went into criminal defense. He built a busy private practice, handling a lot of sex crime cases as well as the La Cava murder case.

Balash was brought into the Bogdanoff case by James Pattillo, the probate attorney whom Diana recruited. He was initially retained by Diana's family, but after the prelim, taxpayers started footing his bill, as they were doing for the other three defendants.

The case was an unusual challenge for Balash in many respects. It was his first death penalty case since La Cava, and it was a rare opportunity to defend a woman—until then, some 90 percent of his clients had been male. It was also his first "battered woman" case. But that was where the defense's problems started.

During the 1980s, domestic violence finally came out of the American family closet. The public was sensitized—by the studies and statistics, the talk shows, TV miniseries like "The Burning Bed"—to a chronic problem that had been hidden away like a skeleton. "Battered woman syndrome" became as much a part of the popular vocabulary as "premenstrual syndrome." In California and several other states, a woman accused of murdering her spouse or boyfriend can now introduce evidence of a pattern of battering to show that she acted in self-defense.

Balash's dilemma in defending Diana was not finding evidence to show she was beaten—McKinley had conceded that as a fact in his opening statement. It was how to use the fact to defend a client who denied having anything to do with killing Phillip, in self-defense or any other manner.

Even more perplexing, if she had admitted she killed Phillip and allowed him to pursue a self-defense theory, there wasn't much Balash could do with that because of the bizarre circumstances of the murder.

In the typical case of a battered woman who kills, she does so in the "heat of passion," when in "imminent danger" of losing her own life at the hands of her batterer. In such a case, the woman clearly does not act with the premeditation necessary for a first-degree murder conviction. The choice for a jury comes down to second-degree murder or manslaughter.

But what could Balash do in a case where the victim was killed as a result of a conspiracy?

Conspiracies are extremely rare in battered-woman cases—in a recent study of forty-two women who killed, only three tried to solicit a third party to kill their abusive partners. A battered-wife theory was invoked in a 1988 conspiracy case in Colorado, but with little effect. The defendant testified that she was so frightened of her violent husband that she asked several people to kill him. Eventually two brothers obliged her. The jury found her not guilty of murder, but the judge still sentenced her to forty years in prison for conspiracy.

Even more of a problem, what could Balash do in a case where the defendant was sunbathing in the nude with her husband when he was killed?

In a landmark ruling in November 1989, a California appeals court set an exacting standard for defining "imminent danger" in cases of battered women who kill. Brenda Aris had been convicted of second-degree murder for shooting her abusive husband five times in the back while he was asleep in bed. A grounds for her appeal was that the victim had recently beaten her and that she was in fear of her life when she shot him. The trial judge should, therefore, have instructed the jury that they could convict her of manslaughter. But the appeals panel upheld the verdict, ruling that "no jury composed of reasonable persons could have concluded that a sleeping person presented an imminent danger of great bodily harm."

In Diana's case, the defense would never establish that she had been beaten between the May 1989 incident involving Frank Dominguez and the murder. Under the most liberal definition, they could not show "imminent danger."

Balash was hamstrung. He had one other hope for saving his client, of planting a seed of "reasonable doubt" that she was not guilty of murder: He could transfer the blame to Stephanie and her friends.

He had aired that theory at earlier phases of the case. "There is no independent evidence that Diana solicited Stephanie to ask Brian to kill Phillip," he said at the prelim. " . . . The conspiracy is to take the blame off the people that did the shooting and put it on Diana." Now he had to suggest to the jury through his cross-examination that Stephanie was the manipulator, the linchpin of the case.

He scored some points during three hours of questioning on September 26; for example, implying that Stephanie had an overpowering hold over the men in her life:

Q: The man that accompanied you down here [on January 15, 1989] to kill Phillip said he was in love with you, correct?

A: Yes.

Q: The man that finally killed Mr. Bogdanoff also said he loved you, correct?

A: Yes.

He also established that Stephanie could have given Brian directions on how to get to Corral Beach without any input from her mother:

Q: Insofar as the call that came in on September 20th at 5:15, it was not necessary for your mother to give you directions on how to get to the cove that she and Phillip would be in, correct?

A: Right.

Q: Because you already knew how to get there?

A: Right . . .

Q: Now did you, after that call or sometime in the evening of the 20th, explain to Brian how to find that beach?

A: I would assume I did.

He probed whether Stephanie had shown Brian the beach during the shotgun trip. "I don't think that is true . . . I wasn't sure if I gone over there and showed them there that day . . . That would be the only time I would have showed him . . . If it was not with Jodie and Calvin on the [shotgun] trip, it never ever happened."

Q: But you will concede, won't you, that it's quite possible you showed him where that beach was?

A: . . . I don't know if I did or not.

Returning to the key September 20 phone call, Balash asked Stephanie if she really did tell her mother that Brian and Rickey were going to Santa Barbara that night. "I'm almost positive I did," she replied hesitantly. " 'Cause she gave me directions and places where she was going to be the next day."

If all this was a recipe for total juror confusion, Stephanie was resolute when it really mattered: scotching any notion that she was implicating her mother to save her own neck. Wasn't she afraid of not getting probation? Balash asked. "I don't want to go to prison, if that's what you mean. But that doesn't alter my answers to any of the questions. The truth is the only thing I can give you."

When Balash used the phrase "testifying against your mother," she interjected: "My understanding is I'm here to tell the truth. I'm not here to testify against anybody." But because of her tender age, couldn't she beat the rap by setting her mother up? "On the thing I signed, it said that I was to testify if I was called by the defense or prosecution," she countered.

On redirect examination, she graphically described the predicament in which testifying had placed her: "As far as saving my own neck . . . if I go to prison, I might even lose my life because I've sat on the stand today and told everything I know, 'cause I'm now considered a snitch . . .

"I just can't see how they can say that I did this just to get out of the trouble I was in, because it's not true. I didn't do this to my mom, my mom did this to me."

On that dramatic note, Stephanie concluded her testimony and returned to her jail cell.

Inevitably, the remainder of McKinley's case was anticlimactic. Another dozen witnesses testified, and the tapes of some of the police interviews were played. But the prosecutor would later say that these last witnesses included his most effective: Tim Gray's aunt.

Tim himself did not make an appearance. After the prelim, he had returned to the Modesto area. He was obviously in desperate straits. He called me collect twice at the end of January 1990 and asked if I could send him a plane ticket to Hawaii or help him find somewhere to live. The following month, he was in Bakersfield, staying at his father's with his two youngest siblings. Just after midnight on February 11, he was found at the residence by his half sister Darlene and his father's girlfriend. He had a gunshot wound to the head, and a .22-caliber rifle was beside his body. He died later that day at the hospital.

After a brief investigation, the coroner ruled that Tim killed himself. Diane Gray would later try to reopen the case, based on statements from Darlene that a party was going on at the house around the time Tim died and that he may have been arguing with his father.

For McKinley, it was somewhat providential that Tim could not testify in person at the trial. The jury would not get to experience his strange demeanor. Instead, his prelim testimony was read to them. But McKinley needed some corroboration apart from Stephanie to show that maybe Tim wasn't crazy. That is where Joanne Smith stepped in.

A plump, jowly woman, Smith was Tim's paternal aunt, who lived opposite Nick Bogdanoff and with whom Tim often stayed when estranged from his father. Testifying on October 1, she looked terrified, her words pouring out so fast, she had to be asked twice to slow down.

She related that some time during the winter of 1989, Tim told her that Diana had solicited him to kill Phillip. He stole a car and went to Santa Barbara but was unable to go through with it. A few days later, Stephanie came over to her house to tell Tim there was a phone call for him at Nick's. When Tim came back, Joanne asked him: "Timothy, who was that?"

"That was Diane. She asked me if I would come back and do it, she would raise the price [by] five thousand dollars."

Knowing his tendency to make things up, she didn't believe Tim at the time. But when she found out about the murder, something clicked. "It was a shock," she recalled. "I felt like . . . something had just yanked the rug out from me. I read the paper and how it was done and I thought, 'I heard this story before.' "

McKinley said later it wasn't the content of Smith's testimony that was so damning but her breathless, edgy manner. "It was such that the jury liked her, the jury knew it was the truth," he said. "Things spilled out in her answers that you could just tell" were the truth.

Something else significant would later be revealed about Joanne Smith: She was "Joe," the WE-TIP informant.

McKinley rested his case on Thursday, October 4. During the prosecution evidence, Diana, whose courtroom attire rotated between a trio of equally demure, high-collared outfits, took occasional notes, whispered to her lawyer, or kneaded a handkerchief. She only showed emotion twice.

On the first occasion, the beach blanket on which Phillip died was displayed to the jury, one corner still blotched with dried blood. Diana sobbed and averted her eyes. Then, on September 27, the jury was given a guided tour of the crime scene. Conditions at the beach that day were quite similar to those of a year before, the tide so high that jurors had to wait for the waves to ebb in order to reach the fatal cove. During the tour, Diana sat in a sheriff's vehicle parked on the bike path. Through the car window, she could be seen wiping tears away.

A Walk in Diana's Shoes

The theory that it was Stephanie who really wanted Phillip dead, that she and Brian went behind her mother's back to commit the murder, dominated the defense's presentation at the trial. Balash expounded on it in his opening statement. The evidence would show, he said, that nobody ever heard "Stephanie Allen say, 'My mother wants him dead,' or Brian Stafford say, 'Stephanie's mom wants me to do it.' " But Stephanie did say, "I want to kill him, I want to teach him a lesson," and Brian did say, "I'm going to kill him because that racist so-and-so had raped Stephanie, and she asked me to do it."

And Diana's role? Balash conceded that she was an "accessory after the fact." When she saw the black guy on the beach, she realized Stephanie might be involved, so she started lying to police to protect her daughter. There was no involvement before the fact. She "never told Brian Stafford to be at the beach or anywhere else."

As his evidence, Balash paraded an extraordinary selection of witnesses. There was UCLA drug expert Ronald Siegel, who was followed by Oildale's Danny Taylor, a drug expert of a different cloth. Modestly attired in earring and black Harley-Davidson T-shirt, Taylor suggested Brian was willing to kill Phillip because "he was giving Stephanie a bunch of bullshit about being with a nigger." Brian said things like, "If the motherfucker keeps it up, he's gonna get his ass blown away." But he never mentioned that Stephanie's mom wanted Phillip dead, Taylor said.

Rosalyn Bookout, Brian's first love, gave a stunning performance, bursting into tears when asked to identify a photograph of Brian. She then described a conversation with Stephanie and Jodie Davis in which Stephanie said she wanted Phillip dead—but Rosalyn "never heard anything about her mother." Stephanie also claimed Phillip had molested her. Rosalyn felt this had set Brian off. She recalled his reaction when he found out about her own alleged rape by a stepfather: "He asked me did I want something done to my stepfather, and I told him, 'No.' And he said if I ever needed it done, or if I ever wanted it done, he would have it done for me . . . He didn't use the word 'kill.' He just said he should be punished for it."

Amy Baca, Stephanie's friend from Visalia, now had nothing good to say about her. "Was Diana Bogdanoff able to control Stephanie?" Balash asked.

"No, Stephanie was a pain in the ass," she replied.

Potentially the most damning testimony against Stephanie was offered by her own sister. Among the women in her immediate family, Stephanie was now the outcast.

Christine Allen was originally recruited as a potential witness for Stephanie. In February 1990 she talked at length with Phillip Shelton, an investigator for Stephanie's lawyer. Shelton concluded: "Christine now believes her mother is responsible for the murder. She admits her mother has been very manipulative . . . She now believes Stephanie was somehow coerced to be involved in her mother's plot."

Christine had come to doubt Diana after her mother gave her two different descriptions of the murder. In the first, told during a phone call shortly after the crime, Diana said Phillip got into a struggle with a man who accosted them while they were lying naked. He managed to wrestle himself free and run down the beach, but the man chased him and, after a second struggle, shot him dead. A few days later in Washington, Diana gave Christine a second story, which featured a black guy and a white guy, and one of them shooting Phillip without a struggle. "She [Christine] knows they both cannot be true, and doubts everything her mother says now," Shelton noted.

But the investigator cautioned that Christine would make a "soft" witness: "In the setting of a courtroom where she may be able to see her mother, or where her mother may have any form of influence over her, [she] may waffle on some of the points . . . She will allow her testimony to become confused by cross-examination rather than take a strong position.

She does not want to offend her mother." Shelton was quite prophetic.

Christine, petite like her mother and with the same angular features and close-set eyes as her sister, looked nervous on the stand despite being sedated on Valium. Her main revelation for the defense involved the phone conversation she had with Stephanie two days before the murder. She had told police in October 1989 that her sister used the words "I'm going to kill him [Phillip]. Mom knows I'm going to do it."

Under Balash's questioning, Christine now testified that Stephanie then added: "And I don't care what she says."

Q: Did she tell you that Mrs. Bogdanoff was asking that this be done?

A: No.

Q: . . . Did your mom ever tell you that she wanted Phillip Bogdanoff killed?

A: No.

Christine also claimed that Stephanie had called her soon after being arrested and said she was going to get out of jail by saying Diana set her up.

McKinley pounced on Christine's testimony in his cross-examination. After she said she never discussed the September 19 phone call with her mother, he asked incredulously: "You never say anything about, 'Hey, Mom, Stephanie told me two days before the murder she was going to do it'?"

Christine could only reply: "I did not take it literally. I've been hearing that she [Stephanie] hated Phil and wanted him dead since they were together. It didn't seem that big of a deal to me . . . You just don't want to come out and say, 'I think Stephanie murdered Phil.' "

Why, McKinley also asked, did she not tell the police about the phrase "And I don't care what she says"?

"I hadn't remembered it then."

It also emerged that it was hardly surprising Diana never told Christine she wanted her husband dead—she never told her that Phillip was beating her, either. McKinley made the most of that, too:

Q: . . . Can you explain why your mom would tell Stephanie about this but wouldn't tell you?

A: They were closer because they had been together longer, and Stephanie was more strong emotionally than I am.

Q: Stephanie was 16 to 18 years old at this time, right?

A: Yes.

Like Stephanie, Christine also didn't know that her mother had only been legally married to Phillip for nine months when he was killed.

While he focused on building a case against Stephanie, Balash tried to tell some of Diana's side of the story. In his opening statement, he invited the jury to "walk a mile in Diana Bogdanoff's shoes," to see what it was like to live through a "daily hell" of spousal abuse.

The principal guide on this walk was "expert witness" Dr. Nancy Kaser Boyd. A psychologist from Los Angeles, Boyd had worked as an assistant to Dr. Lenore Walker, perhaps the country's leading authority on the battered-woman problem. She had testified in several murder cases involving such women, but this was her first in which the defendant allegedly "contracted out" the killing of the husband.

Boyd had spent fourteen hours with Diana, interviewing her in jail and administering a battery of psychological tests. From these sessions, she had concluded that Diana was indeed suffering from the battered-woman syndrome. During nearly a day's testimony on October 10, Boyd revealed that:

- Diana was, among other things, extremely vulnerable, of low self-esteem, paranoid, dependent, self-defeating, and histrionic. "If she had walked into a mental health clinic, she would have been diagnosed with an anxiety disorder."

- The pattern of her relationship with Phillip was "very, very similar" to that of battering couples. He was at first "very nice" and loving, and "their sexual relationship was very good." But as early as 1987, he became abusive, striking her on at least three occasions.

- After they moved to Santa Barbara, Phillip started drinking more and added sexual abuse to his repertoire. That included the sadistic use of dildos.

- Diana did not leave Phillip "because she loved him" and "she felt it was a phase and that he would pass through it and that they could lick it."

- As a battered woman, Diana would have been vulnerable to Al Clarke. She naturally would "transfer her dependency to a person who could get her out of the bad situation." Clarke tried to have sex with her, but she refused.

- Diana appeared to have answered all the test questions in "a scrupulously honest manner."

Boyd also analyzed Diana's relationship with Stephanie and concluded that there may well have been some "role reversal," with Stephanie as the mother, and Diana as the dependent child. She pointed to the episode at the trailer park in August 1989 when Diana begged Stephanie not to drive off and leave her. The child in this case, Boyd said, "is taking care of the mother, is worried about her safety, is telling her what she should do, and so forth."

Despite all this information, all McKinley had to do in his cross-examination was show the jury that the walk in Diana's shoes was a red herring. He did that right away:

Q: . . . Would it be fair to say that Phillip was beating the hell out of Diana, getting drunk and beating her up and that she didn't leave him?

A: I think that's fair to say.

Q: Do you feel there's some question in this case about whether Diana was a battered wife or she was getting beat up?

A: Not in my mind.

Q: Did Mr. Balash give you the impression that that's a contested issue?

A: I wouldn't say so.

But McKinley went further, making it clear that Boyd's testimony had no bearing on the issue of whether Diana should be convicted of first-degree murder. For one thing, Boyd admitted

that she had not even discussed with Diana the key events
surrounding the murder—"I didn't try to evaluate her mental
state right at the time of the offense, nor the factual issues
surrounding the homicide. I didn't see that as my job."

The prosecutor did elicit some opinions about these "factual
issues." But it turned out that, according to Boyd, whatever
Diana said or did—whether she was truthful or not—could be
consistent with being a battered woman.

Take the key phone call from Brian to Diana on the morning
of the murder: Diana had said in the jail note to Stephanie that
he called because he wanted to see the El Camino. She gave
him directions, thinking he "was checking it out to steal."
Assuming that's what really happened, McKinley asked Boyd,
was Diana's behavior consistent or inconsistent with being a
battered woman?

It was possible, Boyd said, that "a battered woman would
express her anger toward her husband in an indirect way . . .
so it could be consistent."

But what if the statement in the jail note was a lie? Was that
consistent with the battered-woman syndrome?

A: I think it could be . . .

Q: So the answer to both questions is, "It could be"?

A: Right.

Q: If it's the truth, it could be consistent with your psychological findings? If it's a lie, it could be consistent with
your psychological findings as to this defendant?

A: I think so. Yes.

McKinley also probed the taped phone call between Diana
and Stephanie on October 6. Does Diana ordering Stephanie to
"totally omit that" sound like "a parent telling a kid something
to do or a kid telling the parent something to do?"

"It sounds like a parent telling a kid something to do," Boyd
conceded.

So had there been a psychological flip-flop now that Phillip
was dead? Had the roles reversed back to normal? "I don't
know you could expect every single behavior on the part of
a battered woman to reflect role reversal."

The expert witness had walked the jury in a dizzy circle.

*   *   *

The fragility of much of Balash's case was exemplified by his last major witness. Judy Chojnacki, Diana's best friend, recalled two potentially damning incidents—one showing Stephanie's violent animus toward Phillip; the other showing how afraid Diana was of her husband. But in both instances, her testimony collapsed under cross-examination.

Testifying with a glassy look and twitching cheeks, Chojnacki said she took Diana to a Visalia hospital in the spring of 1989 to be treated for a dental problem. Stephanie came along, too, and, as instructed by her mother, called Phillip from a pay phone. When she got off the phone, Stephanie exclaimed: "I wish he were dead!"

Chojnacki said she replied: "Don't say that, Stephanie. You don't know what might happen."

"I mean it. I wish he were dead."

But questioned by McKinley, Chojnacki admitted that she had not mentioned Stephanie's outburst to police when they interviewed her on September 26, 1989—before anyone was arrested. How did she explain the omission?

A: They didn't ask.

Q: Were you interested in finding out who killed Phillip?

A: Maybe I hadn't thought about it at that time.

Q: Was it really that they didn't ask, or you thought Stephanie might be involved in it?

A: I don't have an answer for you.

The same thing happened with Chojnacki's other key anecdote. In March 1988, she said, Diana gave her access to a safe-deposit box she had just opened in Visalia. Diana was "fearful that something might happen to her because of physical abuse . . . If anything should happen to her, I was to access the safe-deposit box one time only and be sure that anything that was rightfully due Stephanie go to Stephanie." At Diana's request, Chojnacki said she made copies of bank records showing how much of her own money Diana had put into the Visalia house.

If that was the case, asked McKinley, if she knew Diana

feared for her life in March, did she ask her why she had married Phillip in Reno the previous month? When Chojnacki said, "No," the prosecutor wondered sarcastically: "Was that because she didn't ask you?"

Chojnacki, her glazed expression beginning to crack, then conceded that she also never told Birchim and Ray about the safe-deposit box. Why? McKinley continued, his mellowness rapidly melting.

The answer was predictable: "They didn't ask."

When Chojnacki left the stand, she looked drained and exhausted. She declined to be interviewed for this book without Diana's permission.

On October 18 McKinley tied up his case with a cogent closing argument. "This is an intentional killing, premeditated for years," he told the jury, and using a chart, proceeded to list the key areas of evidence.

Stephanie was at the top of the list. But in California, the testimony of an accomplice cannot be considered by a jury unless corroborated by other witnesses. So McKinley went through the evidence of all the other individuals somehow connected to plots against Phillip's life. "Crazy Tim getting together with Fred Ray and Al Clarke and Russ Birchim and Brandon and Calvin and Jodie and everybody else in here . . . 'Let's all join a conspiracy and make up some stuff against Diana Bogdanoff.' It's preposterous."

He pointed to the importance of *when* things happened in the saga of Phillip's murder. For example, there was the "short honeymoon" after Phillip's second (legal) marriage to Diana. "Less than a month, and Tim and Stephanie were down here, trying to kill him."

He ridiculed the defense case as a school of red herrings. What did Dr. Boyd's testimony have to do with the case? If Diana wasn't going along with Phillip's sexual program, why would Phillip invite Steve Lindgren to make a threesome?

His last category of evidence was Diana's lies to the police. "The white guy did it? Bzzz. Wrong answer." Telling the police on September 26 that she told Kevin Arrowood to sell the El Camino. "Bzzz. Wrong answer."

By contrast, Balash's closing riposte was rambling and disorganized—in fact, he had pleaded unsuccessfully with the

judge for more time to prepare it. Arguing that Diana was only
an accessory trying to protect her scheming, crank-disturbed
daughter, the defense lawyer did raise some pertinent issues:

- Wasn't it curious that Stephanie managed to find two guys
  to help her who were both goaded into action by the belief
  that Phillip had raped her?
- How could Stephanie possibly not remember Brian calling
  her from Santa Barbara on the morning of the murder?
- If the plan was to shoot Phillip at the beach, why did Brian
  and Rickey leave so early? Why did they hang around the
  Caltrans office?
- The Bogdanoffs had a medicine cabinet full of painkillers in their trailer. Why didn't Diana just mix a few
  in Phillip's drink? "That's your perfect murder . . . You
  don't need to run out and get plants and trees and cocaine,
  do you?"
- On the question of money, Phillip's affairs were muddled
  because he hadn't reached a financial settlement with his
  second wife. How could Diana, with no legal training,
  have figured out ahead of time what she was going to
  get after his death?

But some of Balash's other points stretched credulity or
simply did not square with established facts. He suggested,
for example, that Diana asked Brandon McLeod if he knew
any possible killers because she knew about "these harebrained
trips of Stephanie." Maybe she just wanted to make sure that
Brandon wouldn't go along with any of them.

He also attempted to salvage the El Camino lie in the jail
note. If Brian had gone to the Caltrans office on September
21 and seen no sign of the car, it was "quite conceivable"
that he "would call Diana to find out where it was." Then
he could have simply followed Phillip from the office to the
beach on his own accord. But Balash did not remind the jury
that Brian and Rickey were already at the beach when Phillip
left work.

Balash concluded: "We submit to you that all of the evidence is just as consistent with the defendant's guilt only as
to an accessory after the murder as it is if she were involved

in the murder itself. It's all consistent with her overwhelming desire to protect Stephanie . . ."

In his customary fashion, McKinley had hardly objected the entire trial, even to the most obvious of hearsay testimony. As the jury began its deliberations on October 19, he could have been excused such confidence. Most of the trial had gone his way. One of the jurors appeared to be dozing off at times, but they were generally attentive.

Then something unexpected happened. One, two, three days went by, and there was no verdict. The jury asked to be read Jodie Davis's testimony; they asked for a transcript of Stephanie's. Still no verdict. By Wednesday, October 24, McKinley was reduced to a nerve-racking vigil in his office with Birchim. Diana's mother and four of her sisters, who had sat patiently through most of the trial, paced the corridor outside the courtroom.

Finally, after lunch on October 25, the jury trooped out of the deliberation room. They were hopelessly deadlocked, the forewoman announced—ten votes for first-degree murder, and two for second-degree. Judge Gordon had no choice but to declare a mistrial.

According to interviews with jurors, all twelve agreed after only two hours debate that Diana had lured her husband to the beach so he could be killed. The murder was, therefore, premeditated, and that meant a first-degree conviction. But before a straw vote was taken, one juror, a retired college professor named Harvey Young, balked. He couldn't vote for first-degree murder because it might mean the gas chamber.

As his fellow jurors reminded him, the judge had instructed them not to discuss sentencing during the guilt phase of the trial. But Young became more obdurate. He argued that Diana had not planned the murder—it was the idea of Stephanie and her druggie friends. On the final day, another juror joined Young in voting for second-degree.

But the mechanics of the jury's deadlock didn't matter to Diana and her family now. A broad smile on her face, she beamed at her equally jubilant sisters in the spectators' gallery. "We've been through hell, but I'm glad Diana will have another chance for a fair trial," Kathy Markwell told reporters.

"She'll definitely get a more fair trial the second time," said Margaret Ashlock, another sister.

Brian's Story

In late March 1991, Stephanie and Brian went on another "road trip." They traveled two hundred miles to San Diego—in a sheriff's van. It was not an excursion either would remember very fondly.

Stephanie hadn't wanted to go on the trip in the first place. Its purpose was so she could testify in the retrial of her mother, whose case had been transferred to San Diego after the hung jury in the first trial. Venue changes are rare in California—since 1983, the state's courts have granted an average of only fifteen such motions a year. But in Diana's case, both prosecution and defense agreed she could no longer find an impartial jury in Santa Barbara because of all the local publicity.

Stephanie's attitude toward testifying, not exactly enthusiastic in Santa Barbara, had soured in the intervening six months. For one thing, she no longer had the incentive of being a candidate for probation. Such a lenient sentence was a long shot anyway—probation for a murder conviction is almost unheard-of—but Stephanie was still hopeful because of her age, lack of prior criminal record, and a positive psychiatric evaluation.

On January 16 Judge Gordon dashed those hopes. He sentenced her to fifteen years to life in prison and spelled out his view of her culpability: "She certainly planned the commission of the crime. She helped instigate it, she solicited others to take part. I don't subscribe to the proposition . . . she did not actively participate . . . I don't believe she was forced into doing this, that she was coerced into doing this. She did it voluntarily and she did it actively."

The only thing in Stephanie's favor was that Gordon committed her to the California Youth Authority facility in Ventura

County, rather than a much tougher state prison.

Her fate decided, Stephanie just wanted to get on with her life. She certainly didn't want another ordeal on the witness stand in front of her mother. "I felt no anger," she recalled. "I felt no anything. If anything, I felt pity for her. I didn't want to be there [San Diego]. There was no tenseness, there was no 'I'm going to get you' in my mind . . . The second [trial], it was just, 'I don't want to be here, I can't go through this no more, I just want it to be over' . . . The second trial, I didn't care."

Stephanie also wasn't keen on spending time with Brian. At this point, her relationship with him no longer existed. All his talk when they were arrested—about how close they were and how all they had was each other—had turned out to be hollow.

In fact, things had started crumbling as early as the preliminary hearing when Brandon McLeod took the stand and revealed that he and Stephanie were talking about marrying when she got out of jail. After her plea bargain, Stephanie helped the case against Brian by telling detectives about his alleged plan to kill Sean Stanphill on the cow-shooting trip. Until then, none of the other cow shooters, not even Calvin and Jodie, had seen fit to mention that detail.

As for Brian, he had turned back to his first love, Rosalyn Bookout, writing her fervent letters and, on one occasion, enclosing two of his fingernails. "I just don't feel like me without 'em [the nails]," he wrote in his precise, microscopic script. "I feel as if a part of me is gone, but I'm sending them to people I love so they can have a part of me."

In one letter, he addressed her as "Mrs. Brian K.," boasted of how his guards had "built me up bigger than Al Capone," and attached a crude poem about venereal disease. At the end of another letter, he wrote, "PS: You won. Stephanie lost."

Much of a letter dated May 31, 1990, is devoted to Stephanie's "betrayal" of him:

> Just as Sampson [sic] was betrayed by Delila [sic] I have been betrayed and used by women in the same way. I don't know why I am the way I am. I guess I try too hard to help and end up being used . . . It's just not fair that I have to go through this because I wanted to help someone.

But the very next day, he sent a pleading letter to Stephanie in the women's wing of the jail:

> I read about us in the paper, they make us seem so evil . . . I think I would let them say whatever if they'd let you go home and let me hold you just one last time. That's all I ever wanted to do is just hold you and show you that I truly care for you . . .
> I wish you would write me and tell me where I stand with you, because you have me on pins and needles waiting for an answer from you . . .
> I really don't approve of you writing other guys, but I guess in your eyes I have no choice but to learn to live with it . . . Well I guess I should close. I just ask that you'll always remember, "I would die for you!"

Stephanie did not reply to that letter or any others he wrote her. And when they met in the sheriff's van to San Diego, she had an additional reason to ostracize him: He was going to testify in her mother's retrial.

In a sense, Brian owed his deal with the district attorney to the obstinacy of Harvey Young. Although McKinley was not pressing any panic buttons after the hung jury, he made some key strategic changes preparing for the retrial.

On February 6 he announced he was no longer seeking the death penalty for Diana and Brian. McKinley declined to explain this decision, citing office policy. But it is clear that, in Diana's case, the ultimate punishment would have been a tough sell to a jury.

In California the jury in the penalty phase of a capital murder case—when they choose to recommend either death or life without parole for the defendant—must consider aggravating and mitigating factors. Potentially the most aggravating aspect of Diana's case was her alleged plot to have her first husband murdered.

Again, however, the prosecution would have had problems getting the key testimony of Steve and Dwylene Allen admitted into evidence. They needed some corroboration—from whoever was solicited by Diana all those years ago or from someone who heard her make a solicitation. After a somewhat

perfunctory investigation, Washington state police had been
unable to locate any such persons. Without that evidence, it
would have been hard for McKinley to justify the time and
expense of trying another capital case in San Diego.

In Brian's case, the prosecution obviously could not seek the
death penalty for him while sparing Diana. That would have
conflicted with the prosecution's entire theory of the murder
that Diana was the linchpin.

Having taken that decision, it was still more imperative for
McKinley to fill any gaps in his case and convince a jury
beyond a reasonable doubt that Diana was the linchpin. The
key gap in the first trial was the lack of corroboration for the
phone calls Brian made in Santa Barbara on the morning of
the murder.

On January 29, 1991, Brian took McKinley and Birchim to
the Thrifty gas station to show them the pay phone he used
to call Stephanie and Diana. A few weeks before the retrial, McKinley's investigator finally discovered a long-distance
phone bill showing that Brian did call Stephanie collect at 7:38.
There was still no record of the next call to Diana, however.
The only way to present that to the jury was to have Brian
testify. McKinley could then back his testimony up with his
confession, which was not admissible in the first trial. Put that
alongside the jail note, in which Diana wrote about speaking
to Brian, and the result was potential dynamite.

On March 21—just days before the start of the retrial—
Brian signed what was, considering the evidence against him, a
very attractive deal. He pleaded no contest to first-degree murder. But McKinley dismissed the special allegations against
him. That meant a sentence of thirty-three years to life in prison—twenty-five for the murder, plus five because of his prior
burglary conviction, and another three for using a firearm. He
would be eligible for parole in twenty years.

Unlike Stephanie's case, Brian's deal did not include a stipu-
lation that he "testify truthfully if called by any party to this
action." In fact, he didn't have to testify at all. But, Brian said
later, "I wanted to testify so someone would hear my side of
the story instead of the lies that were being put out about me."

Moreover, Brian had given up his constitutional right against
self-incrimination by pleading in the case. So if the worst
happened and Brian refused to testify, he could be held in

contempt and lose all the time off his sentence he had earned during his eighteen months in the Santa Barbara jail.

As they traveled to San Diego, Stephanie wasn't interested in Brian's future. She confronted him about his deal, and he told her he was only going to testify about the key phone call and what happened on the beach. Then he blurted out the fact that he was not even compelled to take the stand. That really lit Stephanie's fuse.

"That shit ain't even funny," she told him. "What are you doing testifying when you don't have to? And you don't have to. That's wrong."

Brian shrugged. "I gave my word to my lawyer I would testify," he told her.

Stephanie was still fuming several months later. "He did not make a deal to testify against my mother; he chose to do it on his own," she told me. "Why anybody in their right mind would *want* to testify is beyond me . . . I was doing the same thing, but I was doing it because I *had* to, not because I wanted to."

In San Diego the case revolved around Brian, and this time Pat McKinley decided to put his star witness on as soon as possible.

Wearing jailhouse blues, spectacles, and a beard, his fingernails again like talons, Brian Stafford appeared in Department 24 of the San Diego Superior Court on April 2. It was only the third day of the trial. The first had been devoted to jury selection, a far speedier procedure than in Santa Barbara since this was no longer a capital case. The San Diego jury also consisted of seven women and five men. This group, however, was a lot more heterogeneous, including two blacks.

As Brian took the stand, the atmosphere was again quite different from that of the previous court proceeding. The pall of the death penalty having been lifted from the case, there was little of the tension that filled Judge Gordon's courtroom. In addition, where the Bogdanoff trial had been the only show in town in Santa Barbara, it was very much a sideshow in the huge San Diego courthouse. None of the San Diego media covered it—they were more interested in the trial of a serial killer down the corridor. The only regular spectators were

Diana's mother, three of her sisters, and a couple of curious senior citizens.

Another notable difference was the personality of the judge. Raymond Edwards, a black Republican appointed to the Superior Court in 1989, has an informal, affable manner reinforced by the mellifluous accent he has retained from his native South. When he starts a court day with "Good morning, ladies and gentlemen," it sounds like he is about to burst into song.

But McKinley was tense enough as he began his examination of Brian. It wasn't just the risk of presenting as a star witness someone who had killed in cold blood, someone who was unlikely to ingratiate himself with a jury. It was also that there was something very unpredictable about Brian. Lawyers aren't supposed to ask any questions in court to which they don't already know the answers. But you really couldn't be sure what Brian would say on the stand. Russ Birchim had interviewed him shortly before the trial, and he had come up with several unexpected answers.

Right away McKinley asked him: "On September twenty-first of 1989 . . . did you kill Phillip Bogdanoff on the beach in Santa Barbara?"

"Yes," he replied weakly.

"Before that date, did you ever personally meet the defendant, Diana Bogdanoff, face-to-face as opposed to talking on the phone?"

Brian fixed Diana, seated at the defense table in beige jacket, black skirt, and patterned blouse, with an intense stare. "No."

"Before Phillip was killed, did you ever meet him face-to-face?"

"Never saw the man a day in my life."

From then on, it was tough going for McKinley. For example, when he asked Brian to describe how Stephanie indicated to him "that her mom wanted you or someone to come over and kill Phillip," he got nowhere.

"I think it was, more or less, like her mom was, yeah, more or less, around in the area," Brian replied.

The prosecutor tried again, but Brian could only recall something like "if the dude was killed in his car, she would get the insurance from the state . . . I guess that's the one key thing that just comes to the top of my head. But it would take me time, and I'm quite sure these people [the jury] don't have that kind of time."

In his testimony, Brian blatantly contradicted common sense or other key witnesses such as Stephanie and Jodie. For example, he maintained that he formed no definite plan to go to Santa Barbara to kill Phillip until he went to bed with Stephanie the night before at around 11:00 P.M.:

> We're laying in bed and we're sitting there and we're talking. You can tell if a person that you care about is hurting about something. And I asked her, "What's wrong?" She was telling me she was worried about her mom. And I thought about it for a minute and I asked her, "Do you really think the dude is going to hurt her?" meaning Phillip Bogdanoff.
>
> And she said, "I just want him to leave her alone. I want him to stop hurting my mom." I said, "What do you want done?"

He didn't say precisely what Stephanie replied. Whatever it was, he told her, "I'll give you that." He then went into the living room and told Rickey they were taking their "road trip."

Of course, this made no sense if Calvin and Jodie had been invited to the apartment some six hours earlier to provide an alibi for him. In an unconvincing explanation, Brian claimed that Stephanie brought them over "without me knowing about it . . . As far as I remember, I don't remember calling for Calvin and Jodie."

Most bizarre of all, Brian now testified that he was not absolutely certain he fired the first, nonfatal shot on the beach. "I know for certain that I fired the second shot . . . But the first shot, I don't remember firing. But I was the only one with the gun, to my knowledge, so it would be me on both shots."

After three and a half grueling hours, McKinley finished his direct examination. Questioning Brian, his own witness, had been like pulling teeth. Now, would Brian drop any more bombshells under cross-examination?

Verdict

Brian's direct testimony had given the defense a ray of hope. For example, the "first shot" scenario might seem a red herring in the wider context of the case—Brian had admitted firing the second, fatal shot. But it could bolster Diana's credibility. Maybe it was true, after all, that she saw a white guy shoot her husband. Maybe it was Rickey who fired the first shot.

Balash went straight for that opening. Referring to Brian's pretrial interview with Birchim, he asked: "Did you tell the officer that you can't understand how you fired the first shot, because Rickey would have been in the way?"

"True."

"And to your knowledge, Rickey was not hit with any bullets, is that right?"

"Correct."

Brian also estimated he was thirty yards away from Phillip when the first shot was fired, marksmanship that was almost inconceivable with a weapon such as a Jennings .22. Balash suggested he was protecting his friend Rickey by accepting responsibility for both shots. Brian denied that.

Continuing his cross-examination on April 3, the defense lawyer reiterated the theory of the first trial—that Stephanie induced Brian to commit the murder without any direct input from her mother. "Prior to September twenty-first, 1989, Mrs. Bogdanoff had never asked you directly to kill Phillip Bogdanoff, is that correct?" he asked Brian.

"That's correct."

"Prior to the twenty-first of September, 1989, all statements concerning either finding someone to kill Phillip Bogdanoff or taking him out or killing him—those all came from Stephanie, is that correct?"

"It came from Stephanie while she was on the phone."

A key part of Stephanie's sales pitch to Brian was supposed to be that she was raped by Phillip. You would kill child molesters, wouldn't you, Balash asked?

A: No, I wouldn't go to that extreme. I just can't stand them.

Q: Would you hurt them?

A: . . . With my hands I'm very capable of it.

Q: Okay. And so anybody that knows you knows that's one thing that will really get you fired up, is that if you believe someone is a child molester, right?

A: Yeah.

Balash returned to exploring the mysteries of what happened in bed the night before the murder, and who fired the first shot. Brian obliged with a combination of obfuscation and improbable detail.

When he told Stephanie, "I'll give you that," what precisely was he going to give her? Balash asked.

A: The thing that she had been asking for, that she said her mother had been calling and asking her for all of this time.

Q: Okay. If you would, would you tell me what was it you intended to give her.

A: I intended to grant her request.

Q: What you intended to give her was the death of Phillip Bogdanoff, correct?

A: Yeah.

He was ready to give her that because, only a couple of months into their relationship, he loved Stephanie so much. "I would have given the girl anything she wanted." He also gave her his "word" during their pillow talk. Once he did that, he was held to it—keeping his word being the third item on his moral checklist.

Even so, when he and Rickey got to Santa Barbara, nothing was certain. "It's not like anything was planned . . . It wasn't like I was trying to have everything set up and prepared to go do this . . . It wasn't set in anyone's mind that the killing was going to take place on that day."

As for the mysterious first shot, Brian now said it may have been fired as he jumped off a rock while the gun was wrapped in his T-shirt. He was in midair when he heard the shot. "I don't know where it came from."

In perhaps the most dramatic moment of the entire trial, Balash, hoping to rattle the witness, had Brian reenact how he fired the second shot. Armed with a toy pistol this time, Brian stepped down from the stand as if he were being led to the guillotine.

As Diana looked away, Balash held up a polystyrene bust of a head. "Let's say this is Mr. Bogdanoff's head. Tell me where to place it, and you show me how you shot him."

"Is it really necessary?" Brian moaned.

Brian pointed the muzzle of the toy at the bust's left temple. "Okay. You put the gun against his head and pulled the trigger, correct?"

He answered "Yes" so feebly that Judge Edwards made him repeat it.

Balash then asked Brian to explain how both shell casings could be found within inches of the body. Another incredible answer: "If the [first] shot was fired while I was in the air, the T-shirt would have still been on the gun. So it could have gotten wrapped in my T-shirt. And when I came up and removed the T-shirt and shot the second shot, it would have fell on the ground."

Again, Brian denied that it was actually Rickey who fired the first shot and who then handed him the gun so he could finish Phillip off.

After some four hours of cross-examination, McKinley used his redirect to discredit his own witness. He ridiculed the first-shot scenario. "It would be a heck of a shot, wouldn't it, to hit Phillip [from thirty yards], and Rickey standing maybe between you and Phillip, correct?"

"I believe in destiny and fate. Have you ever heard—"

McKinley interrupted him. "Yes, I've heard of destiny and fate," he said derisively.

Apart from his lawyer, had he told anyone else—friends or detectives—this story about the first shot? Apart from Diana's statement that she saw a white guy with the gun, was there any other evidence pointing to Rickey firing that shot? On both counts, Brian answered, "No." A few minutes later, he stepped down.

Brian had told his "side of the story." He suggested that he was not a cold-blooded killer, that the murder happened almost by accident, and that he killed for love and honor. But in the process, he lost any credibility.

Certainly the murder was not meticulously planned. In some ways, the conspirators made the "Gang Who Couldn't Shoot Straight" look like professional assassins. The itinerary Brian and Rickey followed in Santa Barbara that day did not make a lot of sense. Why, if the die was cast when Diana called Stephanie on September 20, did they stake out the trailer park at dawn, place the phone calls at the Thrifty station, and then spend four hours making a spectacle of themselves at the beach?

There may have been some method in this madness, however. According to Stephanie, the killers went to Santa Barbara with a menu of options. Plan A was for another freeway ambush, preferably at El Capitan when Phillip left for work. Plan B was to catch up with him later in the day when he was with his wife. In the September 20 call, as Stephanie testified, Diana told her they would "*either* be at the beach *or* the golf course [italics added]." Stephanie also said "they might be going golfing if they didn't go to the beach." Their choice would depend on the weather.

After Plan A failed on September 21, Brian would need to find out from Stephanie or her mother whether he should go to the golf course or the beach. Although he was already supposed to know how to get to the beach, maybe he asked Diana for directions again to refresh his memory or to avoid any further screwups.

Most puzzling is Brian and Rickey's behavior at the beach. In California, lying in wait is defined as "waiting and watching for an opportune time to act, together with a concealment . . . to take the [victim] by surprise." Chasing sand crabs and accosting fishermen certainly doesn't seem to fit that definition. As Brian's lawyer put it in a legal brief, "They were not waiting and watching for the purpose of taking the victim unawares . . . There was nothing in their conduct which suggested secrecy or stealth."

But the way they behaved on the beach was consistent with the way they and their friends had behaved the entire summer. In their fantasy world of drugs, feuding, and cow shooting, they wore a cloak of invulnerability, of freedom from responsibility for their actions. Brian, Calvin, and Gator were all on probation for past offenses, but they violated their probation virtually every day. It was *now* that mattered, not *later*.

James Oliver captured this attitude. "Just about everything we did was on the moment," he said. "Somebody would say, 'Well, let's go do this.' It was like, 'Yeah, why not? Let's go.' We were up and gone."

Brian was up and gone on September 21, wearing his cloak on the beach. Maybe it was the same Brian who, in his burglary case, called a cab to transport the booty, and who showed up at court with marijuana in his coat pocket.

Brian's professions that he simply killed for love of Stephanie also do not stand up to much scrutiny. "He couldn't have been in love that quick," Calvin said. "I find it very hard to believe over a two-month period he loved her the way you'd think he'd have to, to kill for her."

"Love, I would say, had probably absolutely zero to do with it," James said. Recalling the way Brian and Stephanie were together, he added: "If you guys are sitting there and enjoying the evening, and friends come over and they want to take off and go do something, you either ask her to go along or you ask if it's okay if you can go. Brian never did that [with Stephanie]. He was just, see ya, out the door. She would just sit there, fine, 'bye."

Stephanie herself testified in Santa Barbara: "I just can't see him doing it for love. I had that implanted in my mind at the time. A lot of people were telling me that. Well, not a lot of people, but Jodie in particular." She didn't know about "this so-called love" until she was in jail and Brian started writing her passionate letters.

The couple were not "committed" to each other in the usual sense of the word. While they were living together, they

had trysts with their previous partners—Brandon McLeod and
Rosalyn Bookout. In fact, Stephanie told me that Brian even
knew about her attachment to Brandon.

One day, she said, Brandon upset her by kissing another girl
in front of her. When she got home, she told Brian about the
incident. "I told him, 'That really hurt my feelings, because I
still love him.' Brian knew I still loved him, he knew it the
whole time because I told him. It was never something I could
hide from him. It was obvious. Brandon called my apartment
a lot."

If not love, how about money? After all, Brian was originally charged with murder for financial gain. But Calvin's
testimony about him getting half Phillip's estate was unsub-
stantiated, and the El Camino payoff wasn't exactly the most
glittering of prizes. Maybe the most convincing motive for
Brian was power—or the lack of it.

Long before he discovered crank, Brian embarked on a
"power trip." From trying to be a tank boss at the Kern County
jail, he graduated to trying to be a black Al Capone. Possibly as
early as 1988, he was ready to use violence to achieve power.
With crank he was able to make himself the power center of a
circle of less intelligent, less assertive delinquents. The fantasy
was becoming his reality.

But by late September 1989, his power was eroding. Even
members of his "family" had subverted him, their loyalty as
brittle as the crank so many of them snorted. Calvin helped
abort the shotgun trip, and Gator helped frustrate the cow-
shooting trip by taking Sean Stanphill home. When he taped
Calvin's name to a shotgun shell, Jodie just laughed. His mor-
tal enemy, Shalamar Fields, was still hanging around Rosalyn
and Kerisha. And the drug business was crumbling under the
weight of his own excessive consumption and that of his
friends. "He was virtually broke toward the end of all this,"
Rosalyn said. Maybe by killing Phillip, he could reverse the
erosion.

"He was always out proving himself, how good he was, how
much power he had over somebody," said James. "It wouldn't
surprise me at all if he just wanted to do it just to show people,
don't cross him."

What did surprise James was that Brian did the shooting
himself. "I didn't expect him to be the one standing there and

pulling the trigger. I figured it would be Rickey. You could say he was like the boss . . . So I kind of figured Brian would have somebody else pull the trigger."

Stephanie couldn't figure it either. "I never asked Brian to *do* it," she insisted. "I asked Brian for help finding somebody to do it." Rickey was their man—or, at least, so Brian told her. But what if Rickey really had another role?

It may not be coincidental that when Brian demonstrated his power in Bakersfield, he always made sure his friends were there to see it. When he fought Chuck Blankenship, James, and Shalamar, his friends were in the audience. Their reports helped build his reputation. On the beach in Santa Barbara, the "shadow" was his audience. When they returned to Bakersfield and Brian boasted about the murder, Rickey backed him up by showing the blood on the gun.

And when, the night after the murder, Diana talked to Stephanie, she told her that it was Brian who came up to them on the beach and asked for something. What reason would she have to lie to Stephanie if it was really Rickey?

Brian was still clinging to his delusions of grandeur in the Santa Barbara jail. Two excerpts from his letters to Rosalyn highlight this. On May 31, 1990, he wrote:

I also heard that Gator's supose [sic] to be a high-roller now and Mike his brother is now a smoker. Isn't it rather ironic the way things have been happening since I've been in jail? It seems as if I was the one person holding Bakersfield together on all sides.

The following July, he wrote:

Listen, Rosalyn, I love you and my daughter more than you will ever know, and more than words can say, but if anyone was to ever touch you or my daughter, they'd put themselves in a cross, for it would hurt me, therefore my family would get involved, so if anyone does anything to you, just send them to me.

Had Brian done anything to bolster the prosecution's case? After the trial, McKinley himself castigated Brian's performance in a letter to the probation department.

He stated that the "incredible and false" testimony about the first shot "demonstrates that the defendant has not truly realized the enormity of his action in setting out to deliberately kill Phillip, and doing it. These lies . . . seem to me to be simply a pre-trial ploy, attempting to get away from the idea of premeditation and deliberation. Nothing in the facts squares with this ridiculous version . . . At the time of this defendant's arrest, he made no such statement, and in fact admitted his involvement in shooting Phillip twice."

Although Brian had already been sentenced, he wanted the letter included in his probation report "so that in twenty years, when this defendant comes up for parole, the parole board will be aware of the falsehoods contained in his trial testimony following his plea of guilty."

Unless Brian comes "to grips with the fact that he is the person responsible for Phillip's death," McKinley concluded, "I believe he should remain incarcerated in prison forever."

But there were two key redeeming features about Brian's testimony. One was that he corroborated the Thrifty phone call to Diana and described it in detail to the jury. Balash didn't even bother cross-examining him on it. The other was that because he testified, his taped confession was now admissible. "Our whole theory was what [Brian and Stephanie] said on the day of the arrests was the truth," McKinley explained. "His testimony, I think, didn't mean that much. His tape meant something."

The rest of the trial differed little from the first one in Santa Barbara. For many of the prosecution witnesses, it was their third time on the stand, and the novelty had worn off. Al Clarke even told McKinley outside the courtroom that he was contemplating suicide. Stephanie, as expected, was a study in indifference, her answers perfunctory at best.

Balash sometimes seemed to be going through the motions. Where he had cross-examined witnesses at laborious length in the earlier proceedings, his questioning was now cursory. Presenting his own case, he did not risk calling Christine Allen. His new witnesses—the chaplain who consoled Diana after the murder, the golf pro at the course the Bogdanoffs patronized, Linda Swanson—made minor contributions.

He said later that he actually felt the tide turn against him when McKinley dropped the death penalty against Diana. "There's a certain intensity about death penalty cases. The jury pays attention to everything. They have just an awesome responsibility." After the San Diego jury heard Brian's testimony about the key phone call and his taped confession, Balash decided to concentrate on laying the groundwork for an appeal of a murder conviction.

If there was tension, it revolved around whether he would call the defendant to testify. In the immediate euphoria after the hung jury in Santa Barbara, he told reporters he was seriously considering it. Three months later, he had Diana take a lie detector test to indicate how she might fare on the stand. The results, he said, were encouraging. Diana herself was anxious to testify.

But she never did. Balash told me he talked her out of it as the retrial unfolded. "It was a tough judgment call," he said. "We would have destroyed the case as far as an appeal goes if she had testified. Normally, when a defendant testifies, all the other issues go out of the window. It's just, does the jury believe the defendant? The DA's whole case would have been Diana Bogdanoff on the stand."

The jury began deliberating on Thursday, May 2, and resumed the following Monday. McKinley told me he was uncertain about the special allegations, particularly financial gain. The jury could only convict Diana of that if they considered it was her primary motive. The prosecutor thought they might say, "Okay, convict her of this, convict of that, but she was getting the shit kicked out of her, so maybe money wasn't the primary motive for the killing." Maybe the jury would give something to both sides.

It took the jurors only eight hours to make their minds up. At 4:00 P.M. on May 6, they announced they had reached a verdict. "At least it's not a hung jury," McKinley told Birchim as the jurors filed into the courtroom.

The bailiff handed the verdict forms to Judge Edwards. The judge took so long to read them that McKinley feared the worst. "Holy shit, this is going to be bad," he thought, his heart pounding "like I'm sprinting on a bike ride."

At last the forms went to the clerk to be read. McKinley had badly misread the judge. Diana was found guilty of first-degree murder and both the special allegations. All the strategy targeting Diana as the linchpin, all the plea bargaining, all the immune witnesses—it had paid off. The prosecutor felt like running out of the courtroom and screaming his head off.

Meanwhile, Diana dabbed her eyes with a Kleenex and asked the bailiff if she could hug her mother. In the gallery, one of her sisters vented her disgust. "I don't know how you can sleep at night," she yelled at McKinley. That didn't bother him: He and the detectives had got their ducks in a row.

"Without Natural Affection"

The jury's verdict was resounding. Diana Bogdanoff had committed the ultimate crime in the most cold-blooded manner imaginable. It wasn't just the "lying in wait," the way she lured her husband to the beach, spotted his killers, lay down naked beside him, told him to go to sleep, and then watched the whole side of his head go into the sand. It was also the way she calmly ate lunch after Phillip got home from work.

Several months after her conviction, Steve Balash pondered the implications and shook his head. "That's about as cold as you can possibly get," he said. "I find it really hard to believe she could have done it."

"Some people *are* that cold," Pat McKinley said, pointing out how some wives have poisoned their husbands and sat watching as the victims breathed their last.

But Diana didn't do anything in the privacy of her trailer. She could have laced Phillip's drink with painkillers. She could have shot him during an argument and claimed it was self-defense—detectives found a loaded shotgun beside the bed in the trailer. McKinley told me he might not have prosecuted her if such had been the case. Was Diana so desperate, so traumatized by Phillip's battering, that she had to turn to others? Did she have to weave a web of conspiracy that entangled so many others' lives?

Stephanie thinks so. "She was desperate," she told me. "She wanted it done . . . She didn't have it in her to do it. She loved him . . . She didn't have it in her to kill him herself. She couldn't kill anybody herself, just like I couldn't. If you gave me a gun and expected me to kill somebody because he was doing something wrong to me, I would have never killed him. Maybe I would have knocked him out and ran, but I never

328

would have shot him. I mean, that's serious. Having somebody else do it, that's different."

Her father had another theory. The method of Phillip's murder reminds Steve Allen of his ex-wife's penchant for elaborate scheming. "I can see her doing this, the same as I can see her walking into a tavern and saying, 'I'll pay you guys five hundred dollars to knock this guy off,' and never think what's going to happen to these two guys if they get caught. Of course, they would never get caught. She's that smart."

The plot against Phillip might have been the pinnacle of her cleverness. "It was 'I'll manipulate all these people and we'll make it work and I won't even be involved.' Any dumb person can pick up a shotgun and shoot somebody. It doesn't require being clever."

But if Diana did concoct so convoluted a scheme, how does that square with the portrait of a battered woman? As described by Dr. Boyd, Diana was so lacking in self-esteem, so dependent, self-defeating, and histrionic, she could hardly think straight. Either she really wasn't involved in the plot— or she really wasn't battered.

Gary Wymore was unequivocal. Diana would tell Phillip "to jump in the lake and leave" if he beat her, Wymore said. "I don't believe he did [beat her]. I'm not saying he might have not cuffed her one, backhanded her or something like that. But as far as beating her, no, she wouldn't have put up with that.

"I think that battered-wife thing . . . was the only way she felt she had an out. If she had him killed, she figured that would get her off the hook."

Diana could be quite assertive, her second husband said. He recalled an incident when they were at a bar and another woman made a pass at him. After Diana found out, "she was going to take this girl outside. She's a soft-spoken person, but she wouldn't have hesitated to go outside with her."

Wymore's daughter, Stacy Stewart, agreed. "Diana could take care of herself," she said. "She would have just went off and found somebody else if he beat her." Stewart said she laughed when she heard reports that Phillip broke Diana's nose. "Her nose has always been like that."

Some of his friends do not believe Phillip could have been a batterer or an alcoholic. "I know alcohol, I know the stages, I know how the decline starts," said Tommy Byford, whose late brother was an alcoholic. "Phillip maintained his jobs. The last times that I saw him, he would have a beer . . . but not at all in excess." Interestingly, the autopsy on Phillip found no trace of liver disease. Of course, he may have had an unusual metabolism. But it is surprising that the copious consumption attributed to him by Diana and Stephanie left no organic imprint.

There is independent evidence that Phillip beat his wife. Residents at El Capitan heard them fighting, workers on the freeway project saw her with facial bruises, her physician in Visalia treated her for a concussion. Dr. Boyd could not have been completely fooled. What may be closest to the truth is that Diana exaggerated the abuse, at least when she spoke to her impressionable daughter.

By the time of the murder, Stephanie was convinced that her mother was being beaten regularly, maybe as often as weekly, and that her life was in danger. But the defense was unable to find any specific instance of abuse after the Dominguez incident, four months before the killing. Diana never reported any abuse to the police or availed herself of the many services now available to battered women, such as twenty-four-hour hot lines or shelters.

Most startling of all, Dr. Boyd testified that Diana told her Phillip only threatened her obliquely. The psychologist couldn't recall how Diana phrased it. It was something like, "if she told the doctor the cause of her injuries, she might not make it back from the hospital."

"Nothing along the lines of 'If you ever try and leave me, I'm going to kill you'?" McKinley asked.

"I don't believe he made that direct threat."

The San Diego jury found that Diana had a simple reason for putting up with whatever abuse she did suffer. It was money. But what in the marital kitty was so desirable?

The prosecution established that Phillip was a man of modest wealth, who had saved and invested quite shrewdly over the years. But the defense showed that sorting out his financial affairs would tax expert legal minds. He never reached a settlement with Barbara, his second wife, leaving the disposition of many assets unclear, and he apparently never got around to drafting a will. As Balash said at the Santa Barbara trial,

"Diana Bogdanoff is supposed to have figured it out ahead of time what she's going to get, and two lawyers and a CPA haven't been able to tell us yet."

But there was one asset that shone bright through the fiscal fog: the house in Visalia. The stucco bungalow in that small central California town was more than just a house for Diana. It was the incarnation of the material dream she had struggled for so long to realize.

As her history shows, Diana fell off a plateau of middle-class comfort and security into a chasm of hardship and privation. During her first two marriages, she struggled to return to the higher ground, allegedly even scheming against her husbands to achieve that goal. If not a "black widow," she was auditioning to play a gray one. After her divorces, she was left with little or nothing, and by the time she met Phillip, she had reached rock bottom.

Phillip enabled her to regain the plateau. More than that, with the purchase of the old family home, she had something unique, something her sisters didn't have. "That would be her chance to get some respect," McKinley said. "It would be 'I'm not so bad, you see I have a house now,' instead of 'We're living in a trailer and we have to walk down the street to take a shower.' "

Maybe she did at one time genuinely love Phillip. But almost as soon as she got her name on the house, she started plotting against him. By the summer of 1989, she may well have wanted out of the marriage, but the house made divorce a very unattractive option.

Diana had seen for herself what a stubborn and wily divorce opponent Phillip could be. She knew about his battle with Barbara, and she even testified on Phillip's behalf at the hearing in the case on May 26, 1989. As McKinley said, divorcing Phillip would have meant "a long, drawn-out court fight, and fighting for her life over the Visalia house."

But if that was the case, why did she need to have Phillip killed so urgently? If she wasn't going to sue him for divorce, surely she could have taken her time, built up some more equity in the house, and then made her move. Why was she in such a hurry in the summer of 1989?

One possibility is that there was now a danger of Phillip leaving her or throwing her out. Maybe the talk about "She gives it to me too bad, I'll just look for my fourth wife" was serious. Rogena Nutt testified that the incident in which Phillip told Diana she could leave and go live with her daughter happened "just a few weeks prior to the murder."

In the week of the murder, the danger may have been particularly acute. Phillip confronted Diana after learning of her daughter's eviction, and she denied knowing about it. But he was planning to go up to Bakersfield that weekend for his showdown with Stephanie. He would no doubt have seen her landlord to recover the deposit. What if he found out the truth about the eviction? The loss of his trust could have been devastating to Diana.

"He didn't want Diane protecting her [Stephanie] without telling him, he didn't want her hiding something from him," said Chris Norton, Phillip's friend. "Like I said, don't screw him, be right up-front with him."

The importance of the Visalia house was not lost on the jurors in Santa Barbara, who voted to convict Diana of first-degree murder. "The financial part was not so much the money but that house," said Phoebe Klaes. "It was her way of being superior in the family. She was terribly insecure. Her sisters were all good and she was evil."

It was also not lost on her daughter. In perhaps her most remarkable insight, Stephanie told detectives on the day after her arrest: "She always used to tell me that she's getting old and she wouldn't have anything if she left Phillip. She would have nothing. She wouldn't have the Visalia house. And that Visalia house means more to my mother than anything. It means more to her than me."

In an interview for this book, Stephanie backtracked a little from that statement. "I think it's neck and neck," she said. "I think she'd probably let the house burn down before she let somebody burn me up, if it came down to it. But it's pretty close."

Behind that statement lurks perhaps the most disturbing aspect of this case. Diana did let her daughter burn.

Of course, as Stephanie now admits, she could have taken control of her own fate and just said no. "I believe she put me in the position where I was at, but I also believe I was stupid enough to go along with it . . . I could have at some time just said, 'This is crazy, let's just get out of this whole situation,' but I didn't. I just went along with it. That's what got me where I am today, and it's my fault, not anybody else's."

But the fact remains that Diana relentlessly played on Stephanie's sensitivities—her vulnerability, her need for family, her capacity for love—even after Stephanie attempted suicide in January 1989. In the process, Diana turned her daughter into almost a carbon copy of herself. Stephanie also learned to manipulate men she didn't love, Brian Stafford and Tim Gray. The one she did love, Brandon McLeod, she left alone. And she was also ready to commit the ultimate evil.

Then, after the murder, Diana pinned her defense on Stephanie's guilt. Even after she was convicted, she told her probation officer that Stephanie was to blame: "I was a woman who had been severely battered for years by Phillip Bogdanoff. I asked my daughter, Stephanie Allen, for help because I did not know where else to turn. Stephanie and Brian Stafford decided that the best way to help me would be to kill Phillip."

Diana said she "never asked anyone to kill Phillip." The only thing she asked Stephanie to do was "help me to calm Phillip down"; for example, by leading a quieter life-style in Bakersfield. Her daughter was just "very confused."

If the recollections of those who knew her in Washington are correct, Diana was always that cold toward her daughter. But how could she be that way?

Dwylene Allen, one of the most articulate people interviewed for this book, struggled for an answer to that question. As she noted, Diana's background—the cozy embrace of her family, the stress on family of the United Pentecostal Church—doesn't explain it. Dwylene had to turn to the Bible for help.

She pointed out a passage, II Timothy 3:1-3, that describes human behavior in the last days before the Resurrection. You don't have to be a believer to see a certain appropriateness not only to Diana's behavior but to that of many of those involved in the case of Phillip Bogdanoff:

This know also, that in the last days perilous times shall come. For men shall be lovers of their own selves, covetous, boasters, proud, blasphemers, disobedient to parents, unthankful, unholy, without natural affection.

A Last Act of Loyalty

There would be one final bizarre twist in the mother-daughter relationship.

On June 5, 1991, Diana returned to Department 24 of the San Diego Superior Court for sentencing. It was supposed to be a virtual formality. The jury's verdict of first-degree murder with the special allegations had left Judge Raymond Edwards with little room for leniency. The probation officer recommended that "the defendant be committed to the Department of Corrections for the total term of life without possibility of parole."

Steve Balash opened the hearing by asking for a new trial. Diana did not get a fair trial, he argued, because the judge failed to give the jury the choice of convicting her of the lesser crime of voluntary manslaughter. In California the crime is defined as an intentional killing without malice aforethought. There is no malice "if the killing occurred upon a sudden quarrel or heat of passion" and the passion was sufficiently provoked.

According to Balash, the repeated battering by Phillip may have been sufficient to provoke Diana's passion. But Judge Edwards, citing the Aris case extensively, ruled that "it was quite impossible that this could have been a voluntary manslaughter. There was absolutely no evidence that the defendant was operating under some heat of passion . . . that deprived her of her reason at the time of the crime. In fact, the evidence was quite to the contrary."

Rebuffed on that front, Balash now had a chance to present mitigating evidence for his client. For that he turned to the lip-biting girl in the jury box.

Some thought Stephanie was there out of guilt. After all, she had ostensibly testified "against" her mother and helped convict her. But she had always been ambivalent about incriminating her. Moreover, at the first trial, she said she would try to save Diana from the gas chamber—"I know that I can at least say that I do love her, and that I don't want her to die." That same loyalty compelled her to come to San Diego to plead on her mother's behalf.

"I went to make the statement 'I don't want her to go to prison forever,' " she told me. "I was there for the one reason, and the one reason was for my mother . . . I came out of concern and love for my mom."

Balash asked Stephanie only five questions. But she was so nervous that she had trouble articulating her answers. What came out was brief and somewhat predictable.

Her mother was "uncertain, desperate" at the time of the murder, she said; financial gain had nothing to do with it; there was "no set plan as to what was going to happen." What did she think of the fairness of her mother getting life without parole? "I don't think it's fair at all . . . I was more at fault for what I did as the middle person. I knew more [about the murder] than she did."

Balash followed with his final plea. "A battered woman that acts as a battered woman does not deserve life without parole," he said. Diana dabbed her eyes as her lawyer argued that at least a sentence of twenty-five years to life would give her "something tangible," a hope that someday she could put prison behind her.

McKinley was withering in his rebuttal: "My thought on this case is, she should be locked up forever. The only thing that might change that is if she said, 'Yeah, I did it. I was fed up.' She hasn't said that." As far as any remorse, "we don't have that yet."

Diana then got her chance to speak but used it only to reinforce what McKinley had just said. "Do you want to say anything?" Edwards asked. She paused as if about to launch into a speech, but Balash hastily began conferring with her. The conference lasted three minutes, Diana's murmur the only sound in the courtroom. Balash got a five-minute recess from the judge to continue talking to her.

After the recess, Edwards repeated his invitation. Diana's first public statement, delivered in a quavering voice, was brief.

"I don't feel I'm guilty of these charges, and the motion for a new trial should be granted," she said as Balash despairingly shook his head.

"Why don't you feel you're guilty?" the judge shot back. Elaborating, he referred to her phone conversation with Brian the morning of the murder, the testimony of her daughter, of Tim Gray, Brandon McLeod, and Al Clarke.

"I advise my client not to answer," Balash interjected.

As expected, Judge Edwards gave her the maximum penalty under the law—life without parole. He also ordered her to pay ten thousand dollars in restitution. With a curt "Good luck, Miss Bogdanoff," Edwards concluded the hearing.

Stephanie had already departed by then. During the five-minute recess, she was taken back to the holding cells. But on her way out of the courtroom, she was allowed to pause in the doorway leading to the judge's chambers, giving her an unobstructed view of her mother at the defense table. She stared wistfully at Diana, but her mother, deep in conversation with Balash, did not notice her.

"It felt like I would never see her again," Stephanie told me later. "I still feel that way. It's never left."

I asked her what she would say to her mother if she did see her again. Without hesitating, she replied: "That I love her." She laughed and added: "Because I do. I miss her. That's the only person I've ever really known . . . I feel lost a little bit, not having her there, not having her to ask questions, just not having her. It's my mom."

Epilogue:
They Shot Cows,
Didn't They?

Since they drove up Round Mountain Road that September night in 1989, the ten cow shooters have scattered far and wide. Three are serving time in state penal institutions for their roles in the Bogdanoff murder; six of the others have been incarcerated for crimes ranging from arson and assault to drunk driving and drug dealing.

Calvin Monigan was paroled in early 1993 after serving half of his six-year sentence on the arson and child molestation charges.

Gator Bohlinger and **Sean Stanphill** were arrested together in Bakersfield in October 1991. At the time, Gator was driving his car, and Sean was his passenger. Police found crank in Gator's fanny-pack and a loaded .22-caliber pistol under his seat.

In January 1992, Gator was sentenced to six months in jail on a gun charge and put on probation for three years. In a letter to the judge, his parents wrote that his "biggest problem was the choice of company he has kept in the past. Charles has indicated to us that he intends to eliminate any contact with persons who could possibly be a negative influence to him. We in no way agree with some of the people he has associated with in the past, but as his parents will always stand behind him. Charles is not a bad person, but has been in the wrong place at the wrong time, with the wrong company."

Sean also had crank in his fanny-pack when he was arrested. He confessed to police that he had been selling the drug for two weeks. In March 1992, he was sentenced to two years in state prison for possession of crank with intent to sell. He was paroled in late 1992.

Chad Swanson and his brother **Travis** were arrested in Old River in October 1990 after assaulting their parents. At one point, Linda Swanson hit Travis over the head with the butt of a handgun. As he continued choking her husband, she fired one shot over his head. The brothers were sentenced to forty-five days in jail and three years probation.

In August 1992 the Swansons pled guilty to charges involving violence against women. Chad was sentenced to 180 days in jail and three years probation for assaulting his wife and for possession of marijuana; Travis got thirty days in jail and three years probation for threatening a woman.

In December 1992 Travis was charged with causing corporal injury to his spouse.

Rickey Lee Rodgers pleaded no contest on June 20, 1991, to voluntary manslaughter for his role in the killing of Phillip Bogdanoff. Pat McKinley felt he had a murder case against Rickey: "He provided the gun. His presence was some encouragement [to Brian] . . . He drove [back to Bakersfield], fled the area, and got rid of the gun."

But the DA also felt that Rickey had less to do with the murder than his codefendants. "We got the main players, starting with Diana and Brian because he pulled the trigger . . . Stephanie was hitting up on Tim Gray and was involved in this for more than nine months. Rickey just appeared on the scene thirty days before this happened."

Rickey is serving a ten-year sentence at a state prison in northern California. He specifically requested that he not be "housed anywhere close to Brian Stafford as he feels there may be a vendetta involved."

Brian Stafford is serving his sentence for first-degree murder at the Tehachapi state prison, a maximum security facility.

Stephanie Allen is described as a model inmate at the Youth Authority. When she is twenty-five, she will be transferred to a state prison, possibly the women's facility in Chowchilla, near

Fresno, where her mother is incarcerated. She will be eligible for parole in 1999.

Jodie Davis was arrested in Bakersfield in March 1991 for drunk driving. After failing to appear for her original court hearing in April 1991, she pled guilty in September 1992 and was sentenced to serve two days in jail and to attend a DUI program.

When I asked Jodie what she had learned from the Bogdanoff case, she said: "It teaches me well who to trust and who not to trust. People you may think are normal aren't so normal after all." Does that mean her friends were normal? "They weren't that unusual . . . It all depends on which way you look at it."

Compelling True Crime Thrillers
From Avon Books

BADGE OF BETRAYAL
by Joe Cantlupe and Lisa Petrillo

76009-6/$4.99 US/$5.99 Can

GUN FOR HIRE:
THE SOLDIER OF FORTUNE KILLINGS
by Clifford L. Linedecker

76204-8/$4.99 US/$5.99 Can

LOSS OF INNOCENCE:
A TRUE STORY OF JUVENILE MURDER
by Eric J. Adams   75987-X/$4.95 US/$5.95 Can

RUBOUTS: MOB MURDERS IN AMERICA
by Richard Monaco and Lionel Bascom

75938-1/$4.50 US/$5.50 Can

GOOMBATA:
THE IMPROBABLE RISE AND FALL OF
JOHN GOTTI AND HIS GANG
by John Cummings and Ernest Volkman

71487-6/$5.50 US/$6.50 Can

The Best in Biographies from Avon Books

IT'S ALWAYS SOMETHING
by Gilda Radner   71072-2/$5.95 US/$6.95 Can

JACK NICHOLSON: THE UNAUTHORIZED BIOGRAPHY *by Barbara and Scott Siegel*
                    76341-9/$4.50 US/$5.50 Can

STILL TALKING
by Joan Rivers   71992-4/$5.99 US/$6.99 Can

CARY GRANT: THE LONELY HEART
by Charles Higham and Roy Moseley
                    71099-9/$5.99 US/$6.99 Can

I, TINA
by Tina Turner with Kurt Loder
                    70097-2/$4.95 US/$5.95 Can

ONE MORE TIME
by Carol Burnett   70449-8/$4.95 US/$5.95 Can

PATTY HEARST: HER OWN STORY
by Patricia Campbell Hearst with Alvin Moscow
                    70651-2/$4.50 US/$5.95 Can

SPIKE LEE
by Alex Patterson   76994-8/$4.99 US/$5.99 Can